D1807619

Wayward Legionnaire

A Life in the French Foreign Legion

by

James William Worden

ROBERT HALE · LONDON

© *James William Worden 1988*
First published in Great Britain 1988

Robert Hale Limited
Clerkenwell House
Clerkenwell Green
London EC1R 0HT

British Library Cataloguing in Publication Data

Worden, James William
  Wayward Legionnaire : a life in
  the French Foreign Legion.
  1. France, *Armée, Legion étrangère*
  I. Title
  355.3'5   UA703.L5

ISBN 0-7090-3291-9

Photoset in North Wales by
Derek Doyle & Associates, Mold, Clwyd.
Printed in Great Britain by
St Edmundsbury Press Ltd, Bury St Edmunds, Suffolk.
Bound by Hunter & Foulis Ltd.

Contents

Author's Note

The code of anonymity is sacrosanct in the Legion. With the exception of those officers and legionnaires whose names have already appeared in other publications, all characters will only be recognized and identified by those who have served in the Legion.

Illustrations

Practice jump at Cap Falcon
57 mm recoilless rifle about to be fired with evil intent
Ceremonial parade of the 2nd REP
Arriving in France from Algeria, late 1962
Corporal on his way to the brothel
Celebrating the 300th anniversary of the Legion's most popular
  beverage
The 'mafia' of chief corporals at Bou Sfer, 1965
Exiting from a Dakota, August 1964

Map

Credits

All photographs have been reproduced with the kind permission of the Foreign Legion Association. The map is reproduced with the kind permission of Martin Windrow A.R.Hist.S., C.R.Ae.S.

Foreword

by Tony Geraghty

There was once a French general who told the Foreign Legion: 'You legionnaires are soldiers in order to die and I am sending you where you can die.' Other generals said much the same in the years and wars that followed. Not surprisingly many people, most of them French, got the idea that the typical legionnaire was a bull to the slaughter and nothing else. As one such writer concluded in Paris in 1912, the legionnaire was a degenerate personality, while the Legion itself was not just a military élite but also 'a school of expiation and oblivion'.

On the whole, the French do not care for foreigners. (It is no coincidence that Chauvin was a fellow countryman of Asterix as well as a Napoleonic veteran.) Nor, as their history depressingly demonstrates, do the French really trust their own soldiers. So common sense might suggest that anyone who is both a foreigner and a soldier for France must indeed suffer from a death wish combined with the herd instinct.

Jim Worden's account of his life as a legionnaire gives the lie to this bovine image. The notion that legionnaires are 'retread' personalities, simple clones of the men who stormed the heights of Sebastopol a century ago, is widespread and due not only to French prejudice but also to the Legion's own attachment to the idea that it is more than a military formation, that it is a military caste, a family with a powerful collective identity.

Worden and the people he writes about so vividly are no retreads. He is in the same league of military rascality as such 'fictional' characters as Sergeant Bilko and Brigadier-General Harry Flashman. When he describes the disappearance overnight of tons of cement and bricks so as to recycle a police station (as yet unbuilt) as a Legion shower block for which no planning permission exists, he is not just telling a good yarn. He is offering proof that the true legionnaire defies the system. He will do it not by running away but by changing the system a little through the force of his wit and style. And if change is impossible – *tant pis!* – he will make his gesture anyway.

Like the stories Jim Worden tells, his language is full of rich, organic matter. But that also is part of the non-industrial, outdoor nature of the man, his profession of arms and his message. As someone once put it, 'better to live one day like a lion than a lifetime as a lamb'.

Jim Worden's book might have been subtitled, 'The Day Of The Lion'. Its profusion of anecdotes and character should make it a cult book among those who like people, love life and the risk of life, and detest the system.

Those who know the way armies really work will find something else familiar which the armchair strategist will not comprehend. This is that the individual soldier knows intimately only a very few of his immediate comrades. He has no access to the great scheme of things. If he is not an officer or NCO then the chances are that he will not even have a map. Such intimacy with a handful of others helps to make the intolerable a way of life, for whenever he thinks it is safe to take a nap, wash his shirt or empty his bowel, that is the moment the bugle will sound to call him to rush on again, in order to wait some more, only to find that the action is happening a little way off.

Worden accepted the action that came his way and describes with terrible clarity what it is to see young men, friend and enemy, torn apart by flying metal. He was already an 'old' man in his forties, the Second World War behind him, when he fought with the Legion in Algeria. He took no particular pleasure in killing. Veterans usually do not.

The Legion was fortunate to have in its ranks someone whose maturity had not robbed him of compassion or humour, someone intelligent enough to appreciate the significance of small events and through those to record human courage and what one poet described as 'the integrity of danger'. It is, as Jim himself would say, no bullshit.

T.G.

Introduction

Since entry into the Foreign Legion is neither by conscription nor by coercion, it follows that all must be volunteers who are recruited into this infamous, yet little-known, service.

The reasons for a man volunteering to serve in the Legion require some thought. Perhaps only four reasons can be attributed to the Legion's attracting such large numbers of recruits that it can reject more than seventy per cent of applicants: adventure – anonymity – refuge – money. I kid thee not. As an ex-legionnaire, I can tell you that only an idiot would join for the money and, being an idiot, he would be one of the first to be rejected. Anonymity and refuge: yes, the Legion offers refuge from a nagging wife or a pregnant girlfriend, but *not* from the Law. Adventure seems to be the prime reason given by British recruits for their enlistment. However, there *were* many like myself who enlisted for anonymity and refuge.

Many journalists and professional writers have expounded the theory that most volunteers for the Legion are obsessed with a 'death wish'. The more they write on this subject, the more they expound the 'myth' of the Legion. Many have further suggested that the repeated acts of heroism and the willingness of legionnaires to flout danger and flirt with death are a direct result of this inherent 'death wish'. Nothing could be farther from the truth. That the Legion offers constant challenges and opportunities to those who join their ranks to prove their worth cannot be denied. All the attributes and qualities that produce outstanding acts of courage and bravery are contagious, like a disease, and are handed down from generation to generation of legionnaires. Traditions and examples of valour, fearlessness, fortitude and just plain grit and guts are demonstrated to the novice legionnaire by a hard core of grizzled veterans with anything up to thirty years service.

This book has no hero. I certainly was not one. Of necessity it does cover certain incidents in which I became involved, and many of my experiences.

Despite all the trials and tribulations, mostly the fault of my own weakness and inabilities, I found life in the Legion a truly wonderful and satisfying experience: no blood – no sweat – no tears – and no regrets, except that I signed for five years, served for seven and wish I could have completed fifteen.

At the time of my enlistment, I was fortunate in many ways. I was fifteen years older than the average recruit of twenty-one, and considerable guerrilla warfare was still being carried out in the hills and mountains of Algeria.

Perhaps the greatest part of my good fortune was the fact that the majority of the senior non-commissioned officers were of German origin and had served in the forces of their homeland during the Second World War. (Yes, some had even served in the SS). The fact that I had been their enemy during the hostilities did not cause any hatred or dislike. On the contrary, and without doubt induced by the Legion motto of 'Legio Patria Nostra' ('The Legion is My Home'), it caused only a genuine concern about my ability to undertake the rigorous physical effort required to complete the basic training. As one German sergeant commented, 'Johnny, if you manage to complete your training, you'll survive anything.'

I did survive … but many of my friends did not.

1 Voyage into the Unknown

My second arrival at Château Vincennes did not produce a red-carpet welcome. It did produce a handshake from the *adjudant**, once he had recovered from the shock of seeing me again. He then proceeded to lecture me. Englishmen did not enjoy a good reputation with the Legion. Englishmen who volunteered to serve in the Legion were few, far fewer than any other nationality. They further held the highest record for desertion than any other nation, a percentage so high that it was kept secret. But those who did not desert, and some of these he had known, had proved to be very good. Perhaps, but only perhaps, I would make a legionnaire, but he doubted it very much.

The *adjudant* told me that a detachment of recruits had departed for Marseilles the previous day. It would be unlikely that the next detachment would be formed for at least seven to ten days. Should I wish, there was no reason to stay in the barracks. I could return to Paris, stay in a hotel, have a good time and return later. I declined the offer. I was beginning to wonder whether he was going to let me join the Legion. I had a feeling that, should I leave again, he would probably leave instructions at the gate to keep that bloody fool of an Englishman out.

He then told me, fine, since I wished to remain, then tough luck. All recruits were required to carry out simple fatigues during their stay. Since at that time I was the only recruit, I was going to be very busy.

I think I learnt more about the Château Vincennes Legion quarters than any other recruit before me. I found the location of every mess hall, every dormitory, every toilet, every bar, every

---

* To help the reader this rank has been left in the original French as the nearest translation is Warrant Officer (Class II).

staircase, every office and the kitchen. I scrubbed the lot. I also learnt how many uniforms the *adjudant* had – thirteen. I pressed them in my spare time.

I was issued with American-style fatigue coveralls that had probably been made for the largest man in the US Army. I also received a pair of British Army boots, which were obvious rejects from the Guards depot at Pirbright. They had so many steel studs that they seemed to weigh a ton. To add to this, my first Legion uniform was an idiotic green-and-red side cap; since it continually fell off my head, I kept it concealed in my pocket.

So I commenced my new life as a Legion recruit. My first three days at the *château* began with being aroused at 5.30 a.m., being dispatched to the kitchen to obtain coffee and bread for myself and 'Methusula', an old legionnaire of indeterminable age and service, and then proceeding to scrub what appeared to me the whole of Château Vincennes.

I managed to swap my over-large American coveralls for a perfectly fitting brand new set. Immaculately tailored and pressed. I left the outsize set hanging in the *adjudant's* wardrobe. At least it made me feel like a potential soldier – and what the hell did he want with a fatigue set anyway? (Eventually, prior to leaving for Marseilles, when I handed the coveralls back to the stores, I reswapped for the original outsize, just in case!) I know that the *adjudant* was aware they were his set of fatigues I was walking around in. He never said a word.

It was whilst I was at the Château Vincennes that we were sent to a regular French Army military hospital, for what was meant to be a fairly stringent medical examination. It seemed almost identical to that which I had undergone almost twenty years previously, on my entrance to the Royal Air Force, the same stripping to the buff, the same cold floors, the same back and chest tapping, the same parading from specialist to specialist, none of whom was next door to each other. The same dismal attempts to cover with your hand your manhood, which was miserably drooping in the cold. Pissing in the same-shaped bottles as those used by the British services – and experiencing the same difficulty in the passing of water for samples. Whistling in an attempt to encourage one's bladder to discharge – it had not worked twenty years before, and did nothing to help me then. Happily, at that moment one of the young

German recruits came to my rescue and proceeded to fill my bottle for me. Then he had a problem: we were not in a toilet but in the reception area, and he was unable to stop. In the end he helped two other Legion recruits to fill their bottles, and then three French conscripts of the group who were undergoing their medical along with us. God knows what he had been drinking the night before, but it certainly worked a treat, and we all passed that test. A very good man ...

It would not have mattered if I had been half blind during my eye test! It was controlled by a young French conscript. He did not speak English and I, certainly, had at the most only the ability to read a French menu. It quickly became a farce. As I read the first line on the chart, enunciating clearly and concisely the letters in the Queen's English, with one hand over the left eye (the other still protecting my manhood), a complete look of incomprehension fell over his face and he literally shrieked '*Répète!*' Even I realized that he wanted me to start again. By this time, some thirty bods had crowded into the room, all intent on getting a free English lesson, and all starkers.

He pointed to the first letter, 'B'. I quickly responded, 'B' to be followed by thirty voices raised in unison, 'BEEEEE'. Then the next letter, 'D'. Once again thirty voices, all in a very tiny room, following me with 'DEEEEE'. The test ended on the next letter, and it was certainly hard luck on the poor man running the test that the next letter was Y (pronounced phonetically 'egrek' in French). By the time the rest of 'em had tried to follow me on this one, at least twenty were leaning against the walls with tears streaming down their cheeks from laughter. With this episode I was beginning to understand why it was Legion policy to deter British recruits.

The arrival of a French regular army captain did nothing to restore order among what had now become chaos. However, nothing impressed me more than the silence that fell over the whole group, conscripts included, on the arrival of the Legion *adjudant*, who merely stood at the entrance of the room, legs astride, arms akimbo, and said only one word, '*Alors*'. From that moment on, a deathly hush seemed to envelope the whole building.

I later saw the results of my eye test. I'd passed with 20/20 vision!

It was during the medical that I learnt that it did not matter by what name I had been known prior to my enlistment: henceforth I would be known, as all other British Legionnaires had been known before me, as 'Johnny'.

The next day those recruits who had survived the medical and preliminary questioning, exactly twelve in number, received their first military pay. I cannot remember the amounts we received – not a great deal, and the sums varied, depending on how long each had been at Vincennes. I do recall that I received the most and, in comparison with the rest, felt like a capitalist, but in no way did it compensate for the amount of scrubbing I had done.

We were duly sworn in and took the oath of allegiance that morning and informed we would be departing for Marseilles the following evening, on the first leg to our eventual destination, Sidi-bel-Abbès. The swearing in ceremony had a very sobering effect on me and eliminated once and for all any preconceived notions I had that this was going to be 'devil may care' soldiering I was letting myself in for.

I listened to a very sombre and cold English voice clearly pointing out the hazards of life in the Legion and emphasizing that five years in the Legion was a very long time. (Each nationality listens to the same pre-recorded unwelcoming speech in his own language, so that later he cannot declare, 'I did not understand.')

Then came the final address by the captain, the only occasion I had seen him. (It was translated with the assistance of the *adjudant*.)

'You have not been solicited to join the Legion.

'The Legion did not search you out, and ask you to join.

'Each and every one of you has freely volunteered to serve France.

'You will serve in whatever capacity the Legion decides.

'You will each have to WORK harder than you have ever worked in your lives.

'Some of you may eventually become soldiers.

'Should you become soldiers, you may have the privilege of fighting for France, and the honour of dying for France.

'You may leave here now, without signing this contract, but do not return later and try to join again.

'Now, if you have fully understood, sign.'

Of the thirteen of us, only twelve signed the mass of documentation. A young Belgian lad had changed his mind. When he left the room, we were called to attention for the first time in our lives as legionnaires. The tape machine switched on, the deafening rendering of a military band blared out the 'Marseillaise', resounding from the walls of that small room, almost caused the walls and table to vibrate, and certainly hurt the ears. We were in.

The Belgian who had changed his mind about enlisting was not forcibly ejected from Vincennes with a swift kick up the arse. Later, in the barrack room, after changing into his civilian clothes, he was very miserable and dejected and for some reason apologized to each of us who had signed, with tears in his eyes.

It frightened the life out of me when the *adjudant* arrived to collect him, placed his arm around the young Belgian's shoulder, addressed the whole room and said: 'You bloody fools, this is the only one among you with courage and brains,' and then they left. The fears and doubts I entertained were doubled by the realization that the *adjudant* had made this short speech in English ... and only English!

For our lengthy journey from Paris to the Legion fort at Marseilles, we were issued with British-style battledress uniforms, not by any means new, but certainly clean. This, along with a khaki overcoat, almost British style, except for the length, considerably longer than usual, with our boots from the guards depot and the ridiculous side cap, became our uniform for the journey.

'Methusula' produced some shoe brushes and polish, along with a couple of electric irons, for pressing our uniforms. He also informed us that the reason for recruits travelling at night was that fewer civilians might see us and that there was less chance of our being identified as Legion recruits, declaring that, if the French population became aware of the calibre of men the Legion was being compelled to accept they would insist that the Legion be disbanded. I'm sure the Legion deliberately retain these veterans at recruitment depots to deter potential recruits with weak moral characters.

Our escort for the journey was a veteran chief corporal who was returning from leave. During the journey the train made a stop about 2 a.m. and the chief corporal allowed one of our party to leave the train to purchase beer and sandwiches for all of us from the buffet. This individual collected money from all, the equivalent of £10 from myself, and promptly disappeared. The chief corporal received an eight-day prison sentence on arrival at Marseilles. So I received my first lesson in the art of desertion, that it is the man in charge who is punished, not necessarily the culprit. This was a lesson that helped me in later days.

We duly arrived at Bas Fort St-Nicholas, Marseilles, the central gathering-point for all those recruits who had arrived from Grenoble, Lyons, Nice and other places in France where one could be recruited at any police station and provided with a ticket to Marseilles.

We spent some two weeks there undergoing basic induction and even more searching interrogation. It was here that we lost our passports for five years, and there was a final weeding-out of those the Legion had no wish to accept. Yet another medical inspection: X-rays, blood check, innoculations and vaccinations. After the innoculations and vaccinations we were told that for the next twenty-four hours we could relax in the barracks, that none of us would be required for any fatigues or duties. We should relax and take advantage of the Mediterranean sunshine.

I awoke the next day with the very coarse sheets the Legion provided so wet that I first thought I had pissed in my bed. I jumped out without realizing that I was sleeping on the third tier, and collapsed in a heap on a concrete floor. I found that my legs could not support me and that I had a terrific temperature. It was at that moment that I thought what a stupid thing I had done, to enlist in the Legion, and how unfit I was, that I should collapse after such a trivial thing as being innoculated.

My ego was slightly restored, however, when I managed to look around the *chambre* and realized that at least eighty per cent of my fellow recruits were feeling exactly the same as myself. In fact, some were even worse and pitifully requesting the services of a doctor. Unlike the British services, where innoculations and vaccinations are given in 'split' measures, we had been injected with the lot at the same time – tetanus, yellow fever and probably any other spares they had available. I managed to struggle to my feet and get dressed, and did manage to get out to the sunshine, where I felt considerably better. My ego rose as fast as my temperature dropped, at the thought of all those potential supermen who were all in their twenties and still flaked out in their beds. I fully appreciated the twenty-four hours we had been given to recover and, basking in the sunshine, was also very much aware that I could easily have been beaten in a fight with any five-year-old in the vicinity. Like many other things in the Legion, if it is done quick and fast, innoculation does not hurt so much!

Happily it was only a short stay at the Bas Fort – sleeping accommodation was crowded, toilet facilities were primitive and limited. However, there were no restrictions on showers, and ample opportunity to use them.

I found that privacy was now a thing of the past – and one of the most difficult adjustments to make. One cannot make comparisons with recruitment depots in other countries. The Legion is unique in that all nationalities enlist. Different habits – different types of diet – differences in social life: all are cast aside, and one must adjust and adopt the 'Legion way' – or end by becoming a mental wreck and morally depressed.

I opted then and there for the old adage, 'If you can't beat 'em, join 'em.' Even prior to arrival at Sidi-bel-Abbès, I made up my mind that I must adjust. What the hell? It was only for five years.

It was also at Marseilles that I learnt to play poker with thirty-two cards only, Continental poker. This was one adjustment I found very easy. The odds and possibilities playing five-card draw with only thirty-two cards were far easier to calculate than fifty-two. We did not play poker for money – only cigarettes. On enlistment I had been smoking sixty cigarettes a day, but prior to our departure for Algeria I was offering extra packets of cigarettes as a gift to anyone who wanted them, all from my profitable poker playing.

We were required to turn in our civilian clothes, and I assumed they would be stored on our behalf, until such time as we had completed our contract. Since I had known when leaving London that I would be entering the Legion, I had departed with only a small, good leather bag, a very good Harris tweed jacket and first-class tweed trousers. (If I had decided to stay at the Georges V Hotel in Paris, my dress was such that I would have been welcomed as a paying guest, obviously having sufficient funds to pay my bill.) Never make assumptions in the

Foreign Legion … I lost the lot to the Legion quartermaster and was paid the price he valued them at: two packets of cigarettes.

If you had two suitcases, a complete wardrobe, including evening dress (and I did see one lying on the floor), the price was always the same: two packets of cigarettes … I had already given away fifteen cartons of cigarettes. I was beginning to learn.

I had looked forward with some anticipation to our journey from Marseilles to the exotic shores of the North African coast. We were being transported on one of the two sister-ship ferries that had been ploughing their way between Oran and Marseilles probably since the year dot. My anticipation and feeling of adventure changed to despair and depression as we climbed down flight after flight of greasy, dirty iron stairs to the very bowels of the ferry to what was to be our home for the next thirty-six hours.

We were each provided with a filthy dirty deckchair and instructed to form our chairs into circles of ten. The sergeant then appointed the tallest man in each group of ten as *Chef d'équipe* (boss man), thrust him a slip of paper authorizing him to draw rations for ten and beat a hasty retreat to the fresh air of the upper deck and the bar.

Our steel-plated deck was awash with water and the spillage of urine from the toilets. The stench from the toilets of vomit and shit was overwhelming. Even prior to leaving the harbour, at least a dozen of the recruits had thrown up, and they returned from the toilets green and reeling, myself included.

We were lucky in finding a crew member who, in exchange for German marks, English pound notes and anything else he could obtain from us, produced a hosepipe and brooms which allowed us to clean the area. For an extra few cartons of cigarettes, he also found some pungent disinfectant, which contained so much sulphuric acid that it brought tears to the eyes, but at least it made the area somewhat habitable. It was disturbing, however, to hear the constant baas of the sheep, added to the braying and farting of the mules, separated from us only by a low partition.

To obtain food for each group of ten required the climbing of two decks to reach the kitchen. The sight of a thick lentil concoction, with chunks of greasy pork with the stubble of pigs' hair still visible, caused only more visits to the now moderately clean toilets, to throw up again. The food was such that most of us existed on bread, wine and coffee.

We were not at any time allowed onto the upper decks to breathe clean air. On arrival at the port of Oran, it was not a question of marching or walking from the ferry but of eighty individuals staggering ashore, overcome by the strange taste of what appeared to be pure oxygen but which was only fresh air.

That voyage had a very long and lasting effect, so much so that, as I left the vessel, I swore an oath that I would never repeat the journey under similar conditions. If I was successful at completing my five years then, rather than make the same journey, I would desert and make my own way back to Europe. (Much later I found that these conditions applied only on the outward trip.)

Once ashore we were back in the hands of the Legion, swiftly bundled into trucks and driven to a small Legion transit fort in Oran. There we enjoyed welcome showers, an abundance of hot water, and a meal served in the *réfectoire* (dining-room) which, after the sickening mess I had seen but not eaten aboard the ferry, seemed superb and equal to a five-star restaurant, which it wasn't, but I had not eaten for almost two days! It was also the first time in my life I had tasted yoghurt, which was to leave me addicted for the rest of my life. (Not quite all my life, yet.)

We were given the opportunity of purchasing beer, cigarettes, biscuits and any other items from the *Foyer du Légionnaire*, which I had discovered earlier, at Marseilles, did not mean a legionnaire's waiting-room, but the equivalent of the British NAAFI. It was at this small Legion fort that I tasted my first Kronenborg beer – the first, as I calculated after leaving the Legion, of the 10,000 that passed my lips during the course of my service, for which I, like many thousands of legionnaires who had passed that way, offer eternal thanks to the Hatt brothers of Strasbourg, who surely invented this magical brew only for the Legion.

With the going down of the sun, we said farewell to the delightful little fort. There had not been any shouting or harassment by the corporals or sergeants. In fact, the whole fort emanated an aura of relaxed contentment and left me fully unprepared for what awaited us at Sidi-bel-Abbès.

For the train ride from Oran to Sidi-bel-Abbès we were provided with a paper bag containing the longest cheese sandwich I had ever seen in my life, a packet of cigarettes, a bar of chocolate and a bottle of wine between two.

Obviously the Legion was not going to be as bad as we had been led to believe. The boat trip from France had caused my morale to sink to zero but the short stay and reception at Oran had eliminated all doubts and regrets, and I was again looking forward to arrival at the final destination.

Our arrival at Sidi-bel-Abbès brought only the conclusion that I had been an idiot not to have somehow dived off the ferry and swum back to France. The least word to describe our reception is 'hectic'. We disembarked from the train in reasonable order, counted by our escorts, and were led out of the station. Then all hell broke loose. We were descended upon by a multitude of sergeants, shouting, screaming in incomprehensible French, all convinced that the louder they shouted, the more we would understand. I couldn't even speak the bloody language – whisper or shout it made no difference to me. Without doubt all those sergeants had been awaiting our arrival in the nearest bar, consuming large quantities of alcohol, getting stoned out of their minds waiting for the little lambs they were happily going to lead to slaughter. Then commenced their fun. Three trucks had been waiting outside the station. We were ordered to climb in, climb out, climb in again. The slowest climbing in got a kick, the slowest climbing out got a kick. For thirty minutes they played their games, all the time shouting conflicting instructions in a mixture of French and German.

There was one sergeant who pushed me in the chest, and I was fed up to the teeth with this stupid game. I dropped the bag I'd been carrying and snarled at him, 'You touch me again, you fucker, and I'll tear your fucking head off.' I never did find out if he spoke English, but at least he understood the intent from the emphasis and facial expression. They had noticed that I was many years older than my companions. Perhaps this was the sudden reason they dropped me from their game.

It took me two years of service to erase that reception from my mind, and the same period of time to accept that not all Legion sergeants were complete morons, with testicles for brains.

I think the reason we marched from the station to the

barracks, instead of riding in the trucks, was that this band of sergeants needed the march to free their heads from the alcoholic fumes.

I had been in the Legion only five minutes and already was hating all sergeants and praying that some time in the future I would meet again the veteran corporal who had escorted us to the ferry from the fort at Marseilles, the same corporal whom I had plied with drink and cigarettes, the same corporal who had shaken hands and wished me well, the same dirty little shit who told me just prior to embarkation to ensure that I grab a decent deckchair and a good place on the deck, so that I could sunbathe and arrive in Algeria with a sun tan.

That was when my Legion education began, and I little realized then that in years to come I would become a bigger shit than all of them.

On arrival at our destination, the Petit Quartier, in the very late evening, we were marched into a large hall, there to be stripped and searched. Every item of the clothing issued at Marseilles was tossed to the centre of the room, presumably to be fumigated later. The only military items retained were the boots I had received in Paris.

After being hustled in and out of the showers, we were issued with American-style underpants and allowed to select a reasonably fitting set of American fatigue uniforms. The *adjudant* issuing the various instructions (a Hungarian, I found out later) was a complete contrast to the NCOs who had met us at the station. His language ability must have been exceptional, for he managed to make me understand so quickly that I had not realized he was repeating the same instructions and welcome in at least seven languages, and he was not parroting the words, since he also questioned at least six recruits in their own language and spoke to me for at least five minutes. During that five minutes I understood exactly what would be required during the ensuing week, the basic routine. His final 'Good luck', before we were shown to our sleeping quarters, made me heave a sigh of relief, and I slept that night the sleep of the innocent.

Our stay at Sidi-bel-Abbès lasted only one week. Split into small parties of twelve, we were marched to the hospital, for even more medical examinations, then to the dentist. I am the biggest coward in the world when sitting in a dentist's chair, yet I found this dentist far better than the dentist in London who had charged me sixty pounds to repair a broken front tooth. The Legion dentist criticized the repair, the only fault he found in my mouth, and promptly commenced work on my tooth. The result did nothing but improve my natural handsome smile and has remained in place ever since. No pain, no grief. I had not even realized that he had given me an injection to ease any pain.

At the stores we were issued with uniforms for both summer and winter – thirteen of them. Although the uniforms were not new, they were clean, most of them arriving as if from a first-class dry-cleaners. There was also considerable care taken to ensure they were of a reasonable fit, unlike the first uniform I'd received on entering the Royal Air Force, which had been tossed across a counter with the comment, 'That'll do.' We also received the famous Legion *Képi blanc'* (white kepi),which we had seen so proudly sported by all legionnaires already met. The problem was that, although the kepis were brand new, the two covers issued to us were a dirty khaki colour, and nowhere near the brilliant white the veteran legionnaires were wearing. This was later resolved for us by the corporal in charge of our room, at a cost of one beer for each cover. He merely soaked them in bleach overnight and earned himself eighty beers. With recruits passing through his hands at forty per week, it is small wonder that he seemed always to be in a state of blissful oblivion. The *adjudant* checked that each kepi fitted well. Each kepi was very carefully placed on the recruit's head, with the recruit standing rigidly at attention, then the *adjudant* would violently slap the top of the kepi with his open hand. If the recruit did not scream, and his ears were still attached to his head, it was a good fit.

Prior to the fitting of the kepi we had visited the barber shop, a stool perched outside the sleeping quarters, where a veteran legionnaire proceeded to run his electric clippers over the head, not until the hair had been cut but until the head had been shorn. But at least we were no longer required to wear the stupid red-and-green side cap issued in Paris.

Perhaps the greatest surprise at Sidi-bel-Abbès was the education and IQ tests, very carefully supervised and of a duration of two days. We were led to what were obviously lecture rooms, only twelve recruits to a room fully equipped with individual desks and chairs, with no opportunity to take a sidelong glance at any other recruit's work, which, even if opportunity had existed, would have served no useful purpose, since all test papers were in the natural language of the individual recruit. I began to regret that I was the only British recruit in the whole contingent.

Each recruit was handed half a dozen foolscap sheets, with instructions to complete the test in the shortest possible time. On completion of each paper it was to be raised in the air, then to be taken away for checking. We were also told that on completion of all papers we could retire outside for a smoke. That was a bloody lie. I finished mine only to be handed another batch.

During the second day of tests, only five legionnaires had been detailed to continue in the lecture rooms. From the papers I had completed the previous day, it came as no surprise to find that those new ones handed to me included four headed 'Cambridge School Certificate, 1936'. I had not passed my higher School Certificate until 1939. I still swear the questions were exactly the same.

The sergeant looking after us at that time became very upset when, during the completion of the papers, I requested that the French paper be swapped for German, since this had been my modern language at school. How the hell was I to know that he was British, Bill B., now scraping a living as a lecturer at one of the northern universities? He taught me something at that moment: only speak English with an accent in the Legion. Then, when having to give a dirty job to a fellow Englishman, the 'Old Boy' treatment is out of the window, and the idiot receiving the dirty job cannot expect preferential treatment.He had 'conned' me for two days. I would have sworn he was Swiss. Six months later, when I had finished my training, he introduced me to his mother, who had flown to Algeria to see him.

2   Introduction to Legion Instruction

Donkeys do not speak French. Nor, when they first enter the Legion, do the majority of recruits.

Contrary to popular belief, donkeys are still taught with the use of the stick and a carrot. So, in the Foreign Legion, we recruits were required to undertake the same form of instruction, only slightly more sophisticated. The stick was replaced by a swift kick up the backside, the carrot by not getting a kick up the backside.

This method of instruction, with the appropriate reward and punishment, had a remarkably high success rate and certainly gave the recruit considerable incentive in his determination to learn French very quickly. It also ensured that all his attention and a great deal of effort were focused on the absorption of the complex instruction and indoctrination that fell from the lips of the various instructors. If the instructors had spoken fluent French, this would have not, in all probability, have helped the recruit in any way, nor would it have helped, in the remaining years of the recruit's contract, with what would become the most general language, Legion *argot*.

The most frequent expressions in Legion life, which take a very short time to learn but a great deal longer to realize the implications of, were '*Démerde toi*' ('Get on with it'), '*Dépêche toi*' ('Right or wrong, get on with it any way you can'). It was waste of time searching for the meaning of these expressions in a French dictionary, since this did not give the implications. Only the inevitable aid of the boot brought into contact with the arse helped in realizing the intent.

It took only three months to memorize enough French nouns to identify by name each and every item in the barrack block and the contents of my very large kitbag. I could further name each piece of the very efficient MAT 49 (machine pistol) which eventually became my favourite weapon, and the MAS 49/56 (semi-automatic rifle), which required instant recall of twenty-seven different parts.

However, despite having a sore arse, I was still unsure whether or not it was correct to say '*la bayonette*' or '*le bayonette*'. Each time I was questioned on this piece of weaponry (which during the whole of my service, was used only for removing the top from a bottle of beer, opening a can of food or probing for suspect mines), if I replied to Instructor A '*le bayonette*', I received a swift boot, but when questioned about the same item by Instructor B, and I responded '*la bayonette*', I received yet another swift boot. Nothing was more frustrating when, at a later date, I was asked by a German sergeant to identify the object he was holding aloft in his hand and, remembering my previous errors responded '*Ein bayonette*'. That cost me a further boot in a very sore place, plus four days fatigues. This, as the good sergeant explained, was for speaking pidgin German. He would have accepted 'a' or even 'the' *bayonette*, but there was no way he was going to accept '*Ein bayonette*' from an Englishman.

During my first three months at Saida, I made some considerable improvement with my French though I found that while it became quite easy to follow instructions and conversations, I had the greatest difficulty in the formulation and articulation of responses. It took yet a further year of service before I was able to think in the French language, when all became simple, except for an atrocious accent and my ability to bastardize the language with Cockney rhyming slang. One thing is certain: during the period spent at this Legion establishment, a donkey would not have been able to speak one word of French, nor to have mastered the complex arms drill, which, despite allegations by all the instructors, certainly proved that we recruits had more brains than donkeys!

The system of reward and punishment was used for all the basic instruction, varied by constant requests from the instructors to demonstrate the number of push-ups it was possible to complete prior to total collapse. On commencement of the instruction, most recruits as unfit as myself – there were not all that many – would normally collapse after a nominal ten.

Nothing was more astonishing at the completion of my training than to find I could complete fifty, and further, that at the same time I could sing the Legion song '*Le Boudin*'. I was never sure if the frequent requests from the instructors to demonstrate this feat to my comrades was because they admired my voice or if I was overstaying my welcome.

There was an alternative to the ordinary push-ups, probably devised by a sadist. This was to complete the same exercise '*avec musique*' ('with music'). This did not require the recruit to sing, merely to demonstrate the agility to clap his hands between each push-up, whilst in the prone position. Unless the recruit is extremely proficient at this, his face strikes the ground before the hands prevent impact. This could become more difficult, and somewhat of a handicap, whilst wearing a rucksack on your back. But, if your instructor was of a sympathetic nature, he would not insist that the rucksack be filled with rocks – very few were sympathetic!

I think it was the bruising of many Legion recruits' faces, caused by their inefficiency at carrying out these push-ups '*avec musique*', consequently allowing their faces to strike the ground repeatedly, that gave rise to the ill-found rumours that they had been punched in the face by their corporals and sergeants.

A Legion recruit can always take action against his sergeant or corporal should he wish. If the recruit objects to receiving a kick up the arse, and the recruit is fairly tall and considers it anti-social to be treated in such a manner by a diminutive corporal, he has the option of challenging the corporal to a fight on 'equal' terms. Whereupon, even if it be in the middle of the parade ground, the corporal instructor will remove his jacket, upon which his rank is sewn, and gleefully pound the dumb recruit near to death. It is thus that he demonstrates to the other recruits, all of whom have equal opportunity of challenging him but who have been sensibly discreet, the value of the Legion's training in unarmed combat, and the advisability for all in the future of carrying out his slightest wishes.

Meanwhile the dumb recruit who has been damn near beaten to death resigns himself to the fact that a bruised arse is much better than a mouth without any teeth. (I was once that dumb recruit).

Basic training in the Foreign Legion was only slightly different from that of any other army. As with other elite units, the object of the training is to push the recruit to the limit of his endurance and to ensure that he attains a high standard of physical fitness.

At the completion of a recruit's training, it does not matter whether he had finished first or last in his platoon, conditional to his having exerted himself to the limit of his individual physical ability. This is the mark of the *bon volunt* – even the Legion recognizes that all men are not supermen. Perhaps in the Legion recruits learn to adapt a little faster and to march just a little farther, perhaps carrying a little more than recruits in other armies. This may make the training a bit more difficult. But the object of Legion training is not to arrive at a position some twenty kilometres distant with a bunch of legionnaires too exhausted for combat but to allow their bodies to learn to adjust and, more important, for the mind to master any weariness and to dig down for a few more reserves. Not a great deal of training is devoted to parade square drilling. In fact, there was so little of it, compared for example with that of the British Army, that it seemed to be almost negligible, perhaps only some ten hours each week.

In contrast, a considerable amount of training is devoted to the spending of the tax payer's money, in the amount of ammunition expended each week, a regular 200 rounds fired by each recruit from rifle and automatic pistol.

One had to make many adjustments very quickly during the early days of training. Each morning, before sunrise, there was a run of anything from eight to fifteen kilometres – not jogging in unison, but a mad stampede. These runs were always to a halfway checkpoint, attended by a sergeant who would check the name of the recruit against his list as he passed. For the tail-enders, this genial character would attempt to provide additional motive power with that swift kick up the rear. It took only a short time to learn to keep something in reserve at the checkpoint, for with speedy acceleration, evasive action and a little luck, it was possible to leave this character flat on his back when he missed – a delight when this happened, but a question of 'enjoy the moment and pay later'!

Those early morning runners who returned first to the barracks had more time for their coffee and completion of their morning toilet. In the early days, some would even write a letter home before I arrived on my hands and knees.

The most punishing experience was the constant leg weariness. The parade square in the fort was used only for our assembly and dismissal on our return from instruction. Each morning, with the exception of Sunday, which was a complete rest day, we would march out of the fort at a very rapid rate to our lecture room, some eight kilometres away. This would be a forest, a valley or a hilltop, open to the sky, and it mattered not if it was raining or even snowing. As we were to find, the elements were as much an enemy as the Algerian rebels. During instruction you were never allowed to sit: a smoking break was allowed each hour, but at all times you were required to remain standing. After a five-hour session each morning, it would be back to the fort to eat, before returning again to our open-air lecture rooms for a further four hours.

I found the most difficult aspect of the training was getting myself physically fit. At the end of the first week, my calf muscles were rigid and aching, and the thigh muscles felt like planks of wood. During our first time at the shooting range, I actually considered bribing someone with a couple of cartons of cigarettes to shoot me in the legs. Later I was glad I had not, since, at the end of six weeks, I awoke to the realization that my body and physical well being were better than they had been for at least ten years.

I was beginning to enjoy the fresh air and exercise, and no longer had the slightest concern about the regular Saturday long-distance marches of anything up to fifty kilometres and more, where endurance could be demonstrated, preferring them to a sprint run of a hundred metres, where I invariably ended in last position. The ugly and heavy hobnailed boots I had worn since I left Paris had been discarded and replaced by calf-length ranger boots, lightweight and supple, and marching in these was like marching on a cushion of air. It was a further surprise that my appetite was increasing in direct proportion to the weight I lost. My smoking consumption had been reduced to not more than ten cigarettes a day. In a matter of only some six weeks, the Legion had attained a minor miracle in turning me into almost a trained athlete. With the realization that I had reached a reasonable standard of physical fitness and that I was no longer the last man in all the sporting activities, I was really beginning to enjoy the life, except for the combat obstacle course undertaken twice a week.

The combat obstacle courses, though standard throughout the French Army, were usually slightly modified by the Legion, just to make them produce more than a feeling of quivering excitement. In my case, they produced a feeling of dread and an awful lot of respect for each obstacle. There were evil smiles on the faces of the instructors, and an outward glow of anticipation of the accidents they were about to witness, as they announced that a complete morning of instruction would be devoted to 'sport' on the *parcours du combattant*. The only participation of the instructors would be vociferous encouragement during the tackling of the obstacles, and a heavy boot between obstacles.

How these activities could be described as a form of sport, I could never understand. I always considered them an easy means of obtaining access to the infirmary, which they were when a mistake happened to be made – and there were many mistakes made by the unwary, the unsuspecting and in particular the over-enthusiastic, interested only in impressing the instructors with their expertise. Broken wrists, broken arms, twisted ankles were commonplace during every excursion to this playground of 'sport', which provided entertainment for the laughing instructors, agony for those participating, and good practice for those trainee legionnaires selected as medical orderlies. In the days of the Roman Empire, these obstacle course sites would have been described as 'arenas', and instead of lions, the only additional obstacle would be the wild pig stampeding across that had lost its way.

Because of my previous military training, albeit mostly flying, I found I could strip most weapons down and reassemble them much faster than my fellow recruits. Although I rapidly became one of the best marksmen in the platoon, there was little point in becoming an expert marksman if one could not understand the instructions as to which target to shoot at.

There was a time at the shooting range when I received what I thought to be instructions to shoot at the third target on the left. I consequently banged away at this target, some 200 metres away, and knew that I was hitting it well. I even knew that my shots were to the right of the bull, and only slightly high – I was not concerned about striking the bull's-eye, only with obtaining a very good group. At the conclusion of the firing, all eight recruits, myself included, laid down our weapons and approached the targets with our sergeant. Each recruit was required to stand in front of the target at which he had fired, and await the judgment and conclusions of the inspecting sergeant. I became disturbed to find another recruit taking his place at my target – just my luck, a Spaniard, a complete bloody fool who could not understand a word of the English I was using. He could not even understand the basic 'Bugger off, that's my target' that I considered universal. It took quite a lot of gesticulating and hand-waving before my final acceptance that I had indeed been shooting at the wrong target. I subsequently received yet another kick up the arse, and a further twenty push-ups (without music). I was credited with zero results, whereas my Spanish companion was complimented on his expertise, which he never achieved again.

I was somewhat disgruntled and convinced that there was no justice in the Legion, until I reconciled myself to the fact that my own failure to understand was causing most of my grief. It was also obvious that I was going to be of little use to the Legion, or to myself, until I became moderately fluent in French.

From that one incident on the shooting range, the 'Hugo', French in five easy lessons, that I had purchased at Victoria Station prior to my departure to enlist in the Legion, was read and studied at every opportunity until I had memorized the whole damn thing from cover to cover. Then I refused to converse in English with any of the recruits who had studied that language at school and were keen to increase their knowledge. This almost created a further problem. I discovered that, because of its similarity with English, German was easier to understand than French, and I earned a further kick up the backside, and even more push-ups, when I forgot myself one day and responded to a German chief sergeant, *'Jawohl, Major'*. The most urgent requirement for any Cockney enlisting in the Foreign Legion, as I found to my sorrow, is to learn colloquial French with extreme promptitude. The alternative is to finish basic training with arm muscles like Popeye's, aided by frequent push-ups, and your backside a permanent blueish and violet shade, which may look picturesque in the showers but does nothing for your vanity. It does, however, make one grateful that all the instruction is given to recruits whilst they are in a standing position.

Upon reflection, it could be that all those holding high rank in the Legion are of a really sympathetic nature. Realizing that most Legion recruits will be receiving this playful treatment, and further appreciating how uncomfortable it would be to receive instruction sitting on a blue and purplish arse, they insist that recruits receive all their instruction standing, thus alleviating any discomfort and helping to strengthen their leg muscles for marching ...

That learning French is the highest priority can be brought home in many ways. A British – or any other non-French-speaking – recruit is certainly not going to live very long without complete absorption of the language.

In particular, a British recruit is doomed to die quickly if, receiving a shout from his corporal to '*Plongez, Johnny*', he thinks about it and looks around to find the river he is being requested to dive into, while half the bloody Algerian rebel army is trying to shoot his head off. He therefore becomes appreciative of the work he put into the study of the language, so that, hearing 'Dive, Johnny', with the automatic instinct of a born coward and a natural tendency toward self-preservation, he defies all Isaac Newton's laws of gravity and hits the deck with the velocity of a supersonic jet. He also finds that he is able to voice a silent prayer (in French) that his corporal can see where the shots are being fired from, because he certainly can't. He is too busy trying to push his nose and the whole of his body behind or under the longest stalk of grass in the area.

French can be learned very easily when there are two options: learn the language or qualify for a posthumous medal. One is very easy to achieve, the other difficult. Being of an obstinate nature, I naturally opted for the more difficult and learned French. If I was ever to be presented with a medal from the Foreign Legion, I wanted to receive it standing up. All I wanted to be was an old legionnaire, not a dead one.

It is at the training establishments that one is faced with the nightly barrack-room inspections and body counts ('*Appel*') just prior to lights-out being sounded by the bugler – probably exactly as carried out by any other army. The problem was that, in the Legion, these nightly inspections always seemed to be carried out by a sergeant who had been whiling away the hours in the *'pôte-pôte'* (sergeants' mess), no doubt having more than a few drinks with his companions whilst discussing new ways of providing entertainment for the poor bloody recruits, who would be feeling somewhat lost and homesick and wondering what had induced them to join the Legion. And like all senior NCOs at Legion training establishments, being of a kind and loving nature, these sergeants would have been discussing ways to eliminate the recruit's homesickness, like perhaps making him walk barefoot on broken glass or crawl through a roll of barbed wire instead of under it. However, they were limited in what they would have liked to do by the rules. General Rollet, father of the Legion, as far back as 1925, laid down a code of conduct limiting the authority of NCOs.

The problem was that, since General Rollet had died during the Second World War, some of the bastards had thrown away the code of conduct. On these nightly inspections, there was only one safe place to be, and that was in bed. If you were not sleeping, act your heart out and pretend to be asleep. Only two men were required to be suitably dressed and standing to attention at the entrance of the inspecting sergeant. One was the *chef de chambre*, the corporal or acting corporal in charge of the room, the other the *garde chambre*. (No, he was not guarding the room. The poor slob was responsible for the cleanliness of the room and took the kicks if an inspecting sergeant – and they all had 20/20 vision – happened to find a piece of fly shit on the table.)

Each legionnaire would then be safely sleeping (or acting) like thirty-five corpses, their individual *paquetage* (kit) spotlessly clean and meticulously arranged on the shelf above their heads: Their knife, fork and spoon brilliantly polished and standing to attention, boots cleaned, beneath the beds, fully laced and also standing to attention, out of habit.

Then the inspecting sergeant would make his slow tour around the room. If he was Spanish and there happened to be two Spanish recruits in the room, the only sound that would be heard would be that of the Spanish recruits beautifully arranged *paquetage* being thrown the length of the room. If they happened to be sleeping (or acting), near a window, and without too much effort the sergeant could toss it out of the window, then out it went. If the inspecting sergeant happened to be Italian, and there were Italian recruits in the room, boom! same treatment. In my room were twenty-two German recruits. After a visit by a German sergeant, it took no longer than a couple of hours groping around by candlelight for the twenty-two to identify their possessions and remake their *paquetage* for *réveille* the next morning.

Such demonstrations were obviously to prove that national favouritism was non-existent. For almost two months I was the happiest recruit at Saida, for there were no British sergeants there. But those evil sods in the sergeants' mess, had obviously got their heads together and had a round table conference, and all decided that they would become naturalized Englishmen, lest I felt lonely. I had my *paquetage* tossed out of the window ten days in a row until they had all had their turn. The remainder of the room had ten nights of peace. This is only to emphasize that the main qualifications for a sergeant in the Foreign Legion is to have a mother but no father.

There was one night when I had been detailed as *garde chambre*, never a pleasing task but better than that of cleaning the toilets. I had diligently carried out the cleaning of the room and the lining-up of all the boots under the beds, so that not one was a fraction of a millimetre out of alignment. Remembering the old adage that is almost a prayer in the Legion: 'If it's wet, it must be clean', I waited until I heard the approach of the sergeant on a lower floor before I hastily mopped out the room. A further quick check, and it appeared perfect.

The reason for my apprehension was that the sergeant carrying out the evening inspection was a new German from another platoon, who, when he carried out inspections of his own platoon's quarters, usually left them devastated. The rumours about this sergeant were that he had spent quite a few years in charge of the prison at Sidi-bel-Abbès, and further gossip was that Alcatraz was a rest centre compared with that place. I will not say that I waited for his visit with fear and trepidation, just that my stomach felt queasy and I had a sudden urge to visit the toilets to throw up. There were also more recruits in prison from this sergeant's platoon than that of any other …

The sergeant entered the room. The corporal screamed as loud as he could, '*Vous!*' ('Attention!') This shout could have been heard as far away as the town of Saida, not a great distance away from the main gate of the fort, but all recruits in this room, being very good sleepers and of moderate intelligence, used their brains and continued feigning sleep. This was going to be *my* night, and it was my bloody bad luck to be room orderly whilst this sergeant was on duty.

I snapped to attention, trying to ignore my queasy stomach and regretting the supper I had eaten a few hours before, and awaited the explosion.

He very quietly entered the room, saluted in response to the corporal's shouted attention and just stood there surveying the room. This sergeant was very special. He just stood there for three whole minutes (it felt like a lifetime), during which time, in the normal course of events, a minimum of at least two *paquetages* would have made their exit through the window. Then he just raised his hand and pointed to the only bed behind me that was not occupied – mine! When I turned my head to look – shit! I had been so busy checking the room, lining up the boots, that I had left my 5 shilling French-in-five-easy-lessons lying on my bed. I was dead. He actually frightened the life out of me. He did not say a word, but beckoned with his pointed finger, for me to take the offending article to him. This I did with some alacrity. He took it from my hand, slowly opened the pages and appeared to be digesting the contents. He then closed the book, returned it to me and went out of the room, still without saying a word except in response to the corporal's very much quieter '*Vous*', with a further salute, and a murmured '*Bonne nuit*' The moment the sound of his receding footsteps indicated that he had left the barracks, all those budding actors who thirty seconds before had been snoring their heads off were up off their beds, demanding what had happened and why not even one *paquetage* had been tossed out of the window? It seemed a mystery, and as much as we sought for the reason he had allowed us such a peaceful night, we could find none.

Perhaps he was saving surprises for us until Christmas Eve, which was approaching, when instead of the *paquetages* being thrown out of the window, it would be the beds, *or the recruits themselves*!

The next day, whilst engaged on the routine of potato-peeling, having returned from our morning instruction, I was informed by a corporal that I was to report to the office of the sergeant who had carried out the previous evening's inspection. It appeared that I was about to pay for the previous night and would probably be formally charged for the room's having been in disorder (my book lying on the bed). I duly arrived at his office and, for someone with so little service, presented myself well.

'*Légionnaire Worden, matricule cent trente mille, zero trente un, deux mois de service, à vos ordres, sergeant.*' ('Legionnaire Worden, number 130,031, two months service, at your disposition, sergeant.') This whilst standing rigidly at attention, and for someone with the limited French I had, getting the mouth around that lot, two months after leaving Paris, I thought was handling it well.

He said only, 'Relax, Johnny.' He then handed me two books and told me that, if I was going to make a career in the Legion, I would find it better to study these books than that which I already had. The books he gave me were rare indeed – normally, I believe, issued only to officers in the French Army. And both published by the French War Ministry: '*Glossaire militaire de langue anglais*' (*Military Glossary in English/French*), and '*Lexique militaire français/anglais*' (*A Military Lexicon in French/English*). To say I was surprised would have been the understatement of all time.

And I had learned yet another lesson. Ignore all bloody rumours and gossip and judge all by your own impressions, even if these impressions are wrong. What he had given me were the means of compensating for my lack of physical ability in comparison with all the super athletes. And although those books did not make me a military genius, they certainly made life in the Legion a great deal easier. They served me well. They were read and studied as avidly as a priest will read his Bible. For a long time after, I pondered on whether it was possible that this sergeant was human. He was not. The moron blotted his copybook with me later, when I received the hardest kick up the rear ever and *fifty* push-ups, only because he caught me smoking when, and where, I should not have been. Again my own fault really – not for smoking but for the first time allowing myself to be caught. The sneaky bastard had crept up on me.

Frequent visits were made to Saida by officers of the Legion

parachute regiments. It was obvious that their visits were for the
sole purpose of finding the *crème de la crème* of all recruits
undergoing instruction. Recruits were not delegated or
designated for these 'elite' regiments. Those who proved to be
of outstanding athletic ability (it mattered not if they did not
have any brains!) were invited – really, invited? – to join the
Para, on completion of their basic instruction.

I damn near busted a gut in a vain attempt to keep up with
those supermen I had the misfortune to have in my platoon, in
my effort to be on the selection list of those budding
parachutists. I had also worked so hard on improving my
French that I even impressed on the representatives of the Para
regiments that a willing volunteer was surely much better than a
reluctant Olympic sprinter. All I received for my efforts was that
I should consider myself stupid for thinking that I could jump
out of aeroplanes with these 'young lions'. I finally had to resign
myself to the fact that I would find myself in the infantry.

I had been neither stupid nor heroic in my efforts to join the
Para. I had reasoned that the Para would jump into action if not
on top of the enemy, at least reasonably close, and the only
marching would be to their transport at an agreed rendezvous
point, or perhaps they would even be taken out by helicopters.
Certainly a lot better than the infantry, who would have to
march both in and out. Perhaps I had spent too much time
watching Hollywood films. I had visions of parachuting into
combat, wiping out a dozen of the enemy and after the combat
(not more than twenty minutes) lounging around with my
fellow parachutists, awaiting an officer's call on the radio for a
helicopter to fly us back to base, where I'd get decorated by the
colonel. Then it would be out into the fleshpots of the town, for
a night out with the girls. It was an evil satisfaction that I later
derived when I learnt that the Para made very few jumps into
combat and, like us in the infantry, did a hell of a lot of
marching. Served the bastards right. 'Young lions' indeed!

It was exactly four months to the day when we ended our
training at Saida. By some miracle we had been changed from a
motley ragtaggle bunch of non-French-speaking civilians into
some semblance of legionnaires.

Our close order drill may not have matched that of the Guards
at Buckingham Palace but we could have held our own with any

other regiment of the British Army.

There was not a man who had completed his training who could not put ten shots out of ten into a target one square metre in size, at 400 metres distance – naturally not into the bull. I would not have been prepared to stand still at a distance of 400 metres and allow any of them to take even a single shot at me, not even my Spanish companion. Maybe for a million pounds I would have been prepared to do it, but I would have had to have thought about it for a time. As a matter of fact, I would have had to think about it for a very long time.

There was not one of those who had finished their training who could not hit a silhouette target at fifty metres, whilst shooting from the hip, with at least three shots out of six with the very good PM49. (This weapon was a 9mm-calibre automatic pistol, far superior to the British sten.)

All these ex-recruits, even when blindfolded and spun around, until all sense of direction was lost, could accurately aim at a tin can with stones in it that had been tossed at random to a distance of twenty metres, and with only the sound of the tin landing to guide them to the target. They may not have hit the can, but they would certainly have frightened the life out of it.

All these ex-recruits could now do this. Those who could not would not be leaving with us but would continue training with a newer platoon – which was tough! As a matter of fact, very tough.

We had now all become trained *voltigeurs*, a word best translated as 'footsloggers'. But at least we were now able to call ourselves 'legionnaires'.

Prior to leaving Saida, I heard a rumour that all Legion sergeants responsible for training a platoon of recruits who had all completed their final training examination successfully were automatically granted double pay and six months rest and recuperation at a nursing home on the Côte d'Azur.

I had been selected by the other recruits in the platoon to present to our own chief sergeant a silver Dupont lighter (the contributions had been purely voluntary) as a token of his ability to create miracles – well, at least thirty-four out of forty. As I shook hands with this shaking wreck of a man who had devoted four months of his life to trying to teach forty donkeys, I noticed that he had changed during the preceding four months. He had become noticeably thinner, developed more lines on his face and had the suggestion of a nervous twitch. He had done a hell of a good job and had increased my determination that there were two things I would have to remember: one, never to become a sergeant; two, under no circumstances ever to become an instructor. I did have one thing in my favour that would prevent my qualifying as a sergeant: I was not illegitimate.

I had made many mistakes during basic training. Perhaps the most elementary and near disastrous was that which I made on the first route march of any distance.

It was only twenty-five kilometres, but the consistent drizzle of rain and the treacherous underfoot conditions of the thick red mud, causing me to slip and slide, were nothing to the burning sensation in my feet. In my ignorance, I had declined to wear the thick army socks with which I had been issued and had put on my feet my civilian nylon socks. All the lectures by the instructors on the care of one's feet, of the importance of washing them not in hot water but in cold, and that, even after a hot shower, one must ensure that the feet would be further rinsed with cold water: all this I had ignored, and I was paying the penalty before the march was halfway completed.

I ended that march with my feet bleeding from blisters that had burst, and then the friction of nylon against raw flesh, caused an agony almost indescribable. The utter relief when we finally entered the barracks, and the sight of my feet when I removed my boots, made me swear an oath that never again would I disregard advice from those who were far more experienced than I in the art of survival.

I could not remove my nylon socks in the normal fashion, I had to remove them by immersion in hot water (which caused more pain) and soak them off. The doctoring of the unburst blisters by a veteran legionnaire, by puncturing with a needle and thread through both sides of the blisters, cutting off the needle and leaving the threads trailing as drainage, had been standard practice for a hundred years. It still worked. By the Monday morning, feeling very grateful that Sunday had been a day of rest, my self-inflicted wounds were almost healed. Never did I make a similar mistake.

Instruction now completed, we were assembled for our final parade at Saida and informed of our destinations. As I heard the destinations and names being called, seven to the parachute training school, these to that regiment, those to this regiment, I became concerned when all names had been called with the exception of a Belgian legionnaire's and mine. I began to suspect that I would be held back for further training, until much to my relief my own name was called: Sidi-bel-Abbès and specialist training. My relief turned to shock. It was like standing outside the gates of Heaven, taking a step forward and finding yourself in Hell. I would have settled for the infantry. I'd have settled for anything, even a transfer to the Salvation Army, rather than that bastion of the Legion, Sidi-bel-Abbès.

The stories I had been told by many veteran legionnaires of its discipline and regimentation, and of its being a short-cut to the road heading for 'Company Discipline', the 'Penal Battalion' and even 'Devil's Island', and all the other places they had seen at the cinema, for failing to salute even a sergeant 200 metres away, did nothing to make me feel anything less than dejected. I was not a young boy easily influenced by stories exaggerated out of all proportion to the truth, but a doubt was nagging my mind as I recalled the favourite expression of my granny, 'Where there's smoke, there's fire.' Sidi-bel-Abbès was decidedly not my idea of 'home from home'.

With the regularity of Sunday arriving each week, we had all listened to the monotonous chant of the Legion 'Creed', which is inscribed indelibly on the hearts and in the minds of all Legion recruits, not only for the remainder of their service but for the rest of their lives. This Creed is *La Base de la Discipline*. '*La discipline étant la force principle des armées, il importe que tout supérieur obtienne de ses subordonnés une obéissance de tous les instants, que les ordres soient exécutés instantanément sans hésitation, ni murmure. L'autorité qui donne en est responsable, et la réclamation n'est permise à l'inferieur que lorsqu'il obéi.*'

For those reading this who have not served in the Legion, the prime and essential content of *La Base de la Discipline* is simple to understand: 'Any order received from a superior … be it right, wrong, a cock-up or a balls-up, shall be carried out 'without question or complaint.' Should an order be found at a later date to have been an error of judgment or outside the scope of the issuing authority, if the legionnaire involved is not dead in trying to execute or extricate himself from an impossible situation, only after he has carried out the order can he make redress to a high authority, in which case, the fact that he is still alive will give the lie to the fact that the order was stupid, and he will merit the award of the nominal eight days in the prison, for frivolous complaint.

With those words still echoing in my mind, there was the knowledge that I was heading for the place, not only where they practised it but without doubt where they bloody invented it. (I was also remembering, in another time, another place, a certain commanding officer writing on my personnel record, 'A good officer, but NOT amenable to discipline'. When I was required to initial it as being read, he had become annoyed at my 'Get stuffed!') I was definitely on my way to disaster.

Only on my arrival at Sidi-bel-Abbès did I find that, regardless of the fact that I had repeatedly requested that, if I could not be accepted into a parachute regiment, I be allowed to function as an infantry soldier, in their infinite wisdom the Legion had designated me to the most frustrating job I could think of. I was to be trained as a radio mechanic and potential instructor.

The most moving event that took place at Saida was my first Christmas in the Foreign Legion. I was not prepared, nor was I conversant with the traditional way in which Christmas is celebrated in the Legion, and I was taken completely unawares. The overture of Christmas Eve began in the normal way of any other day, and routine seemed unchanged, but for some unknown reason there was an air of excitement and almost bubbling enthusiasm among the young German members of my platoon. Much to my surprise, all instruction ceased at ten in the morning, and we returned to the barracks, then went direct to the kitchen for the normal potato-peeling. But even this was different. The cooks in their spotless white kitchen uniforms and tall white hats – even one with the gold stripes of a sergeant glistening on his arms – with happy smiles on their faces, suddenly appeared with large soup tureens filled to the brim with hot, sweetened wine and a whole basket of glasses manufactured from empty Kronenborg beer bottles, urging us to drink and enjoy the day. It was a most welcome gift on that wintry morning, with the first snowflakes falling from the sky. We were then told to report to the company office to be paid – a week early! After receiving our pay, we dismissed for the day, but we were to assemble in the dining-room in walking-out dress uniform at nine o'clock that evening. Meanwhile the dining-room was strictly out of bounds to all legionnaires.

For the first time we consumed our midday meal in our own rooms, after which it became apparent that a dozen German lads had seemingly vanished into thin air. I was at that time in the depths of despondency, even at my age feeling homesick and very lonely, thinking only of my folks back home and wishing that I had never left, so I occupied myself in writing a letter to my parents, telling them of the wonderful life and joy of being a legionnaire, all the time feeling the most miserable slob in the world and indulging in self-pity.

Nine o'clock in the evening was the normal time for lights out to be sounded by the bugler, but I had by this time discovered that the evening's supper was traditional not only to the Legion but for the French population. Still wallowing in self-pity, by attempting surreptitious bribing of my corporal, I tried to be excused the evening event, to no avail.

We were not marched to the dining-room but drifted there in small groups, immaculately attired in our newly pressed uniforms, as if wandering to some elaborate social gathering.

I found difficulty in believing my eyes on entering. The tables had been arranged in a large U shape, with beautiful white linen table-cloths, adorned with shining glasses, cutlery and plates. As straight as legionnaires on parade, the centres of the table were lined with bottles of wine, champagne and beer. A stage had been erected, and a crèche had been constructed in the corner with more care, attention to detail and devotion than any I had seen in my own church in London. The whole room was ablaze with light, with Christmas decorations festooning it. The walls were decorated with carefully painted posters on which were Christmas greetings in a dozen languages, the largest of which, suspended over the stage, read 'Merry Christmas' in English.

We were greeted upon our entrance by the captain and other officers, with a handshake and the murmured greeting in the recruit's own language of 'Happy Christmas'. Even the sergeants were lined up waiting to shake hands, greeting me with big smiles, as if the bastards had been using my arse as a football only in the line of duty. Christmas being Christmas, I forgave them all and shook hands.

Lobster and turkey in the Foreign Legion? They were cooked to perfection. I enjoyed a cigar presented to me by the most feared German sergeant at the base, the one who had given me the hardest kick up my butt. Then the entertainment began. Legionnaires were being invited – repeat, invited – to the stage to sing in their own language. As I sat puffing on my cigar listening to a Neapolitan giving a rendering of 'Sorrento', with tears in his eyes even before arriving at *'Vide mare quanta bella'*, I found I had lost my self-pity and no longer felt homesick.

I damn near swallowed my cigar as the young German recruits in my platoon began calling 'Johnny – Tipperary.' It had been this group, along with the sergeants, who had spent most of the day preparing the dining-room. Somewhat reluctantly, I mounted the stage, and commenced singing. On my way to the stage I had fully intended to sing 'Tipperary', but to their surprise, and to mine – and it was meant as a thank-you to all of them – what came to my lips was

Vor der Kaserne, vor dem grossen Tor,
Stand ein' Laterne und steht sie noch davor,
So woll'n wir da uns wiedersehen
Bei der Laterne woll'n wir steh'n
Wie einst Lili Marlene, wie einst Lili Marlene.

By the time I finished the song, they had all joined in, singing their heads off, all convinced I had learned the song in German for their entertainment, none of them aware that it had also been the song of 114 Squadron during the war and that I was far more familiar with it than with 'Tipperary'.

After the entertainment came the distribution of Christmas presents. Each legionnaire received a gift handed to him by the captain. The gifts themselves provided further shock, for there was nothing cheap or shoddy. Some received watches, and very good watches, with the faces inscribed *'Légion Etrangère*; a couple received small portable radios. I found a first-class sleepingbag, lightweight, red in colour, of oiled silk and kapok stuffing, a much valued gift to take to the mountains.

At midnight the solemn voices of all in the room joined in 'Silent Night', all singing this most moving hymn in German, the language in which it had first been written.

As we sang this carol at midnight on Christmas Eve 1959, uncontrollable tears streamed from my eyes, and I felt ashamed, until on looking around to see if my emotional outburst had been observed, I saw that it was not only I who was trying to blink away tears, but that all, including the hardbitten veteran NCOs, were busy doing the same.

After the party I returned to my room, destroyed the letter I had written home and by the light of a candle composed another.

I may have left a family in Britain, but I had found another in the Legion. Throughout the remainder of my service, although I felt concern and compassion for my parents, wrote regular monthly letters and sent presents on birthdays and other festive occasions, I never again felt the pangs of homesickness. My Legion education was continuing.

3 Awakening and Reality at Sidi-bel-Abbès

I arrived at Sidi-bel-Abbès determined that, now I had completed my basic training, there would be no way I would allow myself to be subjected to the humiliation I had experienced on my first arrival.

I was informed by the powers that be in the transit company that the training course for which I had been designated would not start for some two weeks. I was a '*bleu*', a novice legionnaire, and as such I realized that I would be carrying out every dirty job and fatigue duty whilst waiting for my new training to commence. However, I was lucky in more than one respect.

I had been assigned to the *Petit Quartier*, which was not part of the main barracks at Bel-Abbès. Nor was I billeted in the recruits' barrack block. It was with a sigh of relief that I found my *chambre* (barrack room) to be part of a newly built single-storey complex, painted white, with all Mod Cons at the end of the block. The whole complex being surrounded with flower beds with flowers in full bloom and an abundance of brilliant colours, complete with a small pond containing goldfish. Adjacent to this picturesque setting was a small parade ground that doubled as a volley ball court for recreation.

The room itself was bright and cheerful-looking, spoilt only by the fact that the beds were double tiered, which, when they were fully occupied, would mean at least forty men in the room. However, after my stay at the antiquated barracks at Saida, this room appeared first class and almost luxurious. Happily, it was only forty per cent occupied.

I had received immediately on arrival at the transit company my *prime*, a bonus for successful completion of basic instruction. This amounted to the equivalent of some £75. At the same time, the paymaster had returned to me the £150 I had on advice deposited for safe keeping prior to my departure for Saida. It was only when I had it returned to me that I realized that it had not been a question of safeguarding the money but to ensure that I did not bribe fellow recruits, with either beer or cigarettes, to undertake any onerous fatigues on my behalf. The advantages that a few hundred extra francs would have offered whilst carrying out basic training would certainly have made life a lot easier. With the cash received from the paymaster, in legionnaire terms, I was a wealthy man.

The corporal in charge of my room, who was also an instructor in radio telegraphy, though dismayed by the fact that I would not be one of his pupils, gave me a choice of fatigue duties for the following two weeks: hygiene detail (this, I was fully aware, meant shit-house cleaning), *planton* detail (this meant general run-about to and from the main barracks as messenger boy) or kitchen detail in the cookhouse in the *petit quartier*. Not being quite an idiot and having developed a ravenous appetite after four months strenuous exercise, it cost me only half a dozen beers to be assigned to the kitchen. This was how I met the astute and enterprising Brockman and heard an amazing story that, if it had not been for the fact that the dates and places were factual, would have stretched the credibility of a wide-eyed twelve-year-old schoolboy.

The chief corporal overseeing the kitchen fatigue squad was in his early forties, obviously of German origin and, although not quite corpulent, had equally obviously been indulging in the good things of life during the preceding couple of years. He was also wearing on his uniform the two inverted gold stripes denoting that he had already served more than ten years service. There was little doubt in my mind that he had merited his present job, and all the extra beefsteaks and wine that must surely have been going his way.

His knowledge of the English language was far superior to my knowledge and ability in French. When, in answer to his probing questions, he learned that I had served with the British forces during the war and had been in the Western Desert, he decided that my only work would be that of helping him improve his English. Even when I told him that I had been flying with the Desert Air Force and spent most of my time bombing the shit out of him and his fellow Germans, he just roared with laughter, and we became the best of friends.

I was plied with cigarettes, wine and sandwiches during our conversations in the English language, and Brockman recounted his story. I had difficulty at first in believing that it had been possible for an individual during the Second World War to have served during the first three years of hostilities under the French-German and British flags and then in 1945 to have rejoined the Legion, but he had.

At the outbreak of hostilities in 1939, he had been serving with the Legion's 6th Regiment of Infantry in Syria. With the collapse of France in 1940, it became the policy of the Legion to terminate the contracts of German, Italian and British legionnaires, allowing them to return to their homelands as best they might if they so wished. This Brockman did. However, on arrival in Germany, he and his Legion comrades were not welcomed with flags waving and bands playing. On the contrary, they were imprisoned for having served with the Legion.

Some few months later the German authorities decided that these ex-legionnaires, with their considerable desert experience, could be utilized in the Western Desert in support of the Italian troops engaged at that time against British and Commonwealth troops. So was formed the nucleus of the 361st Infantry Panzer Regiment, of which two battalions exclusively comprised ex-legionnaires. On their arrival in Libya, they were not thrust into action but engaged as pioneer troops at the port of Tripoli.

As Brockman described it, the ships were unloaded for their Italian allies, with typical Legion efficiency: one case for the Italians, one case for the 361st. (If it happened to be wine, one case for the Italians, two cases for the 361st.) He told me that he was never sure if the 361st were given combat status and sent to the desert because of the loss of stores from the ships and harbour and the complaints from the Italians or because of the rapid advances of the British on Tobruk, Derna and Benghazi. Whatever the reason, the 361st (with him as part of the 2nd Company) went into action completely equipped with captured British transport, their heaviest weapons being mortars and heavy-calibre machine-guns.

By October 1941, he had been promoted to sergeant, wounded and taken a prisoner of war. From the time of his being wounded, he was not aware of his whereabouts nor the fact that he was a prisoner until he regained consciousness at the 13th General Hospital, near Shallufa, on the western side of the Great Bitter Lake. From there he was sent to the POW camp at Kasfareet. (It was his knowledge of the hospital and of Kasfareet that had led him to tell me his story. During the same month, October 1941, I was at the same hospital having treatment for a leg wound – not received in action.)

Within six months of being taken prisoner and with the natural instinct for avoiding hard work that he had developed in the Legion, Brockman had secured for himself an office job, as interpreter. With his knowledge of the German Army, his fluency in both French and English, the fact that he had been imprisoned in Germany on his return from the Legion, and his declaration that he was not a member of the Nazi Party, he managed to persuade the minions of the intelligence branch and inspired confidence in his interrogation officers. He found he had been recruited by one Captain Buck for clandestine operations with one of the long-range desert groups of the British Army. He told me that escape from Kasfareet would have been impossible. Only by stealing an airplane would it have been possible to reach German lines and there were no pilots at Kasfareet. His recruitment was a means to get out of the POW camp, and then see what happened.

On 12 June 1942, there was an attack on Derna Airfield by a small group of the long-range desert group. Two trucks were commanded by a Captain Bray, with a mixture of British-French and Palestinian men and including my new friend Brockman. He was in the truck commanded by a French officer, which was to attack the headquarters building and barracks. The other truck, commanded by Captain Bray, was to attack the aircraft dispersed on the airfield. So they separated.

Since Brockman was familiar with airfield facilities and had been blessed by the British with the rank of sergeant, he was detailed to carry out a reconnaissance alone and on foot. This was the moment when he made his decision and took the opportunity of returning to his regiment. The only semi-illumination was from the control tower which Brockman found unguarded. He entered the control room and politely informed the duty officer that the British had arrived, intent on destroying the airfield and aircraft. (It was somewhere at this point in his story that Brockman could not restrain himself from laughing as he recalled the panic of the duty officer.) Alarmed, somewhat hesitant and damn near pissing himself with fright, the duty officer raised the alarm and then, as Brockman described, frightened the life out of him by waving a loaded and cocked pistol in his face, held in a hand that was trembling with either excitement or fear.

The whole attack was thwarted and Brockman said that regrettably there were only three survivors, all wounded and shipped to hospital. He himself returned to the 361st and was decorated by Rommel for his part in the action. He was later shipped to Tunis on garrison duties, as it was considered too dangerous for him to have any further chance of being captured.

At the time of telling me of his adventures, Brockman was quite concerned because I was making brief notes, and he made me promise that I would not write about him until at least 1966, when he would have completed twenty years service and departed for other places. He was deeply concerned that his name would have been included in a list of war criminals. I told him that I thought this most unlikely, since a mess-up like this, that had been made by the British, would usually be swept under the carpet.

I began writing the story about Brockman in 1965, whilst serving with the 2nd Regiment of Parachutists. I had become friendly with an *adjudant-chef** who had had a distinguished career with the Luftwaffe in the Western Desert, flying fighters. During one of our discussions, I told him the story as I had heard it from Brockman. The *adjudant-chef* looked somewhat startled, then rose from his chair, produced a bottle of scotch from his locker and said, 'We had better have a very strong drink. Then I'll tell you the end of his story.' This is it.

'The night in question is very easy to recall, for a celebration birthday party was being held in the officers' mess and I was one of the officers celebrating. We received a panic signal from the control tower, and the party was temporarily suspended whilst the attack was dealt with – less than thirty minutes. We continued the party and were joined by a very scruffy individual

---

* To help the reader *adjudant-chef* has been left in the original French as the nearest translation of this rank is Warrant Officer (Class I).

wearing British battledress and an Arab headdress. This must have been ''your'' Brockman, but we were never given details.'

The *adjudant-chef* had no idea that Brockman had served in the Legion, either before or after the war, but assured me that, when he next went to France, he would look him up. He did.

It was during my first two weeks at Bel-Abbès, and whilst Brockman was telling me the story of his adventures, that he told me there were several British legionnaires on permanent duty at the Petit Quartier, two of them corporals and good friends of his. In fact, they were more than good friends, they were also drinking companions. He told me where to find them and allowed me to disappear from the kitchen to search them out and introduce myself.

Brockman had made a mistake. Only one was British, Jim Sinclair, a Scot. The other was Donald Thomas, an American ex-marine from Los Angeles. For the following four months at Sidi-bel-Abbès, these two very astute individuals, wise in the ways of the Legion, taught me every trick I had not already learnt in the art of avoiding dirty details.

The first thing they taught me was that in the township of Bel-Abbès there was one special bar that for many years had been a regular meeting-place and rendezvous for all British legionnaires passing through Bel-Abbès. This bar even provided a small board for messages to be attached, allowing one to keep in touch with various English-speaking acquaintances. This was the 'Foot' bar (the 'foot' being an abbreviation of 'football') and the regular meeting-place for the members of the Sidi-bel-Abbès professional football team. (It was only much later that I discovered that Jim Sinclair augmented his Legion pay by playing for this team, and indeed supplemented his income very well.)

Jim and I struck an immediate empathy, perhaps because, like myself, he suffered from that curse of almost complete baldness whilst still a young man. He had joined the Legion in 1957, when the slaughter at Dien Bien Phu was still the main topic of conversation. He was a traditional Scot from Glasgow, very dour, with a dry and sardonic sense of humour, a fairly tall man and a dedicated sportsman and athlete.

Jim's job at Sidi-bel-Abbès was twofold. His somewhat amazing athletic prowess had ensured that he had more or less automatically become a parachutist and at the same time been selected for corporal's training. His duties comprised being an instructor in unarmed combat and a representative of the Legion in the military pentathlon that was held each year. Although the forthcoming event, for which he was in serious training, would be his first, he and the rest of the team at the *Salle de Sport* seemed to live a life of complete freedom, occupied only with keeping themselves in peak physical condition, with exercise and the very special diets provided by the kitchen, supervised by Brockman. Their staple diet seemed to be large, succulent beefsteaks and vast quantities of milk.

It took me only a very short time to arrange that my permanent fatigue whilst at Bel-Abbès would be that of delivering the food for this super band of athletes, ensuring that my good friend Brockman always included an extra ration for myself.

Jim Sinclair was in the prime of his life, at the magic age of thirty. Not only did we become very good friends but he helped me in many ways by allowing me the facilities of the gymnasium and also devoting a lot of his free time – when we were not drinking together – to being my own private physical training instructor. He taught me unarmed combat and the art of knife fighting.

Fighting another man with a short bayonet, particularly one that has been specially sharpened for the express purpose of sliding into the ribs of another, is not in my opinion either entertainment or sport, but it appeared that all these parachutist instructors at the *Salle de Sport* considered it a healthy exercise and a means of keeping fit! It took only a few weeks for me to find that, although Jim and I had become very good friends, he and all his colleagues were very serious about this very specialized means of disposing of an enemy. As far as any of them was concerned, any man facing them with a knife or bayonet was their deadliest enemy, even though they may have been drinking a beer with him the previous evening. It was inevitable that the more skilled I became, the faster the action. Subsequently it became most embarrassing to find myself reporting to the hospital to have a four-inch knife slash in my left arm cleaned and stitched.

I discovered that my troubles had only just begun. The

adjudant in charge of the hospital had some doubt that I had received this wound whilst undergoing instruction and was convinced that it had been inflicted during a real fight. He had even greater difficulty in understanding how an Englishman, even though a legionnaire, could resort to fighting with knives. It required telephone calls to the *Salle de Sport* to confirm that I had indeed been injured during training.

The *adjudant* then demanded what kind of specialized training I was undertaking that involved hand-to-hand knife fighting. With my explanation that the instruction was of a private nature and only for my own benefit and at my own request, he took great pleasure in awarding me four days extra duties. He even explained the reasons for the extra duties: for being old enough to have more sense, for being too slow in getting out of the way and for wasting his time. In the normal course of events the sewing-up of my arm would have required an entry in official documentation, in which case an investigation would have been instituted which would have resulted in someone (probably myself) being awarded eight days prison.

Perhaps one of the reasons for this leniency was that, although at that time the total number of legionnaires in Algeria was almost 25,000, among that number were no more than fifty Englishmen. Therefore an Englishman was not only a rarity in the Legion but a bloody wonder insofar as he had not deserted! This was probably why the British were seemingly far more tolerated for eccentric behaviour than men of any other nationality.

Although Jim Sinclair and I remained very good friends, it came as no surprise to him that I had lost my enthusiasm to become an expert exponent in the art of knife fighting.

So I settled to the routine life at GILE (Groupement d'Instruction Légion Etrangère). The initial two weeks had passed very quickly and I found myself, along with five other novice legionnaires, allocated to a training cadre with the express purpose of becoming expert radio men. The working day of lectures and practical instruction did not commence until eight o'clock in the morning, (surprisingly after the activity of basic instruction). Reveille was at six o'clock, but for morning sport – which can only be described as static calisthenics for a duration of only some twenty minutes – the instructor was the corporal in charge of our room, who seemed determined that the less effort we made would also ensure that his own participation would also be minimal and not in the least strenuous. In fact, our morning sport required so little effort that, despite the fact that I disliked over-exertion, I had no option but to jog around the barracks each evening to maintain at least some part of the degree of fitness achieved at basic instruction.

Our classroom instruction commenced each morning at eight o'clock. The six of us selected for this specialist training would march smartly from our quarters to our allocated lecture room. (We had made the mistake the first morning of casually strolling to it, smoking and relaxed. We were accosted by a sergeant at least a hundred metres away who delighted himself for some twenty minutes having us run, crawl on our stomachs and demonstrate at least a hundred push-ups, and then escorted us to our first day of lectures on our hands and knees, with the recommendation that we be confined to barracks for at least a month. This was for our failure to salute the idiot.)

None of us undergoing this instruction had French as a natural language, and our instructor, a young lieutenant who by profession and prior to conscription had been a teacher of mathematics and radio theory in Paris, had little sympathy for our limitations with the language. During the first week we listened to an almost incomprehensible flow of rapidfire French, during which I gave up any notion of attempting to understand his lectures on the theory of radio and occupied my time with taking of copious notes on the language which flowed continuously from his lips like water from a tap under extreme pressure. We listened to his flow of words, all of us nodding our heads in the affirmative, although none of us had any idea of the subject under discussion. But then, fortunately, he would proceed to set certain mathematical problems on the blackboard that none of us had any difficulty in solving, and our correct solutions must have led him to believe that we had all fully understood the subject. This poor young man was not technically a Legion officer, but was attached to the Legion for the duration of his conscription, carrying out exactly the same function as that which he had been fulfilling in Paris. He even seemed embarrassed when we saluted him, but since he appeared to be satisfied with our correct answers, and since we were allowed to smoke during his lectures, we were all very attentive pupils. It was surprising that, once I had become accustomed to the inflexions of our instructor's voice and the constant repetition of sentences, although at the end of the four months my knowledge of radio theory had not improved one iota, my ability with the French language had rapidly progressed.

At the completion of our instruction, this lieutenant allowed us to study the final examination papers a week prior to the examination taking place. He became quite despondent after the test to discover that I had hopelessly failed to qualify. Yet he failed to realize that, short of being provided with the correct answers to the final test, there had always existed the possibility that I might have accidentally qualified and found myself permanently among the furniture and fittings of Sidi-bel-Abbès, the last place on earth at which I wished to continue my Legion service. For the next six years this young lieutenant always had my sincere thanks.

The afternoons were devoted to practical demonstrations of all types of radio equipment utilized by the Legion, all of American and British manufacture and used extensively during the Second World War. My greatest difficulty was attempting to feign complete ignorance of the equipment, which was quite difficult since, during my service with the British forces, I had qualified as a skilled radio operator and was more than familiar with most of the types. The *adjudant* responsible for the afternoon instruction even provided me with the original manuals for the equipment printed in English. It therefore became quite difficult as time progressed to demonstrate continuously a lack of comprehension. However, I was more than determined that, whatever the cost of failure, there was no way I was going to qualify and spend the remaining years at Bel-Abbès.

I was again fortunate that this *adjudant* was tolerant. He had served in the German Army during the war and then with the Legion in Indo China, where, during the fighting at Dien Bien Phu, he had had the misfortune to lose an eye. This, however, in no way affected his service with the Legion and, as I was to find out during the latter part of the training, he was a damn sight better marksman than most legionnaires with two eyes.

Conditional to the novice legionnaire abiding by the normal formalities of the Legion and at least attempting to carry out the duties allocated to him (if not with a happy smile, at least without reluctance), one could expect a minimal amount of 'bullshit' and quite a considerable amount of humour. However, as time progressed, it became clear that it was also wise to avoid close association with veterans, particularly if they had been celebrating too well and unwisely during a lunch-time drinking session, for then they would unload any frustrations on the nearest legionnaire in the vicinity, who would find himself sleeping in the cells as a punishment for breathing. The next day the *adjudant* would be completely unaware that he had even inflicted the punishment.

I had already learnt my lesson at Bel-Abbès, for on many occasions I escaped prison only by the skin of my teeth. I found myself allocated so many extra fatigues and spent so much time sweeping the roads through the barracks with a palm frond* that my face was becoming over-familiar to many of the permanent *sous-officiers* and some were becoming convinced that my permanent duty was that of official road-sweeper. Because of the continual fatigues, after six weeks at this citadel of the Legion I had managed to visit the town on only two occasions and had disposed of very little of the surplus funds I had available.

It was then that I made a point of saluting everything and everyone at Bel-Abbès. If it had a black kepi, it was saluted, even if it was in the far distance. If a sergeant laughed, I would laugh. If he cried, I would also cry. Most of all though, I practised the art of camouflage. Anyone wearing a black kepi, I would treat as an enemy trying to shoot me. I would blend into the background, melt into the wilderness or disappear into the nearest toilet or washroom. It took me almost two months at Bel-Abbès before I managed to get through a whole week without being allocated an extra duty or fatigue, and then I decided to celebrate the event by inviting Jim, Donald and Brockman out for the evening at their favourite bar. It was a very enjoyable evening, spoilt only by the fact that on returning to my room I failed to report to

* Brushes and brooms were denied those on punishment detail. Palm fronds were very spiky and made the hands very sore. Which was the whole point of the exercise.

my own section duty sergeant, since at the time he was absent from his office. With a large grin, the bastard later gave me four days back on road sweeping, with the full knowledge that, if I had waited until his return, I would have been absent from bed check, which would have resulted in eight days in the cells. Even by that time I had reached the conclusion that, during the training of sergeants in the Foreign Legion, they are fully indoctrinated that in their dealings with legionnaires under their command their first and foremost maxim is that of 'Heads I win – tails you lose!' and that when presented with their sergeant's stripes, they receive the command that they must ensure they assist at least one legionnaire a day in the direction of the cells.

It was whilst at Sidi-bel-Abbès that I participated in my first combat operation. I was surprised to find that there were occasions, indeed many occasions when the whole of the 1st Regiment engaged on these operations, designated as rapid interception groups. It was a complete contrast to the monotony of the lecture rooms, and I was happy to learn from the *adjudant* that I would be included in his combat section as his bodyguard and radio operator. He was prepared to accept my limitations with the French language during any transmissions, in the hope that this would be compensated by the fact that, should any shooting incident take place, at least I would have sense enough not to panic or shoot him by mistake.

I took part in at least three of the standard operations at Bel-Abbès, with the monotony of the classroom replaced by the monotony of a steady twelve hours stomping through the forests, hills and small mountains, terminating in complete weariness and exhaustion and not hearing a shot fired in anger, convinced that the Algerian rebels had all departed to Morocco or Tunisia on vacation and had failed to inform the Legion of this fact.

During my period as bodyguard and protector of my *adjudant*, I had just proffered him a light for his cigarette when a bullet, presumably fired with evil intent, suddenly impacted the ground between our legs, which caused me to disregard completely my function and throw myself to the ground, seeking shelter behind the nearest pebble, leaving the *adjudant*, with his wealth of experience, to determine from which direction the shot had been fired. It was quite embarrassing to find that, once my heart had regained its rightful place in my chest, the *adjudant*, with his pistol in his hand, was more or less standing over me in a protective position. It was even more embarrassing to learn that the shot fired had come not from the enemy but from a fellow legionnaire. This idiot had not placed the safety catch of his semi-automatic rifle on the 'safe' position, and it had been accidentally discharged in his effort to remove the top from a bottle of beer by using his trigger guard as a bottle-opener.

In the normal course of events, this kind of *incident de tir* would have resulted in eight days prison for the culprit. However, the *adjudant* (who had been highly amused at my dereliction of duty and very impressed with the speed with which I had arrived at the horizontal position) did nothing but deliver a mouthful of abuse to the poor idiot and then demonstrated other parts of his rifle that could equally serve as a bottle-opener and which were a lot safer. He took no further action against the culprit.

However, he did punish me. He awarded me eight extra days duties, which once again ensured that my evenings were occupied with road sweeping. As he explained, the punishment was not for my neglect in guarding his body, nor for my speed in taking evasive action. He was quite fatherly as he explained that the terrain we were traversing was flat and devoid of protective cover. If that shot had in fact been fired by the enemy, then even I with my limited experience should have realized that it would have been fired from higher ground. He then emphasized that a standing man at a distance of anything from two to three hundred metres, when being fired at from a higher point, is a target much more difficult to hit than some idiot lying flat on his face on the ground and not in a position to return fire. Being fully aware that this veteran had already won the *Légion d'Honneur*, along with at least half a dozen other awards for bravery, I listened wih respect and absorbed interest, and thanked him for both the advice and the eight days extra duties. Nevertheless during my future service with a combat regiment, although I remembered his lecture and advice, my natural instinct for self-preservation had me dropping to one knee at the first sound of shots being fired, whether or not they were aimed in my direction.

The *adjudant* also emphasized that it was far more honourable to receive a head or chest wound than a bullet up the arse. It was his contention that a bullet wound in the arse would not result in the award of a medal, only in eating standing for a couple of months.

I had already attended the first Camerone ceremonial parade at the Monument aux Morts in the Caserne Vienot on 30 April 1960, whose impact had a lasting effect on the rest of my Legion service. It is the most important anniversary in the Legion calendar commemorating the formidable courage of legionnaires during the Mexican battle in 1863. It was now approaching 14 July, Bastille Day, the last ceremonial parade prior to my departure for my designated combat regiment, the 3rd Regiment of Infantry.

Donald Thomas was an American ex-marine who had served in Korea and had enlisted in the Legion during the latter part of 1957. On completion of his basic training he had been sent directly to corporals' training school. To his utter disgust he received his stripes and found himself assigned as a permanent fixture at Sidi-bel-Abbès as a small weapons instructor, demonstrating to and instructing not novice legionnaires but senior sergeants and chief sergeants undergoing instruction at BA II, without which no senior NCO can become an *adjudant*. His specialities were the US lightweight carbine, the M16, and the MP 38/40, the sten gun and the British Lee Enfield rifle, many of which were widely used by the Algerian rebels and all of which had been captured.

Donald did not appreciate his sinecure at Bel-Abbès, a room to himself and a lecture room that was sacrosanct and free from interference, but he was doing a damn good job and was very popular with the senior cadre at that bastion of the Legion. He acted as my private instructor on all of these weapons, in exchange for my buying the beer at the Foot bar. His sense of humour was demonstrated by three large posters which he had designed himself in large Gothic script and distributed around the lecture room in three languages, headed:

RULES OF WARFARE

1. The soldier fights chivalrously for the sake of national victory. Atrocities and needless acts of destruction are unworthy of him.

2. Every combatant must wear uniform or specially authorized and clearly visible insignia. Fighting in civilian clothes or without such insignia is prohibited.
3. No enemy who surrenders must be killed. This also applies to irregular troops and spies, who will receive their just desserts from the courts.
4. Prisoners of war are not to be abused or maltreated. Weapons, plans and documents must be confiscated, but no personal belongings may be removed.
5. The use of dumdum or explosive bullets is prohibited, nor must any normal ammunition be converted.
6. The Red Cross is inviolable. Wounded enemies are to be humanely treated. Medical personnel and military chaplains must not be prevented from carrying out their medical and pastoral duties.
7. The civil population is inviolable. No member of the armed forces shall engage in looting or wanton destruction.

These rules intrigued me and, like all others who entered his private domain, I was challenged by Donald to determine from which country they had originated. Like all others challenged who were not of German nationality, I naturally plunged for British or possibly American. Naturally I was wrong. They were in fact the German soldier's creed, and from those I met in the Legion, I could see that they were honourable men and very brave soldiers.

Two days prior to my departure from Bel-Abbès Jim Sinclair brought me news that Donald had deserted. I could not believe it. I knew he had not been happy at Bel-Abbès, and that he had been envious of the fact that I had failed my instruction and been transferred to a combat regiment, but with his sense of pride in being a legionnaire and a citizen of the United States, it had to be impossible for Donald to have deserted. I began to wonder if perhaps it was my fault, with my frank delight at having 'beat the system' and heading for the best infantry regiment in the Legion. Maybe Donald had become pissed off and resigned.

It was not until two months later that I received a letter from him along with a few photographs. He had indeed deserted – not, however, from the Legion but only from Bel-Abbès. With the ingenuity of an 'old soldier', he had taken off his corporal's stripes and joined a group of novice recruits heading for the 5th Regiment of Infantry on the Moroccan frontier, a regiment in almost daily contact with the enemy. The colonel of the 5th, yet another of those legendary Legion heroes, had inflicted on Donald eight days prison (which he did not serve), placed him in a 'cream' combat company and, despite all requests from Sidi-bel-Abbès for his return, decided that Donald's type of deserter was the type he liked. Prior to the end of the Algerian campaign, he was made a sergeant. A character impossible to forget ...

So I bade a temporary farewell to Sidi-bel-Abbès, Jim Sinclair and Bill Black and set out for the regiment that would become my home for the next 2½ years, totally unprepared for the fact that the 3rd Regiment did not sleep on beds or mattresses, but on the ground. Perhaps three nights a month one could indulge in the luxury of sleeping on a camp cot ... after six months in the regiment even the camp cot is discarded!

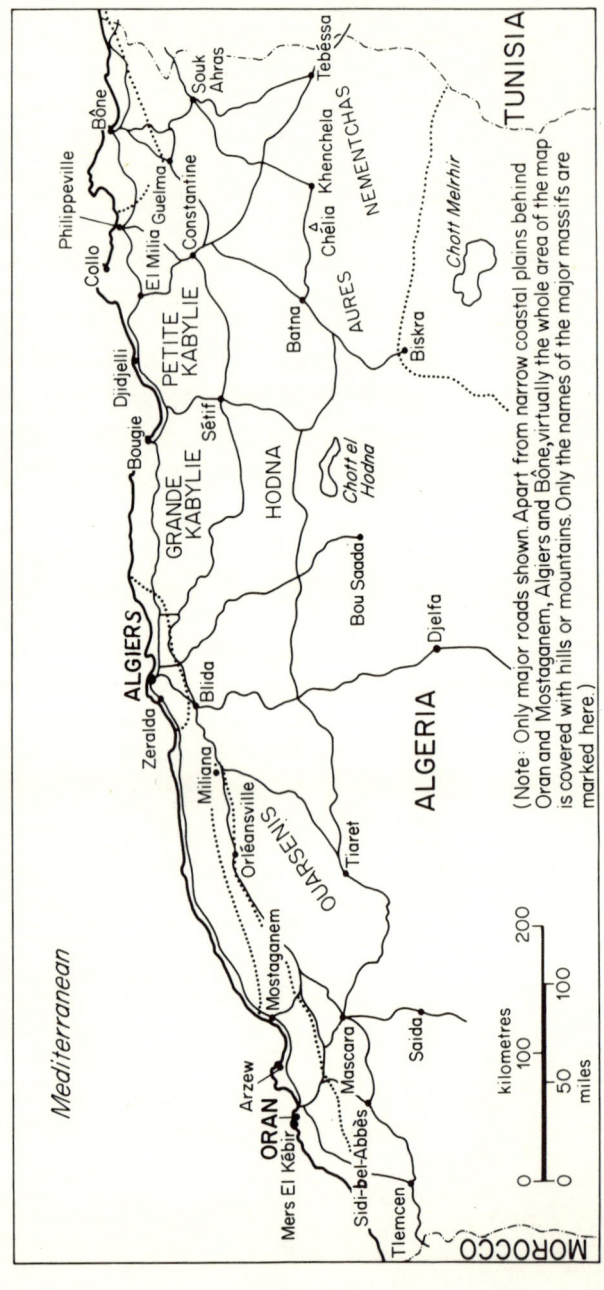

(Note: Only major roads shown. Apart from narrow coastal plains behind Oran and Mostaganem, Algiers and Bône, virtually the whole area of the map is covered with hills or mountains. Only the names of the major massifs are marked here.)

4 Misadventure with the Infantry

I have neither the practical experience to write of company tactics nor the facts needed to write of regimental events during the 2½ years I spent with them.

Like the majority of legionnaires in the regiment, I was only ever vaguely aware of our exact location, whilst being led through the endless mountain ranges, on our guided tours of the natural beauty of the Algerian interior. Algeria certainly does have a natural beauty. We came across many places with Roman ruins and hot water springs, and probably washed our socks where Roman legionnaires had washed their bodies 2,000 years before. And we innocent legionnaires were enjoying these guided tours at the expense of the French Government and still receiving our daily ration of free wine, our monthly ration of free cigarettes and being paid for it! When I expounded my views to members of my section, that tourists would pay a fortune to do what we were being paid for, it did nothing but increase my vocabulary in additional swear words in German, Italian and French.

It was whilst on these guided tours that the Regiment carried out its 'search and destroy' missions against the Algerian ALN (Army of National Liberation), generally referred to as 'the Fell'. The greater part of these missions comprised a hell of a lot of searching and very few opportunities to destroy. Like the Scarlet Pimpernel, the rebels were very difficult to find: 'We sought them here, we sought them there, we searched for the bastards everywhere.' However, when find them we did, they died!

The 3rd Regiment was mobile in more than one sense. It was reputed that our base was at Khenchella. This could possibly be true, but in the time I was with the regiment, the whole 2½ years, I spent a maximum of only some ten days at that base. I heard rumours that there legionnaires were even provided with beds and mattresses to sleep on, but this was probably only a rumour and I did not see any.

For myself and, without doubt, for the rest of the legionnaires of the 2nd Battalion, base camp meant only a location where our trucks were parked, and among these trucks would be our mobile kitchen. Wherever the mobile kitchen was parked and operating, with the food prepared by a very competent and able German cook, there was our base, our home.

Among the convoy would be our own truck, containing all our belongings and personal effects, neatly packed in two large kitbags. Each truck would have attached to the rear a very sturdy trailer containing the tents, electric generators and all the accoutrements required to establish a mobile base.

At these rest area bases we would quickly erect our eight-man American-style tents, and into these we would pile our kitbags and camp cots. These bases would be established in no more than a couple of hours, including electric lights in each tent, and telephone lines run out between the various companies. The selection of the rest area sites was always good, for which the senior officers of the 3rd Regiment will always have my grateful thanks. They were secluded, always with an abundance of fresh water from a nearby river or stream, or perhaps an abandoned farm with a fresh-water well. 'Bullshit' at these rest areas was kept to a minimum. Like the fatted calf, we were well rested, well fed and fattened up for the kill, for cases of beer, cigarettes, wine and beefsteaks descended upon us like manna from Heaven.

The moment the camps were established, so were the inevitable poker schools, which were strictly forbidden. Happily those tents where poker schools were held quickly became known to the sergeants, who would make a point of avoiding them like the plague on their required inspections. Any legionnaire who, like myself, remarked that the various senior non-commissioned officers in the Foreign Legion were a brainless lot of morons, was wrong and failed to realize that many years earlier these same individuals had also served as ordinary legionnaires and had never forgotten all the tricks in

Top: The author (rear left) whilst with the RAF, 1945. *Bottom left*: The author as a very novice recruit at Sidi-bel-Abbès, March 1960. *Bottom right*: The same man as a Legion veteran parachutist, 1965

Top left: The dreaded 'escalade' – descending from Fort Monte Christo overlooking the harbour of Oran. *Top right*: Anti-tank practice. *Bottom*: The captain demonstrating how it should be done

Lecture on instinctive night firing at Bou Sfer, 1964

Commando instruction

The regular eight-kilometre forced run with the lieutenant in the front row

Training in 1964: the Legion being welcomed aboard a French naval vessel

The required form of departure

Standing to attention in the front row, third from right, is Corporal Donald Thomas who 'deserted' from Sidi-bel-Abbès and joined a combat regiment

The author waiting nervously to jump

The inevitable screwed up landing in the only tree for 500 metres

The reason why all legionnaires of the 2nd REP are experts with *plastique* explosives

All legionnaires are Boy Scouts at heart

avoidance of duties and fatigues. Some of these tricks we had yet to learn.

To carry out our combat operations, we merely climbed into our now empty trucks and were speedily transported to the sector where Fortune, God and Colonel Langlois (in reverse order) decreed we should carry out our missions.

During the 'missions' carried out in the 3rd, the ordinary legionnaire would only know that he was somewhere near the Tunisian frontier – or near Miliana – or Affreville, but he always knew when he was in the Aurès, a region of mountains and breathless beauty (the breathlessness coming after a climb of perhaps 7,000 feet getting to the top).

No matter how heavy the bergen sack you were required to carry, no matter the thirst you might be suffering from, no matter how tired or utterly shagged out you felt, it was a wonderful feeling to know that your officers were equally suffering – probably worse, since they had more access to the fleshpots of Algeria than we common legionnaires. The officer carried no less weight than the ordinary legionnaire. Perhaps his only advantage was that, instead of carrying a rifle or pistol *mitraillette* (small sub-machine-gun), he would carry a pistol at his waist. But even this advantage was counterbalanced by the fact that a pistol is a useless sort of weapon for the type of guerrilla warfare carried out in Algeria.

After struggling for perhaps five hours to reach the apex of a crest and be one of the first to arrive, there is no feeling in the world equal to that of looking down to see all the other silly bastards that still have a further eighty metre climb to reach you. By the time they do arrive at the top, you have fully recovered and immediately offer a light for their cigarette, whilst they stretch out in a comatose state. Doing this on a regular basis was not a means of endearing you to your own captain, but small doses certainly boosted the ego.

It is a wise legionnaire who knows his limitations. I think I should perhaps emphasize that each officer carried his own bergen sack. It would contain his own rations, lightweight sleeping bag, change of socks, toiletry kit, water bottle and any other items required for survival. If we carried two water bottles, they carried two water bottles.

It is true that the officers' batmen would also be 'in the hunt', but the batman's primary function was as a legionnaire and to participate in combat when required. He would perhaps only find a suitable sleeping area for his officer and scrape a slight mound for his hip, then in the morning prepare the officer's coffee, along with his own. The only 'perks' a batman would receive on the march would be half shares of any beer or luxury cheese he was prepared to carry on behalf of his officer. It seemed to be an unwritten law that 50/50 was standard. Further compensation was enjoyed by a batman in being placed on the hourly sentinel roster at night so that his relief for sentinel duty would be his own officer. What small pleasures can be enjoyed by the thought of an officer being awakened from his sleep by his batman and, instead of receiving coffee, being told it is his turn for guard duty!

Swop a batman's sack for his officer's sack, and the only difference in weight would be that of four Kronenborg beers. I was never a batman, but there were occasions when I carried as many as eight beers, strictly on a 50/50 basis, for my own *adjudant*. I also developed many devious ways to encourage him to drink his share as quickly as possible, thus reducing the weight of my sack. I always managed to get him to drink his share of the beer after no more than four hours of marching. After eight hours, I always still had two beers in my sack. I considered I was being fair minded and just when I offered to share these last two with him, in exchange for his presenting me with a further four beers when we reached our trucks. Both he and I were happy with the arrangement, and I was quite sad when he left the regiment, having completed twenty years service.

He tolerated me well, taught me a lot, and the respect I gave him did not prevent a certain friendliness. However, he was still a bastard, since he was responsible for sending me to a corporals' training platoon.

My life in the 3rd Regiment was closely entwined only with the very few individuals upon whom my very existence became dependent. There was a particular chief sergeant of German origin, very tough, very rough, a very good legionnaire, and an excellent *chef de section*, Sergeant Kruger, also German, also a bloody good legionnaire who, like myself, believed that rules and regulations were strictly for the guidance of wise men, but for blind obedience by the ignorant. Like myself, Kruger also completed more than seven years service without that most popular of Legion punishments 'eight days in the cells' ('huit jours en tôle').

My companions for the whole time I spent with the regiment were 'Minny', a veteran of Dien Bien Phu, who had received his parachute wings for his first and last jump into that calamity, and Jacques, a Frenchman, also with experience in Indo China. These two had over twenty years service between them, and had received more than ten citations for bravery. With all their service, both remained privates. They also had the capability of drinking more beer, wine or scotch than any other ten legionnaires like myself, which was why they remained privates. (Yet no matter what they had drunk the previous day, they could also march faster than any other ten legionnaires like myself.) They both became my mentors during my early days in the regiment, and I reaped the benefit of their experience.

Then there was Menon, who was Italian and spent all his time translating for Raphael, who was Spanish and, after nearly three years in the Legion, spoke less French than I could speak when I joined. Last but not least, Pasquale. Italian, he believed that rules were strictly for breaking. Eight days prison never deterred Pasquale. (Many years later when I met him at Aubagne in France, he had only five days service to complete his contract but six days of his current prison sentence to complete.) These legionnaires were without doubt the most disreputable bunch that ever existed, but all of them were recipients of the *Croix de Valeur* for bravery. A citation did not bring extra wine or rations; it did, however, allow an individual legionnaire to pinpoint accurately where he had been when it was earned. For example, I know that on 14 October 1960 several rebels were found and killed at Djebel Taktiout (secteur d'Arris, zone sud Constantinous), but I have no idea where this is.

I spent a whole year in 1975 visiting locations where I had served as a legionnaire, perhaps with a morbid curiosity. I found many other places where the 3rd Regiment had carried out operations. These are easily found by the monuments erected by the Algerian Government to the 'martyrs', fallen in combat, for the Liberation. There are many of these. I had no idea that the Legion had been so successful. Unless, of course, they have been erected as additional tourist attractions, to show that independence was won by combat?

It appeared to be standard procedure in the 3rd Regiment that, for each period we spent marching and sleeping rough in the mountains, at whatever spot we arrived at one or two hours before dusk, a proportionate period would be allowed us at the temporary base rest areas we had established.

Therefore, if we spent a continuous ten days in the hills on hardtack rations and water brought to us by the courtesy of the French Air Force helicopter, we could be assured of at least five days of rest and recuperation. Perhaps periods out operating and the proportionate rest time did not always balance, but I never saw a legionnaire evacuated for exhaustion by the helicopters. Normally these were strictly reserved for the wounded and those who had unluckily been killed. The bodies of the Fell were left where they had fallen, after they had been searched and photographed for intelligence purposes. However, if the enemy had fallen on a track or path, and the legionnaire was aware that his commandant or the colonel would be following along immediately behind, the bodies would be pulled to the side of the track to allow the commandant or colonel free passage. (Captains and lieutenants would be expected to step over the bodies, if not on them.)

As to our 'hardtack' rations, the term is a misnomer. They were one-man daily ration packs weighing exactly one kilogram, in a waterproof small oblong box known as a *pacifique*. They were far superior to the American-style K rations. They contained small but adequate cans of various meats, cheese, sardines, sachets of powdered soup, coffee, sugar, salt tablets, water-purifying tablets, cigarettes, toilet paper, nougat and chocolate. The ultimate joy was a small bottle of *eau de vie* – brandy. Awaking in the mornings, at first light, in the bitter air of freezing mountains, how better to start the day than with a large cup of piping hot coffee and brandy! The small group to which I was attached never really appreciated the full beauty of the sunrise, as the sun climbed over the horizon, and the luxury of coffee and brandy whilst enjoying this magical sight. I do not think any of them forgave me for the continual repetition of this wonder each morning as we arose to continue the hike of the day.

There were occasions during these operations when one could sense a feeling of anticipation and excitement and judge by the activity around the portable radios that some Fells had been spotted, so we were on the right track. There would be a rapid acceleration in the march rate, not on any given instructions but simply from those legionnaires who, along with their sergeants, happened to be in the leading section, fearing they were not sharing in the hunt with the rest of the company. The other sections would also be trying to overtake whoever was leading, since they also wished to take part in the action. There were many occasions where some of these sections could have easily won a well-run half marathon whilst carrying their weapons and sacks, and they became simply rat races. There were also times when some of these front-running bastards would really cheat. They would discard their sacks and even their water bottles, and really get down to hard running. The poor Fells never had a chance.

The most annoying fact on these occasions was that the section following these self-appointed Olympic sprinters would be obliged either to carry their sacks for them or to stack them together and sit guard on them until the sprinters returned. Then their only participation in these events was to listen to the distant firing. When trapped in such a situation, our own small group opted to wait and guard their sacks until their return by ensuring that our radio suddenly developed a fault, we could not receive the order to rendezvous with the sprinters, and we would patiently relax and rest and await their return. They were always unappreciative of the dedication and devotion we gave to the guarding of their sacks, to which our response would be for them to 'Join the bloody Para.'

When I first joined the Regiment, I was told by my own sergeant that I should go along to the 5th Company, where I could meet an Englishman who at the time of my arrival had served with the Regiment for a couple of years. That is how I first met John H. (I have no intention of mentioning his surname – not because he had, or has, some sordid detail in his past to conceal, but out of respect for him, since I discovered by accident that his family were 'connected' to some of the most respected people in the United Kingdom. I was often asked to take his mail to him, and crested envelopes revealed the relationship between him and his constant correspondent, for the crest and the motto were easily identifiable.) John was a very tall man indeed, and his physical build matched his height. He had two distinctive features: red hair and a gold earring in his left ear. (The earring itself was unusual in that it was tolerated by the Legion hierarchy.) The other thing about John was his guitar playing. He told me that when he left Cambridge he had spent two years 'bumming' around the South of France, paying his way with his guitar playing. (His mention of Cambridge slipped out in a normal conversation, along with the name of the college.) John had been a 'hippy' before the term became accepted in the common language.

David Fireman was the para medic of the 6th Company. (I see no reason not to state his name or anything about him, since he was fully aware some fifteen years ago that it was my intention to write about the Legion and that he would be included. His only comment has been that he would accept a copy as a gift – but he would never pay to read it.) He was very young, one of twins, and a Jew. He also came from a well-known family, one that owns quite a few of the better-class London furniture stores.

One of David's disadvantages was that he had been educated to such a degree that he spoke better French than many of his officers, and it constantly led him into trouble for it became almost automatic for him, without being aware of it, to correct the grammar of his superiors – even the captain. David's usual punishment was to go on missions denied the right to carry his pistol and carrying a dirty big stretcher, on which his captain slept every night. The other medics carried only bandages, morphine and dressings.

John H. had an extraordinary ability and endurance during the long, dreary marches. His speciality was as a *tireur élite*, an expert marksman – to put it bluntly, a sniper. His rifle was kept immaculate, with the butt and stock finely sandpapered and unpolished. His telescopic sight was untouchable, without risk of a broken arm. He kept this rifle wrapped in parachute silk, further wrapped in plastic. He also secured the muzzle from dust, with the misapplied use of a rubber contraceptive. (He had an unlimited supply of these from David.) One would have been safer trying to fondle John than to touch his rifle.

I do not think I have known anything more demoralizing than, when climbing a very steep hill at what I considered a very reasonable speed of progress, to have John suddenly come striding past and overtaking along with the rest of his *équipe*, carrying not only his rifle but, hoisted across his other shoulder, a heavy calibre machine-gun that was generally shared by two legionnaires. It was at moments like this that, although I am moderately tall, I wondered what the hell I was doing there, trying to emulate a legionnaire.

Only one particular incident relating to John remains permanently in my mind. We had been out searching a range of hills for more than ten days. There had been neither sight nor smell of any Fells for the whole period. I think everyone, including the officers, was becoming frustrated with the bad weather, the coldness during the nights and the unsuccessful attempts at flushing out Fells from where they had been reported, but of whom we found no trace. And as good as the field rations supplied by the helicopters were, I think we would all have swapped our month's pay for a well-cooked meal. Our small group arrived at the crest of a hill in the late afternoon to find John's section accompanied by his company captain, who had secured two prisoners trussed with ropes and well guarded. These were two plump mules that had obviously been roaming in the hills for a very long time. After some considerable radio traffic, and much discussion between the various officers, an attempt was made to lead these two mules to our agreed rendezvous point. It quickly became apparent that the mules not only spoke and understood French but had made up their minds that there was no way we were going to lead them anywhere. I think some idiot had used the word barbecue, and it was this that caused the mules to become so aggressive.

When we arrived, they were calm and docile. The moment the word barbecue was introduced, they became fighting maniacs, and within a matter of minutes, with flying hooves, had about a dozen legionnaires lying on the ground, one with slight concussion, the rest in a state of shock. Our combined efforts were made absolutely useless against the mules' determination to stay exactly where they were. There was then more radio traffic, which led to the rendezvous being changed to the place we were at. (The prophet Mohammed could not get to the mountain, so the mountain was coming to us.) The mules were forthwith slaughtered and cleaned, skinned in an expert fashion and then barbecued. Our group was invited to share a well-cooked supper of beefsteak (well, French beefsteak anyway), with ample supplies of fresh spring water, followed by coffee. (There was a stream only a couple of hundred metres away in a downward direction. This was the first time I saw any legionnaire utilize the salt tablets contained in his *pacifique*.)

I had been with the regiment for ten months before the opportunity came to go into the town of Miliana with John and David, for a meal in a restaurant. I was somewhat shattered, since this was also the first time I had seen John in his walking-out dress, to find that he was not only adorned with the *Croix de la Valeur* but had won it three times – the Legion was never over-generous with these. In all our discussions, John had never mentioned these citations to me.

John left the Legion early in 1962 and I heard nothing more from him until I picked up a French newspaper the same year to see his picture and a front-page story describing how he had gone to the rescue of a French taxi-driver in Paris who was being beaten up and robbed. John had received stab wounds in his chest and back, with of all things a spear, in an attempt to intervene. Five years in the Legion, a lot of combat experience, never having been wounded and then to be beaten nearly to death by a gang of Parisian thugs! John was not aggressive by instinct, but his nature would not allow him just to stand aside as an observer whilst an innocent victim was being beaten and robbed. He was a gentle giant and a gentleman. His five years in the Legion had merely been a passing experience, as had his two years 'bumming' around with his guitar.

Three years of my life in the Legion were spent in very close association with David. We first met in 1960 at Sidi-bel-Abbès, where he was training as a paramedic at the Legion and military hospitals. He was quite a small man, less than average height, but he made up for it by his physical courage and endurance. Any man prepared to carry a long bulky stretcher which, apart from being cumbersome and heavy, served no useful purpose, other than as a bed for his captain, had to have an awful lot of restraint and patience. (I would have thrown the bloody thing off the highest mountain.) David had qualified as a parachutist, something that had been denied to me.

Colonel Chenel, who at that time was at Sidi-bel-Abbès, was also a parachutist, older than myself and, following his appointment at Sidi-bel-Abbès, commanded the 2nd Regiment of Parachutists. Like all colonels in the Legion, he made a point of trying to get to know every legionnaire under his command. I had previously met him when he was touring the base at Saida, when he had spoken to each legionnaire. I had pleaded my case at Saida, that I wished to enter one of the two parachute regiments, but he said I was too old – and he said this in English. I politely told him that he was obviously older than myself. He, with equal politeness, pointed out that he was a colonel, and rank had its privileges. Those senior sergeants and officers who understood English were waiting for the order to be given to march me away to the cells for my impertinence, but he just grinned and dismissed me.

At Sidi-bel-Abbès, whilst I was sweeping the road in the Petit Quartier on punishment detail, a jeep roared past, suddenly stopped about twenty metres away and quickly reversed back to where I was standing. As I pulled myself to attention, I realized it was Colonel Chenel in the jeep – the same colonel that I had spoken to, only for five minutes, and that three months previously. He merely returned my salute and said again in English, 'You are still too old for the Para, but you'll be going to the best infantry regiment.' As he drove away, I could not believe he had recognized me, but as I found out later, he had a reputation for such actions. He was yet another gentle giant and a gentleman. (Lest it be thought that I use the term 'gentleman' in excess, I do not. Not all officers were gentlemen – some, perhaps many, but certainly not all. I was lucky from the day I joined the Legion. All the colonels I served under in the 3rd RE and later in the 2nd REP, where I eventually finished, despite Colonel Chenel, were all gentlemen – bastards perhaps, but still gentlemen.)

A couple of days later, when I was having a beer with David and relating the casual meeting with Colonel Chenel, David told me his story about the colonel and why, although he had recently qualified as a parachutist, he too was destined for an infantry regiment. Despite his somewhat small stature, David was an exceptional athlete. It was whilst completing his basic training at Mascara and because of his natural ability to finish in first place on the military obstacle courses, and always first in the twenty-five-kilometre runs with full kit, that he had been selected for parachute training. But while undergoing this training and after completing his first jump, David realized that parachuting was not his *métier*. As he pointed out, when he had enlisted, he had not even been aware that the Foreign Legion used parachutes. He had thought they used mules and camels. He had been quite willing to join the Legion and be a legionnaire. He had been quite willing to do his best whilst completing his basic training. He had further been quite willing to carry out his parachute training – until his first jump!

David told me that when he left the aircraft, it was not a question of being scared or frightened, it had terrified the shit out of him, and when he landed, he just shut his eyes, attempted to curl himself into a ball and landed with a thump. He refused to do his second jump. In consequence, he spent eight days in the cells. Then he was again detailed to continue with the required jumps. He again refused, so, back to the cells. David spent twenty-eight days in prison. He decided that after serving his twenty-eight days enough was enough, and he carried on to complete the required jumps to qualify. His system of jumping was different from that of any other parachutist. On leaving the aircraft he would firmly close his eyes and not open them again until he felt the ground strike his body. That he managed to survive without a broken arm or leg was probably due to the prayers he would murmur to himself on the way down, and his belief in the Jewish faith!

He was again fortunate in that he had received his parachute brevet from the hands of Colonel Chenel, who had been told about this *very* reluctant British parachutist, and of his long prison sentence and of his very good knowledge of the French language. A reluctant parachutist is no good in any army. David was therefore destined for the infantry and to be trained as a medic. (Being a medic is not a sinecure in the Legion: when the shooting starts, the medic is always right up with the action. A thought to ponder: how, when medics take no part in any actual shooting so many of them get decorated?) David had therefore become grounded, without further punishment, and good fortune had taken him to serve in the same battalion as John and myself.

There was one occasion when we suddenly found that we had been deposited at the Tunisian frontier, between Fort Lamy and Souk el Aris. As we established our temporary base camp, on the crest of a small hill, we could see below only a matter of two hundred metres away, the barrage or Morice line which ran from the coast to as far south as Negrine. On either side of this electrified fence, which was reputed to carry as much as 5,000 volts, were tangles of barbed wire to a height of some three metres. Within the barbed wire, scattered very liberally, were a whole stack of mines, some booby-trapped, some visible and many more not visible. Bordering this formidable defence line was the tarmacadam road between Lamy and Souk el Aris. This was the closest, as far as we were aware, that we had been to Tunisia. Here was an ideal opportunity for any legionnaire who wished to desert (some spent the whole of their five years talking about it but never did). All that was needed was to get through the barbed wire, avoid the mines, not get electrocuted and you were home free! It had to be easy – the Fell had been doing it for years. The total number of legionnaires who deserted from the 3rd Regiment at that time – zero.

It was claimed that, should you spit at this electrified fence, the recoil would knock you on your back, but I won a case of beer from my sergeant by reaching out and grasping one of the strands of wire.

The previous day I had been on escort duty with the French engineers responsible for the maintenance of the fence. They told me that it was switched off from dawn to dusk. The good sergeant bet me that it was 'live' for twenty-four hours a day. He bet that it was on. I was betting that it was off. I had faith in the engineers, since they had demonstrated in the same manner to me. A fool I may have been, but not quite a bloody idiot. And I did win a case of beer. It took Sergeant Kruger quite a while to reason that there was no possible way he could have won this bet anyway. If the fence had been alive, he would have had extreme difficulty collecting a case of beer from a burnt corpse.

In our ignorance, we had assumed that whilst we were at this temporary base it would be considered a 'rest area'. The Fell, who had established several training camps in Tunisia, frequently entered Algeria through this protective barrage. It seemed to us ordinary legionnaires that they were hardly likely to pass the barrage whilst they were aware of our presence. Nor, we thought, would we be called upon to make forays into Tunisia. Therefore, as far as we were concerned, this was to be a semi-vacation – even more so, since we could see with the aid of binoculars at about two kilometres the other side of the wire a military camp where Tunisians or Fells, or both, were actually playing football.

To our disgust and surprise, Sergeant Kruger suggested that we had better dig slit trenches. I thought he was bloody mad. A slit trench? Where the hell did he think he was, back in Indo China? Or perhaps he thought this was where World War III was going to start. It was with some reluctance that we started digging out the rocky surface with our entrenching tools (purchased secondhand from the US Army surplus stores). They, like us, were useless at the job. After some two hours, without exhausting myself, I had succeeded in digging to a depth that when I laid in it would have left my posterior exposed. That was enough. Among the five of us, none of whom had made any real effort, not one trench was deeper.

Within two hours of sunrise the next morning my trench was so deep that, when I stood in it, I could just manage to see over the top. The rearpart was covered with logs, and again with earth. It had also been so well camouflaged that it could not be seen from five metres away. It was no longer a slit trench: it had been converted to a well-constructed atomic bomb shelter. The rest of our group had built similar funkholes. All of this had been done on a voluntary basis without any urging from Sergeant Kruger. His only comment when he saw them was to ask if we had struck water?

The reason for all our flurry of activity was that the previous night, whilst peacefully wrapped in the arms of Morpheus and dreaming only of the days ahead without the monotony of climbing mountains, we had received visitors in the form of British 81 mm mortar shells, which had landed slap bang in the middle of the camp. There could only have been some twenty or thirty, but we would each have sworn to hundreds. They had been launched from the other side of the wire, if not by the Tunisian military, then by the Fells whom they were instructing. What followed was even worse. The French artillery commenced laying a barrage of shells from their 75s. Their ear-piercing whistling and shrieking and the crashes of the impacts, only some 400 metres in front of us were not good for the nerves. (That night I would have declared they were only fifty metres in front of us!)

The colonel and commandant may have had confidence in the accuracy of the artillery barrage. We did not. Not only that, but Kruger spoiled my day by suggesting that the British Army were probably instructing the Fells in the use of British mortars. Could be – someone was, and they were accurate!

We did penetrate this famous electrified fence – the whole regiment – though not to invade Tunisia, since I believe the actual frontier was a river running through the middle of the slight depression in the terrain about a kilometre away, on the Tunisian side of the wire.

We were clearly visible to any Tunisian or Fell observers, and we were making enough noise. Someone said there were good fish in the river. All one could hear for the next couple of hours were the explosions of grenades as they were thrown into the river. A lot of mud, but no fish.

We found where the artillery shells had fallen. There were no bodies, no scattered pieces of equipment, no tattered remnants of uniforms, and not the slightest trace of where the mortar shells had been fired from. All we managed to find were a couple of dead forest rats which from the position of the bodies, had died either in an ecstasy of copulation or of fright from the sound of bursting artillery shells. It was the redoubtable Sergeant Kruger who remarked, 'What a wonderful way to die.' I received *quatre jours consigne* (four days confined to camp) – *confined to camp?* – for telling him that if he decided to stay where we were for the night, he could easily find himself a forest vole, enjoy the same copulation and wait for the same artillery barrage.

I think it was the next day, when I was still in the tent, 'resting', when I should have been elsewhere, that Kruger caught me and demanded what the hell I was doing there. I explained that I had placed myself under arrest and confined myself to my bed and my tent for four days, 'as he had instructed'. Lucky for me, Kruger had a sense of humour and decided to call it a day. Once again there was peace between us. He did however promise me that, if and when we ever arrived or established a base where there was a prison, I could be assured I would be the first for the *huit jours en tôle* (eight days prison). During all my time with the 3rd Regiment, a prison was never established, nor was I ever aware that one even existed. Those who received this punishment had their heads shaved and dug a latrine trench at the most. Since I was almost bald at the age of twenty-eight and regularly used a razor on my head, the only loss would have been the eight days pay – big deal. I dug the latrines anyway!

We did carry out more operations, whilst in this sector, mostly motorized. I found it somewhat strange that we should have established ourselves on the frontier and should then make the inevitable searches for the Fells in a westerly direction. Which again proved to me the reason I was only a legionnaire and that the officers in the 3rd Regiment were a bloody sight more intelligent. The regiment did have considerable success in finding more Fells, thereby increasing the number of Algerian widows. They were caught both going and coming.

It was whilst we were on another motorized patrol, somewhere south of Souk el Aris, that we came across a track that for some reason was suspected of being mined, and that the mines used were anti-tank mines. How, why or where the Legion officers of the 3rd Regiment received their intelligence, they never confided in me, for I was little more than the regimental regular shithouse cleaner But on this occasion I was carrying out the duty of bodyguard to the commandant, along with five other legionnaires of my section, with as usual the watchful eye of Sergeant Kruger boring into my back. Our position was on the second vehicle, a small six-by-six US Dodge truck behind the commandant, who was leading the convoy.

The whole convoy halted whilst two legionnaires were detailed to use the American World War II mine-detectors. They were brand new and had obviously been untouched by human hands since they left the makers, many years before. They still had the manufacturer's handbook in the carton. All my explaining to Sergeant Kruger that I had never seen one before in my life, that I had no idea how they worked and that, although I spoke English, I had not finished school and therefore could not even read English, proved to be of no avail. I found myself delegated as a mine-detector specialist, to read and digest the handbook and to instruct (instruct!) my companion Minnie in their use. I managed to get the darn things assembled – eventually – and proceeded to the front of the convoy to search for these mines. It was only after I had taken the first few steps that Minnie called my attention to the fact that I had forgotten the headphones.

Minnie and I proceeded on our way. Meanwhile the whole battalion, at the rear, had climbed down from their trucks and were lazing about at the side of the track, smoking, making coffee and generally leading the life of Riley, enjoying the welcome break in the morning sunshine. We steadily plodded along the track, swinging these mine-detectors from side to side, keeping them at the correct height above the ground exactly as directed in the handbook which was sticking out of my top pocket. Sergeant Kruger walked a good fifteen metres behind – as he explained, 'just in case we were successful in finding one with our feet, instead of with the detector'. It had cost the Legion too much money for him to be trained as a sergeant for him to be blown up by a stupid legionnaire who stepped on a mine.

It did nothing to my confidence when Minnie told me that in Indo China mines had been of carton and plastic, which could not be found with a mine-detector. At that moment I would have been far happier in the mountains humping my sack. In fact, I would have been far happier anywhere than on that track. (I had merrily marched along other tracks that had been mined but only aware that mines were in the vicinity, when some poor bugger behind had stepped on one.) The thought also came to my mind that perhaps Minnie and I had been allocated this job because we were the oldest in the section, and therefore the most expendable.

We had traversed some sixty metres when I struck gold in the form of a whistling in my ear. I had found a mine. Sergeant Kruger then joined us, well pleased at our success, and told me to dig it up. There was further discussion as I explained to Kruger that, although I had been instructed on how a mine could be removed from the ground, whilst at basic training, the instruction had been oral and without a practical demonstration, and there had also been warnings about booby-traps and grenades under the mines that would result in a headache when the mine was removed. Sergeant Kruger then showed what

Legion sergeants are made of. He borrowed my bayonet and got down on his knees to start probing for the mine. He was most upset when Minnie and I told him that, whilst he was getting the mine, we would return to the trucks for coffee. He was so upset that both Minnie and I further increased our vocabulary of German swear words. We did not return to the trucks but certainly kept well clear of Kruger. As we moved away, he passed a remark about courage and again became upset when I informed him that the reason I was keeping away was only that I was wearing a freshly laundered combat uniform and had no wish to have it bloodstained, unless the blood was mine.

The anti-climax came when, after all the very careful probing and scraping the surface with his bare hands, and his meticulous removal of the loose soil, the mine was suddenly exposed – and proved to be a rusting sardine can that had probably been there for several years. Minnie and I quickly picked up our made-in-America mine-detectors and carried on, moving as fast as we could to keep out of the reach of Sergeant Kruger. Our problem was, that neither of us could stop laughing.

We had completed another fifty metres when we had another 'contact'. After the previous fiasco, I had no hesitation in digging down and probing around. I produced yet another sardine tin.

It had taken almost twenty minutes for Sergeant Kruger to dig up his sardine can, only fifteen minutes for me to produce mine.

The futile search, the time consumed and the sight of some 400 legionnaires lying about in relaxed attitudes, some even playing poker, proved enough for our officers to call off the mine-detecting, order everyone back in the trucks and get the convoy rolling. We then proceeded on our way.

I had lit my first cigarette and was describing to the rest of the bodyguard the gentle care shown by the good Sergeant Kruger in the extraction of a sardine can when there was a most horrific explosion from the second truck behind us, as it tried to leap in the air. We had found our first mine without the aid of a detector. The truck that blew up was the fifth vehicle of the convoy, and all vehicles were steering in the wheel tracks of the vehicle in front, so it was obvious that the mines used by the Fell were sophisticated, probably British made, so as not to explode with the first vehicle that passed over them – ideal for setting up ambushes. Without any orders being given, we were all out of our trucks, on either side, setting up for what I, anyway, thought was sure to be an ambush. Nothing.

In the truck that had blown up there were no serious injuries to any of the legionnaires, though they were shaken without doubt. When I walked back to find them being attended to by David, the medic, I actually heard one of them trying to bribe him to fix it so that they could have at least four days *repos* (rest), with suspected concussion. I know that it was shortly after this incident that David seemed to have unlimited sources of beer.

All that had been seriously wounded was the truck, and the senior officers, again in their infinite wisdom, called the whole operation off, and we returned to our temporary base. Victory that day rested with the Fell, although the mine probably cost more money than the damage sustained by the truck, which was repaired in a matter of days. And the Fell had the thanks of a few hundred legionnaires for what can only be described as a day off.

Life was becoming more and more enjoyable in the 3rd Regiment. On another occasion when we carried out another motorized search for Fells, we went on 'half tracks' with regular French Army drivers. These were tracked vehicles, open to the skies, very heavily armoured around the sides – in this convoy there were even tanks. The philosophy of the senior officers of the regiment was, why have Legion trucks damaged – let's have regular army vehicles blown up instead. (At least that was the opinion of all of us riding in these vehicles.) We saw a lot of the countryside, but I became very concerned when we were ordered to dismount and proceed ahead of these trucks, on foot and in open order *in case we were attacked by the Fells*. So we dismounted from these bullet-proof armoured vehicles and commenced plodding on in front of 'em, feeling quite happy that we had managed to drink all the wine that we found lying about inside the vehicles. (I doubt it, but it could have been possible that the regulars had really brought the wine as a gift. We never found out.) We kept plodding on in a straight line for some twenty kilometres, lost sight of the tracked vehicles in the rear and never saw them again – strictly a 'one-off' exercise. Pity, it was better than marching.

We eventually departed from that temporary base camp,

taking great care to fill in the funkholes we had dug, a lot more hard work but strictly on a volunteer basis. We had learnt that another regiment, the 13th Demi Brigade, would be taking over. Legionnaires they may have been, but we did not love them, and they did not love us. So far as we were concerned, let the bastards dig their own bloody holes, along with the hope that they would have exactly the same reception from the other side of the wire as we had received. Such is the perverse nature of your ordinary legionnaire.

It was back to the mountains, in yet another sector, with this reputed mystical permanent base at Khenchella still beyond reach. I was quite content. I had found out that they had a prison there and, according to the *adjudant-chef* and Sergeant Kruger, once we were there I would be permanently incarcerated within, not until I had completed my five years but until I died of old age.

I am surprised that the 3rd Regiment was never called the Gypsy Regiment. I certainly felt we were living the life of gypsies. *But* lest the reader think we were suffering, we were not. The food provided by the cook was superb and of very good quality. We may have eaten out of messtins for more than two years, we may have, at the most, sat down at a table to eat no more than a dozen times, but no one in the 3rd Regiment ever collapsed through hunger. Also each month, when we received our free issue of cigarettes, we would also receive one or two pairs of first-class woollen socks. (When I left the regiment for corporals' platoon, I gave a dozen new pairs away.)

Not all the operations carried out by the 3rd Regiment were done the hard way. It came as a pleasant surprise on several occasions when, during a march of only an hour, helicopters would descend from the sky for no other purpose but to transport us as quickly as possible to a location where Fells had been spotted.

My first experience of this, and at first to my great delight, was during the latter part of 1960, when some dozen of us crowded into a Sikorsky Banana. Only the officers had been aware that this form of transportation would be available, and although it was easier than marching, I became slightly uneasy as I listened to the doubts expressed by those among us who had previously taken part in similar operations. None was concerned at being unloaded in close proximity to the Fell. In fact, most were looking forward to it. The dominant factor was the duration of the flight. Each ten minutes of flying time also represented a distance of forty-five kilometres. Would we be returning with the helicopters to the location of our trucks? Or would we be required to march even longer distances than normal, after whatever combat we were fortunate enough to find – if we found any?

In the section to which I was attached, the concern was only the distance and terrain we would have to traverse in the return to our trucks. Any meeting with the Fell would be a short, sharp confrontation, of which the outcome could be predetermined. It mattered not if there were thirty or a hundred Fell, the result would always be the same, and the provision of helicopters must surely have meant that more than the normal *faoudj* (eleven men under a corporal) had been spotted. Although we ourselves were only twelve, we had seen another two helicopters being loaded at the time of our departure, so no matter where we were eventually dumped, we knew that other members of the battalion would be in the vicinity. Although still a novice in the regiment (one is considered a novice for the first three years), I had learned already that the only means of survival in a hostile territory is a naturally developed instinct and a hell of a lot of apprehension. Legion training had helped in the development of instinct, and reliance on my comrades had overcome any apprehensions.

After only some twenty minutes of flying time the helicopter began its descent. Minnie and I edged our way to the door of the aircraft, determined to be first out. Minnie, with his usual unflappable aplomb, sought to cover himself with glory; I had no idea of winning any medals but the knowledge that any outbreak of shooting on arrival would surely be directed at a dirty big helicopter, rather than two isolated legionnaires. It was also my intention, once I arrived, to put as great a distance as possible between myself and this dirty big target.

Somewhat anxiously I watched the terrain approaching, concerned mostly with looking for an unpleasant welcoming committee. My inward qualms eased as I saw no signs of hostile bodies. The intended landing area was a small hilltop covered with thick underbush, with limited open spaces, and was obviously going to provide a difficult place for the pilot to land. The helicopter hovered some five metres from a small, flat surface about fifty metres below the brow of the hill, whilst Minnie and I, in our innocence, waited for the wheels to touch prior to our departure.

The French Air Force dispatcher, a complete bloody moron, was doing his utmost to eject us forcibly whilst we were still hovering. The doorway of a Sikorsky may be only two metres above the wheels, but the wheels were still some four metres above the ground, and as I looked down, I would have testified that it was at least twenty metres. Despite our reluctance, we were encouraged to jump by the abuse falling from the lips of our *adjudant* somewhere at the rear, and his rash promises about our future lives being made very miserable by our hesitancy, so we made our exit.

I made my target a large bush below and launched myself into space. I was carrying on my back at least fifteen kilos in weight, my faithful automatic pistol firmly gripped in my right hand, fully arrayed and additionally weighted with eight spare chargers in the pouches attached to my webbing harness, a few grenades, my water bottle and all the incidentals a legionnaire is required to take into battle. The weight of all these items does nothing to inspire one's confidence when falling into space, even though the space is only four metres. (It still looked twenty.) As I left the helicopter, I had placed my left arm across my face to protect it from injury that might be caused by my fall into the bush. In spite of the velocity of the descent, instinct made me adjust my sense of values and switch my left hand to protect my crotch. A few bruises or even a scar on the face would have been acceptable, but accidental castration certainly held no future.

Although the bush cushioned my fall, the force of impact must have addled my brain. I rolled out of my bush, hurriedly disentangling Minnie from the bush he had landed in, and we both took off at a run for the crest of the hill, flopping on our faces on arrival. I was well and truly shattered from the force of the landing, and certainly incapable of fighting should there have been any Fell in the area. If there had been a dark and dusky maiden, nude and willing, waiting on top of that hill, I could have done little more than raise my beret and wish her a pleasant day.

As we both looked back down the hill, expecting to see the rest of our group following, it was disconcerting to see the helicopter veering away looking for a better landing zone, and even more dismaying to find we had been abandoned. Minnie and I had been the only ones to jump. The rest of the group had stayed with the aircraft. I felt most despondent as I watched our own helicopter, along with two others, discharging their cargo of eager legionnaires on a perfectly flat and ideal landing ground some 500 metres away.

As I lit a cigarette, for a moment I thought I had pissed myself, as I felt a very discomforting trickle of wetness running down my leg. I was not in the least relieved to find that I had not, when close inspection revealed that it was blood. My leg had been gashed by the unfriendly bracken thicket I had chosen to fall into, and my camouflage trousers were turning not a shade of red but black. The proof that my brain had been addled by the impact was the fact that I had run fifty metres uphill and not even noticed.

Minnie and I decided that it was in our best interest to link up with the rest of the section with utmost speed. I did not attempt to inspect the damage my leg had sustained. I had already run fifty metres, and it was hardly likely to fall off before we joined the section. So, wrapping my field dressing round my leg, we made our way to the main party, where I was sure I would be welcomed with open arms, sympathy and evacuation by helicopter, direct to the hospital in Algiers, there to meet a beautiful nurse who would wipe my fevered brow and spend the rest of the night in my arms. (I think this is the ultimate dream of all legionnaires, who, contrary to popular belief, do not join the Legion looking for adventure but with the hope of being slightly wounded, very highly decorated, finding a beautiful nurse in hospital, with very wealthy parents, and quitting the Legion with glory to live a life of luxury in blissful happiness.)

I should have known that my *adjudant*, whom I had always considered a kind and friendly soul, would not be in the least sympathetic, when he looked at what was in my considerable opinion a severe gash and dismissed it as a slight scratch. To add to my misfortune, the only available medic was David, my supposedly best friend and fellow Londoner. For the preceding few months David had abused my hospitality with his frequent visits to our bivouac area, ostensibly to collect fresh medical supplies but in reality to consume vast quantities of my treasured stocks of beer. It was this friend who ripped my trousers to inspect the damage, poured out liberal amounts of my precious water to cleanse the 'scratch' and declared he could fix it. Offers of free, unlimited beer for the next few months, conditional to my leaving with the airborne taxi service, brought only rejection and a large, stupid grin.

David did fix my leg. He produced from his medical sack an ordinary needle and thread that, in the normal course of events, would be used only for the treatment of blisters. Then he added insult to injury by carefully moistening the thread with his lips before threading it through the needle and proceeded to sew up my scratch. Not one stitch – four. Up to that point, if it had not been for the fact that I felt the blood on my leg, I would not have noticed the injury at all (probably my force of impact earlier had acted as an anaesthetic) but when he began his amateur needlework, it felt as if he was doing it with a rusty nail. He may have had medical training at Bel-Abbès but he had certainly skipped the instruction on hygiene and needlework.

When the *adjudant*, later that evening, enquired if I was OK and even produced a beer from his own sack and gave it to me, it was better than receiving a medal from the colonel. Anyway, who wants to be kissed by a giant?

As early evening approached, we went through the section's usual routine: the lighting of fires prior to sunset for the preparation of hot soup or coffee from our ration packs, then, with the declining sun, the fires extinguished, then the selection of sentinel posts for the night guard. All members of the group would complete only one hour of duty during the night. The guard's concern would be surveillance in only one direction, the security of his sleeping comrades and, most important, the location and sleeping place of the relief at the end of his hourly stint. The sleeping place of the relief sentinel was of the highest priority since, if you were unable to find him, you had a very big problem, along with a cold and lonely all-night vigil on your lonesome. Wake up the wrong man, and you could end up with a rifle butt kissing your lips, especially if that unfriendly individual had already completed his stint of duty.

We remained a further two days in this sector, and the most pleasant surprise was the short distances we were required to traverse. It is doubtful whether even forty kilometres were covered.

The helicopters returned on the second day – not the original Sikorskys but the British Westland type. Regrettably these were not to provide a means of transport but had brought cardboard and aluminium foil water-containers, each containing about ten litres, and more hardtack rations. Much to our disgust and displeasure, the hardtack rations were of the Moslem type, devoid of that most vital sustenance, essential for the well-being of all legionnaires, the small bottles of *eau de vie*. As far as I was concerned at that moment, the whole operation was a screw-up.

It was David's bad luck that he arrived with his section, to find that I had been designated to ensure the fair distribution and strict allocation of the water. We had all been without water since the early hours of the morning, and I had suffered the most. Too much from my water bottle had been used by David in cleaning my leg the day before. I had been sucking a pebble since early morning, trying to allay my thirst. It may have worked in adventure stories, but it had not helped me in the slightest.

As I sat there, the lowliest legionnaire in the regiment was suddenly the most popular: I had the water, my leg propped out in front of me, the bloodstained bandage for all to admire, looking sadly at the helicopters flying away in the distance. David received the full blast of Cockney verbiage for denying me the right to a few days in hospital and for being the probable cause of what I was sure would be a first-class packet of gangrene prior to the completion of the operation, and for that the bastard would be last man to receive water. I received a burst of applause from all those dozy, idle legionnaires standing around with nothing else to do. They may not have understood the English language but they were fully conversant with the flow of invective. Even the *adjudant* somewhat sarcastically came over, shook hands and murmured: 'Quite right, Johnny. If you can't trust an Englishman, who can you trust?' Needless to say, David and I shared our soup and bread that evening.

This operation ended on the third day, and it was a pleasant relief to find our trucks waiting for us, after a march of just a few hours, to transport us back to our current bivouac. This was only one of the few times when one of the trucks had cases of beer on board, thanks to the organizing genius of our own Sergeant Kruger, who had purchased them *en route* from his own pocket. It could have been that those who had accompanied the trucks to the rendezvous had been aware of our severe water shortage or that the very gallant Sergeant Kruger, despite all my assertions, had not been born out of wedlock.

I still remember that my own consumption of beer was five bottles in as many minutes, causing anxiety to Kruger when I informed him that my money was back at the bivouac, but when I tried to pay him later, he refused to accept it. This gives the lie to my constant declarations that all sergeants were bastards.

Information about operations we had taken part in was always limited. We would know if a legionnaire of another company, or even another section, had been killed only on return to our bivouac, and only then if we were required to participate in the burial ceremony.

Despite the numbers of legionnaires involved in this operation, we had seen only members of our own section, except for the brief visit of others to collect water. With the aid of binoculars we had seen a certain amount of activity, with the helicopters descending and rising again, after depositing other members of the battalion. It was only a few days after our return that we discovered that the operation had been fairly successful and that a considerable number of weapons had been recuperated from the Fell. I had not even heard the sound of a shot being fired in the distance. However, we also found that during this operation a very popular chief sergeant had been killed, along with another legionnaire. The only compensating factor was that, since 'a considerable number of weapons' had been recovered, for each weapon a very dead Fell would have left yet another lonely widow.

My own arrival at our bivouac base was followed by my immediate call on the doctor, escorted by David. I expected to be greeted with warmth and compassion, competent surgery and dispatch to hospital. Disappointment. The doctor merely gave my leg a cursory inspection, during which time I thought the ash from his cigarette was going to fall in the wound, and told me I could have forty-eight hours rest. Big deal. The whole bloody regiment was on three days rest. Meanwhile I had to listen to him congratulating David on a first-class sewing job and telling him to remove the stitches in a few days. Ten years later, at my home in London, where David did most of his courting prior to his marriage, he informed me that this incident resulted in his receiving a commendation. With friends like him in the Legion, who needed bloody enemies?

The year 1961, although it brought little change in the normal functions of the 3rd Regiment of Infantry and the routine of the endless searching for elusive Fell, brought considerable changes in myself. I found myself fast becoming more of a legionnaire than I had ever dreamed of. I was beginning to love my regiment, my company, even the bloody sergeants. I loved the Legion. My comrades were no longer just friends, they were my brothers. When I was born, so many years earlier, I was born an instinctive survivor, almost a coward with a tendency for self-survival. Yet, if it had been required, I would have been prepared to risk all for a fellow member of the Legion. If I had beer and they had none, it was shared. If I had cigarettes and they were without, they would be split. Money, food, wine, anything was theirs. They were brothers. The only thing I would never offer to share with a fellow legionnaire would be *his* eight days prison.

I also discovered that I had fallen in love with the natural beauty of Algeria, even though most of that discovery had been made whilst marching through it. The awe-inspiring depths of the Aurès, the rugged windswept peaks of the Atlas mountains, the high plateaux found where least expected, the ever-changing flora and fauna, always with the breeze bringing the sweet smell of the yellow Algerian flower, standing on the edge of an escarpment and admiring the view of magnificent gorges and ravines – a sight that can be equalled only in the Grand Canyon in the United States: I had learnt to love all this, despite the uncertainty, whilst appreciating the beauty, that some stupid Fell might be aiming a rifle at my head from the other side of the gorge.

Perhaps one of the factors responsible for my changing outlook was that, whereas in the early days I was obliged to carry out duties or orders because this was the *réglement* in the pecking order of hierarchy, now I had thrown away the 'book' and saluted officers, and felt privileged to do so, because I respected them as individuals. I carried out instructions no longer as instructions but as requests given by someone I respected. This respect was not something I had found by accident or picked up from the ground: it was merited by the officers' and sergeants' attitude, behaviour and love for the Legion. I had reached the conclusion that any army without discipline was no longer an army but a rabble. Me, I wanted to be a member of the élite.

I loved the Legion. I loved the country. But I hated bloody fatigues, so still avoided them whenever possible.

I may have changed, I may have learnt something, but there was still a long way to go and a lot more to learn.

Much has been written about the mystique and myths of the Foreign Legion, undefinable and seemingly inexplicable.

It is true that the majority of recruits do not speak French when they enter the Legion but they very quickly learn to do so. A considerable part of the oral instruction that all recruits undergo during their basic training is the constant repetition of the battles the Legion has fought, the names of various officers and legionnaires who have died in combat whilst leading their men, always in the front, and invariably the first to die. Equally revered are the names of those legionnaires who have sacrificed themselves for their comrades or for their officers. And there are many of these. During the battle of Camerone Legionnaire Catteau threw himself in front of Lieutenant Maudet to protect him and received nineteen balls and a medal for the effort.

Recruits learn of combat during the First World War, when a whole Legion regiment was decorated by the Americans. Even today each legionnaire in that regiment wears on his breast the award that has been inherited.

They learn of the Legion's participation in the Battle of Narvik during the Second World War, and of Bir Hakeim in the Western Desert, where so many legionnaires still lie alongside their British allies.

They learn also of the calamity of Dien Bien Phu, in French Indo China, and of the 10,000 legionnaires buried in that country, lost in a hopeless war, unheard-of until the Americans inherited the responsibility and called the country Vietnam.

It is through learning by constant repetition the history of the Legion, the names, the battles and the events, that the recruit absorbs the French language.

When the legionnaire has completed his basic training, he may still have no idea who is the Minister of War in the French Government, perhaps not even the name of the President of France, but he will be able to recite the history of the Legion, though possibly not word perfect, nor with the correct accent, and will have absorbed, even in the early days, that if he is called upon to make the ultimate sacrifice, it is to be done in the tradition of the Legion, facing the enemy!

It is at this time that the almost fully trained recruit realizes that, although on enlistment he swore an oath of allegiance to the French flag, that flag is wholly represented by the Legion, and only the Legion. He may be termed a soldier but he is not part of the French Army, and for him there will only exist the Legion and his officers. The French regular army is as remote as the man on the moon, and will not even exist in his mental make-up.

The next factor in the mystique will be the regiment, and it will not matter to what regiment the recruit is transferred after his training. Ten legionnaires may have completed their training together and have been indoctrinated in exactly the same manner, they may even have been born of the same mother, but these ten legionnaires, on arrival at any of the regiments, will each, in the shortest time imaginable, be convinced that God has helped him in the selection of that particular regiment. His regiment is the best in the Legion. His colonel is second only to God, and the best in the Legion. All other regiments are inferior in all aspects to *his* regiment. They may call themselves legionnaires in other regiments, but they are worthless.

Then there is the newly qualified legionnaire's company. It will matter not which company it is, he will be convinced that it is the best and only worthwhile company in the regiment. His own company captain will be the only true gentleman in the regiment, and the best officer who ever left St Cyr. Then will come the senior non-commissioned officer of the section to which he now belongs, who may be an *adjudant* or chief sergeant. This man, he will be convinced, is the most brutal and sadistic bastard who has ever served in the Legion. At the first opportunity this swine will be killed in a shooting accident. The legionnaire will spend night after night with his newly found friends in the section planning how they can destroy this sadist, not with an easy death but with bullets placed everywhere except the head or heart, thereby ensuring that he will suffer a lingering death. Part of the mystique becomes apparent when the legionnaire is given the opportunity to go to a different section, thus ridding himself of this bestial section chief forever: he will fall on his knees in front of his captain and beg to be allowed to stay with his *own* section.

Other sections will also find to their cost that any criticism of a particular brutal and sadistic section chief is a prerogative allowed only to those legionnaires who serve under him, for this is the same brutal swine who, with the realization that as the end of the month approaches, his legionnaires will be without funds, will send them a case of beer from the sergeants' mess. The arrival of a case of free beer will in no way deter the recipients in their planning of his future demise. Even if they spend three years with the same sergeant, they will forever discuss how they can successfully kill him. Meanwhile the flow of free beer will arrive each month with the regularity of the new moon. Inexplicably, after a year with this individual, they find themselves shaking hands with him each morning, saying '*Bon jour, chef*', but still spending the evenings planning his death. (This stupid band of idiots, myself included, could, during the course of any operation that included a fire-fight, have let the odd shot go astray. Then would come the pensive thought that, during a fire-fight, we needed him a lot more than he needed us.)

When this brutal and sadistic swine, with the vagaries of life in the Legion, finds he is obliged to leave the regiment, his legionnaires discover that, if it were not for the fact that, like all members of the Legion, they suffer from emotional constipation, they would say farewell with tears in their eyes.

Much to the surprise of most legionnaires, they find that towards the end of the second year of service they have absorbed all the traditions: they have achieved a loyalty to the regiment, the company, the section, the officers, even the bastard NCOs. But most of all, they will have discovered a loyalty to their comrades, and a kinship, as a brother, to them all.

5   The Year of Shame

Legion historical records probably do not include a skirmish that took place in March 1961 near a small village called Morsot, twenty-five kilometres from the Tunisian frontier. Yet this operation is to me a vivid memory, not because of my participation (I only cocked my weapon when the shooting had ended) but because it was the only close-up panoramic view witnessed from beginning to end of the destruction of a complete unit of the Fell. The whole shooting match was completed in less than ten minutes, at a distance of only the length of a football pitch from where I was standing. Not a legionnaire was killed or wounded. As far as I am concerned it was one of the most successful operations carried out by the second battalion of the regiment.

The 2nd Battalion was, to the best of our knowledge, on stand-down after we had arrived at Morsot only a few days before, and constructed our bivouac area surrounded by a single strand of barbed wire, within walking distance of the village. Ample supplies of water were available, and an easy air of relaxation permeated the whole camp. For one of the few times we were near civilization, even though that civilization was just a small village.

Reveille that morning had not been until seven o'clock, all my laundry had been well washed and was hanging on the fence to dry, and I was seriously considering walking to the village and seeing if it had anything to offer when, shortly after nine o'clock, someone hit the panic button. Someone shouted that we were on combat status, to be ready in five minutes, with weapons, ammunition and water bottles – rations, food, sleeping bags *not* required: MOVE!

We were ready for departure in three minutes; within five

minutes we were already trying to sort out our equipment, in the back of a truck where we had thrown it, making full speed for the frontier.

I had never known an operation where I would not be marching without the weight of a sack on my back, and I felt only half dressed. The truck turned off the road and began climbing a cart track towards the heights. Within thirty minutes of leaving our bivouac, we were dismounting and heading for a hill that led to a small plateau inclining upwards. After only thirty minutes march at a fairly rapid pace, we arrived at the edge of a small escarpment.

I had been under the impression that it was only the one company escorting the headquarters group involved in the operation. Arrival at the edge of the escarpment showed this not to be true. Only some twenty metres below was a small, narrow valley about 150 metres in width. As I looked down, there came a burst of fire. For a moment I thought it was my own section that had opened fire, then in the valley I saw a group of figures running, two carrying an AA 52 light-calibre machine-gun, the rest carrying rifles and pistol machine-guns. Looking at them, I noticed they were all wearing brand-new camouflage uniforms, and felt envious as I thought of my own sun-bleached and tattered uniforms hanging on the barbed wire, which would probably be stolen by the time we returned.

I was still wondering where the shots were coming from and who they were directed at (no splats had come in my direction, and though I could hear the firing, I wasn't dead) when I realized that it was the running figures that were the target. They were not legionnaires. They were bloody Fell, dressed as we were. I saw the three with the AA 52 cut down by a sergeant who seemed to appear from nowhere, slightly above and at the most only ten metres from them. It was like sitting in a cinema watching the action take place on a wide screen. It was only then that I saw other legionnaires on the opposite side of this small valley come into sight and commence sweeping the area slightly to our right.

I had been standing next to our captain when the shooting ceased, he asked me for a light for his cigarette, and I was in the process of lighting both his and my own when a man stood up in the undergrowth only some thirty metres in front of us, with a carbine held above his head in a gesture of surrender. He was a Fell officer wearing stars on his shoulder straps. *That* was when I cocked my weapon for the first time. I was restrained by the captain as this Fell officer threw his weapon to the ground and again raised his hands in the air. I wanted to shoot him because he had obviously sent his men on and then laid down and hidden himself. This individual and heroic 'freedom fighter' had heard the clack as I cocked my PM, watched as I started to raise it and, rather than approach us, walked towards another group of legionnaires. He had noticed the hand of the captain pushing the muzzle of my weapon down. I still think I should have shot the bastard, despite the captain. But ...

We then began to descend into the depression, in search of any odd Fell who had slipped through the screen, but we were then informed that the operation was over and that we were heading to the rendezvous with our trucks. I was surprised to find that the small depression led to the edge of yet another escarpment, where looking down one could see, some 500 metres below us and only a kilometre away, the barbed wire of the Morice defence line. As we passed the bodies of the Fell, by this time being dragged together for photographs, I could not help but notice that their lightweight canvas boots were brand new, their uniforms as if just issued from the stores, the ammunition from their pouches sparkling shiny like polished brass, everything as if it had been issued from a well-stocked stores only the day before, which it probably had. These poor fools had probably crossed the frontier the night before; they certainly had not got far.

Arrival at our trucks, which could not be seen from the top of the escarpment, brought a further shock. There were over a hundred trucks apart from ours, containing at least a few thousand regular French Army and conscripts, all spread out, most of them looking slightly nervous and placed there to prevent the Fell now lying on top of the escarpment returning to Tunisia.

We were back at the bivouac by early afternoon, and the cook had excelled himself in keeping our lunch fresh and hot. He even earned a few beers from me for having collected my laundry from the barbed wire.

Not a legionnaire wounded nor killed, brand new weapons

captured, the whole operation completed in a few hours, and I had not marched more than a few kilometres. Who the hell wants an office job nine till five? This was the right way to fight a war. Leave after breakfast, see some action, back for lunch. Stuff the Para, this was the way to live.

Perhaps the reason why this is the most vivid operation I hold in my memory is that it was the easiest. Problem was, it was the only one like it.

Even today I have no idea of the total effectiveness of the 3rd Regiment, for my own life revolved completely around the 2nd Battalion, and within that battalion I knew only a few legionnaires in the 5th and 6th Companies, and then only by sight. Most of those I got to know I found at the inescapable poker schools that convened at the end of each month. These poker schools would be established within hours of the pay being distributed, held in the back of a truck or, should the eight-man tents have been erected, then poker would be played in five out of six. If neither trucks nor eight-men tents were available, five legionnaires would crowd into a one-man tent. It became almost habitual that, month after month, at least fifty per cent of the pay made to any one company would find its way into the hands of that company's expert poker-player. By some coincidence, these were almost invariably Italians. The only exception was myself.

I made it a strict rule not to play poker until at least a week had elapsed after the distribution of the pay. This allowed a sifting process of the big winners of one section or company, playing against other big winners. Only then would I commence playing poker. I did not play with any of my own section – I played poker with their money! We formed a monthly syndicate, and I would play on their behalf, profit being distributed equally. During two years of playing, I lost all our pay only once; at all other times we made a profit. During December 1960, after playing over twenty hours continuous poker, our food brought by our various well-wishers, I arose from the table having won more than £2,600. As we were quite near Algiers at the time, all members of the syndicate had a very merry Christmas.

It was during this period, when the whole of the 2nd Battalion were only about two kilometres from Bou-Farick and thirty kilometres from Algiers, that I visited the capital city on two occasions. The first visit was in the company of Jacques, a good friend, a member of the syndicate and one of my mentors in the ways of the Legion. Jacques was quite knowledgeable about the city of Algiers for during his service he had spent many months there. (Regrettably his previous visits had been in happier times, long before the violence, riots and bombing of hotels and cinemas that had become almost a way of life since 1958.) It was like the visit of two country boys who had never moved out of their village in all their lives, visiting London and ending up in Soho, or paying a visit to New York and, instead of finding themselves in Manhattan, arriving in the Bronx.

We started off well. Both being flush with money, we decided to have lunch at the Alletti Hotel, our first mistake. I had forgotten that on my previous visits it had been as an officer in the RAF, and we were very abruptly refused entry. Since the officers who objected to our presence were of the regular army, we argued, and I, with my fluent vocabulary recently acquired, produced every French swear word I had learnt. The speed with which Jacques and I left the hotel by way of the window, with a drop of some six metres from the balcony of the restaurant, directly into flower beds, was brought about by the appearance of a captain dressed in Legion uniform – since we both recognized him as being from our regiment, it was time for a hasty retreat. Jacques could easily have been identified by the value and quantity of ribbons he was wearing, but as the day wore on, it was obvious that no search for us had been instigated.

We settled for lunch at a restaurant near the harbour that specialized in seafood that had been spiced with aphrodisiac. It had to have been spiced with something, for although we had consumed at least three bottles of wine and two of champagne, within five minutes of lighting his cigar, Jacques insisted that we visit the casbar and the best brothel in Africa: the Sphinx. Although I was somewhat dubious about entering the Arab quarter, my misgivings were dispelled by his description of the delights to be found at the Sphinx. But I wished at the time that I'd had sense enough to bring at least a grenade.

Although the entrance to the Arab quarter was guarded by police, they must have assumed that we were on duty – at least, they let us pass without question. We wandered about the casbar for at least an hour, and although we eventually found the Sphinx, it would have been easier finding a Fell in the mountains. We also found that we were being trailed by at least thirty Arabs, none of whom appeared in any way to be of a friendly nature. It was with some relief that we finally gained entrance to this 'Palace of the Near East'. It cost £30 to gain entrance, and after two hours of tasting its delights, it cost a further £150 to get out. On contemplating the cost, I thought the money could have lasted a lot longer at our own regimental brothel, but I resigned myself to the fact that it had been the profits made from a poker game with the 1st Battalion before Christmas that had paid the expenses.

Our problems started when we left the brothel. The number of Arabs waiting outside must have been at least fifty, all looking very unhappy at our intrusion into their territory. The winding streets of the casbar, only wide enough for four people to stand shoulder to shoulder, must have been designed many years before with the express purpose of allowing legionnaires such as Jacques and myself to abstract ourselves from what I can only describe as a very delicate situation.

When we arrived at the exit to the casbar, our uniform tunics had been ripped to pieces and for some reason we were laughing our heads off. Jacques had collected two ugly-looking knives, with which an attempt had been made to slice his head off, and I found myself holding an American Colt .45 automatic that one of the Arabs, who had broken his arm, had insisted on handing to me. We had left at least a dozen of them requiring hospital treatment, and a further six who would certainly not be demonstrating their sexual prowess to their wives for at least a week.

As we descended the steps of the casbar, for the first time in my life I was happy to see some of the regular military, even though they were pointing their weapons at us, awaiting our arrival and wondering what the disturbance was about. (They had not cocked the weapons.) We had both managed to retain our kepis despite the fracas, but there was no way we could return to our camp with our tunics looking so disreputable. The regulars, for once in their lives, did something useful. They obtained two new tunics for us, in exchange for the two knives and the .45 automatic. The officer in charge seemed a little reluctant to let us leave without our giving our names and signing a statement, but he seemed content when we asked his name and said we would report the incident to our own officers on our return to the regiment. Very gullible.

My second visit to Algiers was with the positive thought that there would be no repeat of previous incidents and strict avoidance of the Alletti Hotel and the casbar. I invited David and a diminutive Spanish legionnaire, only a few days before Christmas, to come with me to have a traditional English Christmas dinner, with turkey and all the trimmings. David was selected because he came from my home town, the small Spanish character to keep me out of trouble. (To the citizens of Algiers, three fairly tall legionnaires would be the same as waving a red flag at a bull.) Since both my companions were of small stature, we would obviously not be looking for trouble ... I hoped.

It may appear to have been ridiculous logic to assume that traditional British meals would be served at the Hôtel Angleterre, just because of its name, but I had been right in my assumption. The hotel was run by two British ladies and, although both were very charming, they were rather reluctant to allow us to enter – not because it was for officers only but because they were doubtful of our ability to pay the bill. I was required to produce a very large roll of cash from my pocket and, being rather annoyed, proffered it all as a deposit on the purchase of the hotel. This gesture was not really appreciated, since the conversation was in English, during which I utilized my cultivated British officer voice. With apologies, my cash was returned, we were given one of the best tables and had the staff scuttling about as if we were visiting royalty.

Nothing pleased me more than the expression on these two ladies' faces when one of our own officers entered the restaurant with his wife and son, and, as we stood up at our table, as a compliment to him and his lady, watched this captain salute us and wish us '*Bon appetit*' and take a table adjacent to ours, in preference to others. We enjoyed our meal. I had enjoyed playing one-upmanship. I expect these ladies were talking for the next few years about the curious sight of a Legion captain who, on our departure, had risen from his table to shake hands with each of us and wish us a 'good day'. 'Good Day!' If only he had known ...

Prior to entering the hotel restaurant, I had noticed a small bar quite near, and serving behind the bar were two very nice-looking Vietnamese girls. It was here that we had decided to spend the next few hours, in the hope that one of us would be lucky enough to end up in bed with one or the other, or in my case preferably with both. While David and our Spanish companion were engaged in playing the stupid bar table game of football, I did my best at the bar with the girls, being polite, charming, gallant, generous and drooling, and was convinced that within the next hour I was going to be invited upstairs.

Then I heard a disturbance behind me and, when I turned, I found David and our Spanish friend either fighting or dancing with an ugly-looking large Algerian character. I ignored them completely. The odds were more than enough, and to even them up I would have had to join in on the side of the Algerian, so I carried on trying my damnedest with the girls. At a sudden shout from David, behind me, of 'Jim, he's got a gun,' when I turned this time I saw six hands high in the air trying to gain possession of a dirty big American Colt .45 automatic. I spilt my drink as I wondered if this was the same bloody gun I had handed in just a couple of days ago. Without even having to leave my bar stool, I had only to lean over and pluck it from their hands, and laid it on the bar. They continued to dance and fight, and I carried on with the girls.

Some stupid bloody fool had telephoned the police. A half dozen jeeps arrived outside the bar, with some regular army conscripts, all waving PMs and revolvers and, it seemed, all pointing at me because of the gun on the bar. The owner of the bar declared that I had taken no part in the fracas, only those three, pointing at David and our Spanish friend, both sitting on the head and chest of the poor Algerian character, now flat on his back. All three were arrested and taken away. As I handed over the gun, the officer in charge (looking at the girls) told me I could pick David and our Spanish friend up in a couple of hours, when I had finished my business. This would give them the chance to tidy their uniforms. When I collected them, at five o'clock, they refused to believe that I had spent all the afternoon at the museum.

We quit the town. I then decided that it was my final visit to Algiers. It was too bloody dangerous, and safer in the mountains.

I had been in my regiment for slightly more than a year, and in the Legion for two years, when I realized that though the Legion had achieved a minor miracle in developing my body into peak physical condition, my mind was beginning to stagnate.

I had learned the French language, along with a smattering of German, Italian and even Arabic. Through the aid of some very helpful officers obtaining books for me from France, I was making a study of French military history, especially those items that concerned the Legion. I was a voracious reader. But even this was not satisfying my appetite to do something constructive with my mind.

It was then that I decided to keep a notebook. It was not going to be a diary; it would not contain the intricate details of combat. Within the regiment there was an official historian, far more intelligent than myself and, since he was an officer, with access to far more facts than would have been available to me. Nor did I wish to keep a record of: 'Tuesday: Killed two Fell. Friday the 13th: Killed four more.' So I decided not to write about heroic deeds, or heroic legionnaires, only about incidents which had interested or amused me, and a few that occasionally sickened me. This I did throughout my service, recording only the items that would never appear in any official history of the Legion.

There were such small and insignificant items as the story of the captain who for more than a year had noticed, but not remarked on the fact, that I always volunteered to carry the additional weight of the spare battery of the radio, thus easing part of the weight that Jacques, the radio operator, would normally carry. It took the same captain a year to discover that during operations, even if a fire-fight was taking place, a small piece of paper would be passed between Jacques and myself, either from Jacques to me, or me to him. The whole thing stopped when the captain intercepted one morsel of paper, on which was written 'Q F 4'. It was at that moment that the chess games being played on miniature chess sets between myself and a friend in the 5th Company came to an end. I spent an hour explaining to the captain how to code a chessboard, reduce the radio transmission to a minimum and make it undecipherable if overheard. I also explained how my move of the Queen to F4 placed my opponent in check.

My use of the captain's radio was terminated, but I continued to carry the spare battery for Jacques and later felt affronted and annoyed to learn that the captain was now playing radio chess with a colleague of equal rank. Although the captain had been slightly peeved to find that I had been using his radio as a private telephone service, he treated the episode as a huge joke, and I received a warning and a lecture but no reprimand. This demonstrates that a legionnaire has nothing to fear from his officers. One is not punished in the Legion for breaking rules, or disregarding orders, only when caught, and not always then.

I wrote of how, feeling weary and distressed, after hours of steadily plodding through the mountains, one could stumble across Paradise – of how, ludicrous as it seemed in a remote, almost secret valley with lush undergrowth, carpeted with wild flowers, concealed high in the mountains, one might find three orange trees bearing fruit. These trees had not been planted by any hill farmer, for the whole sector was devoid of any cultivation. They were denuded by my section as quickly as they would have been by a swarm of locusts, had locusts ever reached such a height. They were not as sweet as the oranges planted in the groves of the lower coastal regions, but they did have a certain succulence halfway between a lemon and an orange and tasted like pure nectar to thirsty legionnaires. At least they assuaged our thirst for the next few hours.

I wondered if perhaps, some years earlier, another legionnaire had sat in the place where we had found those trees, eating an orange he had taken with him, and if the pips he had spat out had become those trees. I've wondered since, who will be the next wanderer to find them? Those remote mountain areas were only for fighting, not for exploitation or tourism, and no roads existed, only animal tracks and the natural paths of melting snow turning to water, finding the easiest descent to the valleys.

I wrote to my father telling him of the wild orange trees, of the beauty of the valley, and of the near conviction that we had stumbled across the Garden of Eden. Then I received from him, in each of his monthly letters, a packet of British garden flower seeds, with instructions to plant them during what he referred to as my excursion trips. I carried out his instructions, using my bayonet as a hoe, turning over the earth at every stop we made whilst carrying out our operations, carefully planting each seed and even allowing a slight trickle of my precious water to help them on their way.

Whilst at first the sight of me carrying out my gardening duties, attempting to plant seeds in the lower reaches of the Aurès mountains, raised a lot of laughter, and invited ridicule, it was soon excused by my section, since they all considered me mad anyway. When I later saw a hardbitten German sergeant, one of those who had led the laughter, secretly planting garden seeds he had received from Germany, I invited him to 'join the club'.

I had obtained a very small frying pan and, marching in the mountains with this hanging from my bergen sack, was declared an idiot by my comrades, since towards the end of a day's marching each gramme of weight unnecessarily carried feels like a brick. But at the evening halt they would crowd around my small fire, the saliva dripping from their mouths, as they savoured the rich smell rising from my frying pan of the can of meat from my hardtack rations blending with that of a small onion I had taken along. Then, as I added the final touches, a sprinkling of salt and pepper from between thumb and forefinger, in the fashion of a cook preparing a very special dish, I would watch tears running from their eyes as they begged the use of my pan. Then I enjoyed their exasperation at the approach of the commandant's batman, who conveyed the compliments of the commandant, who had also fallen victim to the aroma, with the request that he borrow my pan to prepare their supper. At least I had my priorities right, for I not only loaned the pan but also presented an onion. I've often wondered since if perhaps it was for this reason that I was sent to corporals' training school.

I wrote of a young sergeant who had deserted while we were in the hills near the Tunisian frontier, after a tiring day of fruitless searching for Fell. He had been foolish enough to have taken his weapon with him – if he had departed without his weapon, it is unlikely that the regiment would have bothered chasing him but, intercepted by the Fell, his weapon would have been used to kill other legionnaires. If he had crossed the frontier, his weapon would have been confiscated by the Tunisian authorities and given to the Fell enjoying the sanctuary of that country, resting between forays into Algeria. Deserting without his weapon and then running into Fell before reaching the frontier, death would have been welcomed, for they were not kindly people.

The sergeant's own section was sent to track him down and bring him back. This they did. However, in his foolishness he had opened fire as they approached and was consequently killed. They then had the onerous task of carrying his body back as evidence of the completion of their mission and that they had not fired a few random shots out of sight. The sack of the sergeant contained his letters, family photographs, slabs of chocolate purchased from a souk, and a spare water bottle. He had therefore planned his departure. When offered, I declined to share the chocolate.

I wrote in my journal of 'Black Thursday' and the reluctant Fells. I witnessed the incident only because I had escorted a lieutenant from my own section situated two kilometres away. A small group of a dozen Fell had been intercepted by members of the 5th Company, and three of them had been killed in the first flurry of fire; the remainder had thrown down their weapons and surrendered.

Prisoners in the almost inaccessible heights of Algeria can be neither fed nor watered The rules of the Geneva Convention and gentlemanly warfare did not apply between the Fell and the Legion. The most gratifying gift allowed any legionnaire captured would be death, but legionnaires were never captured.

After being interrogated, for which purpose my lieutenant had come, they were searched and relieved of all their possessions. Looking somewhat dejected and miserable, they sat crouching and squatting, their hands firmly clasped on their heads about ten metres away. No effort was made at guarding them. The section responsible for their capture was sitting drinking coffee, and I had been invited to join them, at the same time giving an admiring glance at the new watch now adorning John's wrist.

The section sergeant approached the Fell and told them to 'pee off', but none showed any inclination to depart, despite his repeated shouts, and it required none too gentle kicks even to get them on their feet. Then, rather reluctantly, they began to edge away. None of the legionnaires sitting drinking had a weapon in his hands; all were only interested in making the most of the break offered. At a distance of thirty to forty metres, the poor bloody Fell broke into a panic-ridden mad stampede for what they mistakenly thought would be their freedom. Without even standing up, the group of legionnaires with whom I had been sitting simply picked up the weapons lying by their sides and opened fire. None of the Fell survived. None gained a greater distance than sixty metres away. All were reported as killed whilst trying to escape.

I had not taken part in the shooting. That was not because of my high principles as an Englishman. John, whom I had joined to drink my coffee, was far more English than I, had higher principles and had demonstrated these higher principles and marksmanship by shooting with only his right hand, whilst still holding firmly on to his coffee with his left. I had not opened fire because it was not my party, and I had not been invited to shoot. Yet I was happy to rejoin my section, happier still that I had not participated in the pigeon shoot, and I slept well that night.

Yet another incident recorded in my journal. This was of a legionnaire who had deserted from the 13th Demi-Brigade almost six months earlier. He was picked up by one of the sections who had intercepted a few Fell. He had been with the enemy for the whole period since his absence from the Legion. He was court-martialled, prosecuted and defended by the same captain within thirty minutes of being captured. All legionnaires were called close to witness the execution, which was carried out by the same captain. He was made to kneel, given two minutes to make his peace with God, and shot in the back of the head with a revolver.

The bodies of the Fell were never buried, at any time, but the concession to this ex-legionnaire was that at least he was buried, albeit in an unmarked grave. He had been a fool, he had made a mistake, he had been executed, but he was buried by his family. Come what may, at one time he had been a legionnaire. Once …

Regardless of the physical and psychology tests inflicted on Legion recruits on enlistment, there were none that could predict the most dangerous malady of a legionnaire operating in hostile territory, that of sleepwalking. For more than a year prior to my arrival at the 3rd Regiment and eventual section, a form of security to protect Raphael from this malady had been established.

On combat operations in the mountains, each legionnaire does sentinel duty. His only job is guarding his comrades for a duration of one cold and lonely hour. There is no guard commander to disturb his lonely vigil. There are no breaks to disturb the eerie silent darkness. No relief will come until he wakens the next sentinel. Anything moving in the vicinity will be shot without the formality of a challenge. A very dangerous situation exists for the sleepwalker.

Raphael had a comrade who for a year ensured that he would not be killed by a weary but vigilant sentinel by sleeping wrapped in, not lying inside, his sleeping bag, his feet tied to those of Raphael. Raphael could never complete just the one-hour duty which was always followed by his comrade Menon. If he ended his duty and returned to his sleeping bag, there was always the possibility of his wandering off alone, still asleep. And if he was not shot by Menon, he might be shot by another sentinel posted nearby. So when Raphael had completed his own hour, he stayed for the next hour along with Menon.

When I arrived in the section, I found no difficulty in accepting that I too would be responsible for Raphael and that, in the absence of Menon, it would be my feet tied to those of Raphael. It was slightly difficult to adjust for the first month, and very disquieting to be awakened by Raphael, who seemed to be the only legionnaire in Algeria determined to go hiking on his own at night.

Happily they both finished their five-year stint in 1963 and departed to make their fortunes in the Amazon. I've often wondered since if Raphael would be taking his night walks in the jungle – even more dangerous than Algeria.

A whole company moving slowly forward in new and hostile terrain might find evidence of predecessors in the form of a freshly opened tin of sardines (standard rations for the Fell), which had been discarded by one of the careless enemy. (They would normally bury even their cigarette butts.) Ahead of the company, at the spearhead, was the duty section. Ahead of the section were five lonely men of the forward scouts.

On one occasion the five were proceeding in arrow formation, with the regulation distance between them, the leading man in a deep gully winding its way through the hills, his friends spread out to either side. A sudden clatter at the bottom of the gully, a cry of '*Merde!*' from the leading man, and his comrades quickly rushed to his aid, full of concern.

He had embarrassed them all. At one of the turns in the gully, he had come face to face with a Fell who was acting as point man for his own group. Both hesitated, and for both of them the world stood still while each deliberated that, 'He'll not shoot if I don't.' Finally the Fell dropped his weapon, turned about and fled, the guilty legionnaire still standing, with a look of shock, his suntanned face turning a shade of green, as his comrades joined him.

The legionnaire in charge of this hero, and the rest of 'em, had a problem. He now had a captured weapon without a body. With a weapon and a dead body came a medal and a few days rest, without the body at least eight days prison for failing to shoot. A way out of the dilemma was found by hastily burying the captured weapon, first removing the breech block and spring and placing them in the sack of the non-hero, with instructions to throw them off the highest mountain later. The incident was not reported, but at least the message was passed back that they had sighted the movement of Fell, some distance in front of them but out of range. How did I learn this story? I was one of the five! But which one?

A prisoner handed over to the authorities on return from an operation was a thirteen-year-old boy, the only survivor of Fell who had been responsible for killing one of our sergeants. The boy had not been armed but insisted on carrying on the war by hurling rocks, one of which hit me in the mouth. I felt no animosity but a silent respect for his courage. When told to 'get rid of him' by the captain, I enquired if we were now killing children. My reward for such impertinence was to be made responsible for him during the next three days, and we were a long way from 'home'.

The first day I allowed him to walk by my side, sharing my very sparse rations, drinking my very precious water, I was surprised to find he was a very heavy smoker. (Cigarettes have a high value in the mountains.)

That night I was awakened by the feel of a stealthy hand attempting to slide my fighting knife from my waist. If he had been successful, it would not have been used to give me an early morning shave.

The second day he walked in front of me with his hands free but now secured by a length of rope attached to his waist, still sharing my food, water and cigarettes. The second night I tied him securely, to ensure there would be no repetition of the previous night. Waking at dawn, I found he had spent the night trying to free himself, and had almost succeeded.

The third day I marched with him not secured by a loose rope but with the rope looped around his neck, continuing down his back and tied tightly to his hands. This was no longer a boy I was escorting but a dangerous wolf.

My unvoiced thoughts as we marched were that he would attempt to break away and run for it, thereby giving me the chance to shoot him legally. Even if I missed him, he would fall over the edge of the escarpment. With luck the rope would be caught up, and he would hang himself. The third day he went hungry, thirsty and none too gently propelled forward with the aid of my boot. The cynical glances I received from the captain, when he sarcastically asked if I was thirsty, when he was fully aware that my water bottle had been empty since the previous night, did nothing but induce from me that 'compassion' was a word I was going to delete from my dictionary.

The pure relief at meeting up with the regular army and handing over my boy wolf to their custody! And their surprise at seeing a prisoner!

Later, as I greedily supped a beer, I realized that a weapon in the hands of a thirteen-year-old would kill me just as dead as one in the hands of a man. He was the last prisoner I ever pleaded a case for. I still had a lot to learn.

There was this one morning, after another night of sleeping in the hills, when, having packed my sleeping bag in my sack, ready for the next march, and drunk my coffee and brandy, in the beautiful clear air of the wakening dawn I went to the toilet. Rather than expose my posterior to my comrades, more out of modesty than for fear of offering them temptatioin, I descended only a matter of ten metres from my friends down the slight rise that had provided us with our beds and shelter for the night and concealed myself behind a bush. Kicking the earth with the heel of my boot, to make a small hole, so that I could later conceal the evidence of my visit from any of the enemy who would be passing that way, I laid down my trusty pistol machine-gun quite close, resting upright against a small shrub, stood over my hole and lowered my trousers and slip. As I crouched over my hole, awaiting my body's discharge of the surplus residue of my stomach, admiring the distant view and the morning sun beginning to rise over the mountains, with the clear sky heralding yet another wonderful day, I began to experience winges of constipation and found difficulty in completing my task. Then to my horror, I saw on the path below, only fifteen metres away, the passage of two Fell. Both of them, who had probably just completed the first of their traditional five daily prayers, were at peace with the world, completely relaxed, smoking a cigarette, their rifles casually resting on their shoulders. It was a temptation to call and wish them 'Good Morning'. Both were very unobservant, since neither had seen me. It was as if they were engaged on a leisurely stroll.

It was then that my stomach deserted me. Whereas I had been suffering the cramp of constipation, it now erupted with a sudden burst of flatus, like a clap of thunder, probably the loudest fart ever sounded in the mountains, so loud that I waited for the resounding echo. At the sudden explosion, they both looked up at me with signs of shock on their faces. My raucous fart had been followed by an outpouring and uncontrolled involuntary attack of diarrhoea. For one of the few times my weapon was out of hand's reach, and in spite of the situation I had no wish to dive for it and soil my slip and trousers, which I was sure would soon be buried, with me inside them.

Being very good little Fells, indoctrinated that discretion is the better part of valour, they charged into the undergrowth and took off at full speed in their now changed direction. It took me some while to recover my composure. It took me a bloody long time.

I climbed back up the hill to my section and told my sergeant what had passed (including the diarrhoea). The stupid bastard almost fell about and rolled on the ground, unable to control his laughter. Then he showed good sense in not taking up the chase, since we knew at midday we would be keeping the rendezvous with our trucks, then going back to our bivouac and rest. His only comment to me was *'M'en fous!* There is always another day. They'll still be around when we get back.'

A nineteen-year-old novice recruit of the Fell was happily striding along a small track in the hills, a few hours after midnight. His almost new American carbine was perched jauntily on his shoulder, and his newly issued backpack contained a nice new freshly issued handtowel, a bar of toilet soap still in its wrapper, and a fine new spare pair of blue woollen socks. Pushed through the shoulder strap of his nearly new combat jacket was his military brown and green side cap. In his breast pocket were his newly issued identity card and photograph, giving his number and company. In the bright moonlight the pathway was clear. It was a wonderfully mild night that made his march a pleasure, on his way to meet his comrades. Suddenly he saw a dark figure emerging from nowhere at the side of the track, only fifteen metres in front of him, and the night erupted with the frightening sound of the crash of the bolt of a pistol machine-gun being armed. Instinctively he shouted 'LAH! – NO!' and tried to throw himself off the track, but he was too late. Only a short burst of six rounds had been fired, but all had made contact between his groin and chest. It was then he started screaming and pitifully wailing.

Foolish young man! Over 300 legionnaires had been sleeping on either side of that track, waiting for first light to go after his comrades. He had walked into the arms of an alert sentinel who was in no mood to challenge or take a prisoner. I had been sleeping only some three metres from the sentinel, for I was due to be his relief. We dragged the body from the track to where I had been sleeping. I had a flashlight in my sack, and with the light provided the medic attempted to dress his wounds and ease his pain with precious morphine. He would not respond to questions, and his constant screaming and wailing in the still night air could have been heard a good kilometre away. The shot in his head with his own weapon was not murder but a merciful killing, so he was put out of his misery. Then those who had had their rest disturbed got back to sleeping. It had not been the sound of shots that had awakened me. It had been the shout of *'LAH!'*

April 1961 brought the four blackest days in Legion history, and this only ten days before legionnaires celebrated the anniversary of the Battle (of Camerone) that had brought them fame. A Legion regiment had spearheaded the *putsch* in Algiers. The 1st Regiment of Parachutists of the Legion, along with other regular colonial and para regiments, were disbanded on the direct orders of the President of France, General de Gaulle. The remainder of the Legion, although they had taken no part, were forbidden from that date to participate in the 14 July parades in Paris, although they had earned the honour of leading the parade.

At the time of the revolt, the 3rd Regiment were still in the vicinity of the Tunisian frontier. Despite orders from our own officers when we received news of the *putsch* that as legionnaires we should not discuss politics, or involvement, there was an air of excitement, anticipation that our own colonel would join in. We legionnaires were hoping that he would join the rebellion, crash through into Tunisia, wipe out the bloody Fells who did their training there and take over the whole damn country. Like our fellow legionnaires of the 1st REP, who had happily followed their own commanding officer, we would have followed our colonel to Hell, or any other place he had wished to lead us.

I listened to every news bulletin flashed from Algiers, Paris and London, most of which seemed contradictory. Then came the solemn desultory voice of 'Charlie' himself, addressing all soldiers of France and declaring: 'They did not have to obey the orders of their officers!' A very easy statement for 'le Grand Charles' to make from Paris! That evening, as we sat around a flickering fire, each with a cup of wine or a bottle of beer, discussing a situation that was far out of the control of ordinary legionnaires, we took a vote between ourselves, to elect the first individual of the section to accept Charlie's offer of refusing an order. After three hours of discussion, a hero could not be found, but we all agreed that the next morning we would not attend rollcall. Came the dawn, and each of us, somewhat bleary-eyed, attended the morning parade, all pledges made the previous evening completely ignored, all of us waiting for some indication from our officers as to which path we would be treading.

The *putsch* had commenced in the very early hours of 21 April. In only a matter of four days it was over. *Kaput!* Four hundred of the 1st Para faded into the wilderness; the remainder were quietly absorbed into other regiments. My own sense of uncertainty, along with those others in the company, had brought not a feeling of relief with the knowledge that it had been abortive but a sense of being 'let down' by those who had failed to allow us to participate.

Very shortly after this rebellion, along with other members of the 2nd Battalion, I found that our trucks – which had belted along in a westerly direction from dawn to dusk at a very high speed – had deposited us at Zarelda, the headquarters of the 1st Regiment of parachutists who had spearheaded the revolt. My section was not in the barracks but camping only a kilometre away, detailed as guards for the regimental brothel that the remnants of the 1st Regiment had failed to take with them. This duty was not a popular one. We soon discovered that it brought neither hospitality nor rewards unless paid for in ready cash. The girls failed to appreciate that our duty required the laying down of our lives for their protection, and as much as I waxed loquacious about defending them to my last breath, it did not do me a bit of good. Those girls were without heart or feelings. They did do my laundry for free, and after only three days I was being supplied with sandwiches and wine, but their honour was sacrosanct. You either hired it at the going rate or went without. After five days I weakened and decided to do some hiring. Before I knew where I was, I was not only having my laundry done but all my uniforms were being pressed. Sandwiches had turned to beefsteaks. Nadia not only began to mother me, she bloody near smothered me. I was very pleased when we upped stakes and departed. Three more weeks of that and we would have ended up getting married!

Again we were on constant desolate country searches for the Fell. We had now taken over the sector normally swept by the 1st REP. It was here that again I had a panoramic view of a fire-fight, this time not all in favour of the Legion, and on this occasion we were supported by helicopter gunships.

We had found a whole band of Fell between a row of small

hills on the left with a whole Legion company on the crests, a small valley heavy with undergrowth. The small hills opposite had yet another company on the crests. A Legion section was in the valley commanded by a chief sergeant. A few sections were sprinting along the crests of the hills, to form an ambush as the Fell were driven along the valley. The section in the valley had already opened fire on them, and they were returning the fire with interest. Then the air force gunship helicopters swooped into action. As we looked (and I had Minnie's binoculars glued to my eyes) I watched as the gunship opened fire with dirty big .50 calibre Browning machine-guns. I felt sick as I watched the strikes of the bullets not among the Fell but among the Legion section. I could even see the chief sergeant as he jumped onto a rock and began to wave his beret at the helicopter, with the strikes all around him. Then the first gunship pulled away, and the second made its attack. As I watched, the very gallant chief sergeant still did not take cover but, wildly waving his beret, indicated to the whole bloody world that he and the target were legionnaires. I watched his arm severed from his body, and the shock of impact knocking him to the ground. Meanwhile the whole group of Fell had evaporated. The rest of the day we pushed on to the coast, still looking for the elusive enemy, eventually arriving at sunset on a cliff edge looking down at the sea. All of us were disturbed by what we had seen, and this was one of the few operations that was not freely discussed.

Even more disturbing, that night, was a discovery made as David and I looked for a sheltered sleeping place, away from the wind sweeping in from the sea. We saw, only some thirty metres away, what appeared to be an animal pen, surrounded on all four sides by a wall only a metre in height and only about twenty-five metres by twenty-five. This would be protection for the whole section. I was surprised to see in the centre a tomb – not of marble or granite but of concrete, with a rather dirty plaque set in cement on top. Curiosity killed the cat. I could not resist the temptation. I cleaned the plaque to see with whom the section would be sleeping that night. It was almost dark when we read the plaque, and after the day's events there was no way I was going to sleep there. The plaque read; 'Unknown English sailor washed ashore at this spot, July 5th, 1941.' David later wrote a letter to the British consular office in Algiers, requesting them to inform the War Graves Commission, giving details and location.

We continued the endless searching for the elusive Fell – far more elusive than those in the eastern part of Algeria. On 14 July 1961, a day when elements of the Legion should have been marching in unison down the Champs Elysées in Paris, we were tucked away in the hills not too far from Algiers. As usual, we were in a temporary bivouac but since today was Bastille Day, celebrated by the Legion as much as by the French population, tables had been laid in the open, so we would all be sitting down to our usual sumptuous celebration lunch. As always at these times, there were ample bottles of beer and wine in the centre of the tables, and everyone was festive and becoming merry.

We were just beginning to eat when there came a cry of 'Alert! Everyone is to pack. We are invading Tunisia!'. I thought at first it was a joke, until the food and drink at the table were abandoned and there was a flurry of packing. The eight-man tents were pulled down, and trucks appeared from nowhere, and were loaded with all the accoutrements of the bivouac, except one lonely tent in the centre.

I had packed all my equipment ready to load when the *adjudant* told me that I would not be going. I, along with Sergeant Kruger, would be staying to pack the residue of the equipment, repair the single truck that was being left and take charge of the spare ammunition, grenades and all the bits and pieces. These were to be loaded into the truck, which we were to guard until informed where we were to go.

I got down on my knees and begged the *adjudant* not to leave me behind. If we were going to invade Tunisia, I wanted to be along. He told me that he did not know when the regiment would be returning to Algeria, and both Kruger and I were due to be sent for training at Sidi-bel-Abbès, I for corporal's training, Kruger for advanced NCO training. Within two hours, they were gone.

As I looked around the now isolated and deserted bivouac, surrounded by a single barbed wire strand, cases of ammunition and grenades stacked in the centre, one eight-man tent standing all on its ownsome, I looked at Kruger and enquired how the hell anyone could let us know where to go. We had not even got a radio. Kruger really made my day by remarking that if the Fell found out that we were alone with all that loot, meaning the grenades and ammunition, we would go down in history in the Legion by fighting a two-man Camerone.

As the convoy pulled away and I looked at the now devastated area, I reflected on what Kruger had said. The realization hit me that we really were alone in hostile territory, without transport, without radio. I had visions of my father admiring the posthumous medal received with the compliments of the Foreign Legion, which without doubt he would treasure. Meanwhile I would be lying on some hill in Algeria, not buried but cut into small pieces and left to feed the wild pigs. More annoying, I knew that Kruger would be looking forward to any Fell visiting us, already contemplating a visit to the tailor to have new medal ribbons sewn on his uniforms. Of all people to have been left with, why Kruger? If we were attacked, he would want to lead a two-man charge with bayonets.

However, both Kruger and I worked like beavers – two men pushing a dirty big six-wheel unserviceable truck over open ground, Kruger with his natural strength, I with the strength that comes to a naturally lazy character hit by panic. We managed to get the truck and ammunition nearer the tent, and I hastily reduced the perimeter surround of barbed wire down to a tighter circle of what I felt sure was going to be General Custer's 'last stand', without the benefit of his presence. Then I hung small cans filled with stones on the barbed wire, to act as an alarm system during the night. Kruger really made my day with the comment that he had seen the same film at the cinema, and it had not made the slightest difference: those who had established this type of alarm system had all been wiped out anyway.

These inspired words from Kruger, which did not stimulate my confidence and certainly reduced any feelings of friendship I had for him, only led to my working harder and faster towards what I was already considering to be the highest priority: my own self-preservation.

I had my normal complement of eight chargers for my pistol machine-gun, each containing thirty rounds of ammunition, which I had already checked that morning, as I had checked them every morning for two years. The rate of fire of this most wonderful of weapons was reckoned to be about 130 rounds per minute, when fired by some cold, methodical and calm legionnaire. At that time I was certainly neither calm, cold nor methodical, and if needed to use my weapon there was little doubt I would have hit the cyclic rate of 600 rounds per minute. Therefore my defensive firing power was going to last only some thirty seconds. With all the surplus ammunition available, I loaded a further ten chargers. If nothing else, at least I'd make a lot of noise, even if the barrel of my weapon did burn out.

When I asked Kruger if he wanted me to load some extra chargers for him, he told me that his current weapon was an American carbine. It was his own private weapon, 'found' in the mountains and previously carried by a Fell officer. I knew darn well that he had only thirty rounds of ammunition for the thing – a perfect weapon for shooting a wild pig and having a pork sandwich, but in the situation I envisaged it would not have proved much use. If it had not been for my faint-heartedness of being left on my own, I'd have shot the bloody idiot and buried him.

I then began opening a couple of cases of grenades to prime them, only to find that they were not defensive grenades, which could give attacking forces a severe headache even when the head was no longer attached to the body. Made of cast iron and placing anyone within thirty metres in extreme peril, what we had been left were offensive grenades, in a two-part lightweight aluminium casing. They would make a loud bang and produce a headache, but the only damage inflicted on an enemy would be to blow his hands off, and only then if the idiot caught it in his hands and stood looking at it!

As evening fell, there came the sound of approaching vehicle, and with relief I saw it was one of our own, a small six-by-six with some half-dozen legionnaires and our own *adjudant*. Problem was that they had not returned to keep us company, only to bring the spare parts for the vehicle, but they had also brought some rations. Up to that time I had not even bothered to check on food and drink, and only then did I remember that this was 14 July, and whereas there should have been at least a few bottles of wine and beer, there was not a darn thing. All those good friends of mine, all my comrades, all those men I called brothers, those thieving bastards of my own section had taken every drop of beer and wine available, that gallant band of brothers who, as I had bid them farewell, not with the usual handshake but with a hug round the shoulders, brave and heroic soldiers going off to war and glory. The bastards had left me to die of thirst. It was fortunate that the legionnaires escorting the *adjudant* were not from my own section. If they had been, a minor battle would have taken place even before they arrived in Tunisia!

The *adjudant* stayed only half an hour, giving a sardonic look at my prepared defensive position, the spare chargers neatly arranged, two dozen grenades close to hand, the tin cans hanging from the barbed wire. Then, shaking his head sadly, he really spoiled the day by shaking hands and saying, 'I'll arrange for someone to come tomorrow to collect the bodies.' I am convinced that at the training cadres for very senior non-commissioned officers in the Legion, at least three months instruction is in the art of sarcasm and ready wit, a compulsory subject. And this was the man who had conned me into corporal's training!

After the *adjudant* left, Kruger came over to see me and, with a grin, laid down in front of me the PM49 (pistol machine-gun) that the *adjudant* had left with him. If I'd load an extra ten chargers for him, he said, he'd buy me a drink – where the hell was he going to buy me a drink? We were in the wilderness. Even so, I was grateful that Kruger had begun to appreciate our situation. At least with two PM49s we could now cause a lot of problems for unwelcome visitors.

Kruger decided that, in the failing light, the repair of the vehicle could not be commenced until the next morning and suggested that we remove the side flaps of the tent and stack them in the truck, and that the tent be shared as a base and sleeping quarters. Also, from the tent with flaps removed, we could observe all directions. It was with some delight that I saw in the tent two large cases that contained all the reserves of the sergeants' mess: cases of beer, bottles of rum, vodka, brandy and *Ricard*, cans of Nescafé, cheeses, loaves of fresh bread. At that moment I was quite happy to have been left behind. The speed with which I volunteered to prepare a meal, build a fire, arrange a small table, and a couple of seats from old boxes, surprised Kruger. He was even more surprised with the quality of the meal: omelette with mushrooms, canned meat and potatoes, a few oranges, washed down with a couple of bottles of good-quality wine, all looted from what had been the sergeants' mess.

Warmed by the fire, blazing cheerfully in the darkening light, relaxed with the wine I had allowed him to share equally – one glass for him, two for me – we began to discuss what precautions we should take during the night. Should we keep the fire burning or allow it to die out? I proposed that we should keep the fire, even although we were only two. For the preceding week at this bivouac there had been no restrictions on fires, and if any of our friends the Fell had been observing the activity, it would be doubtful that they would realize how few in number we were. It could have been the wine or the supper but this was one of the few occasions on which Kruger ever agreed with anything I suggested.

I appreciated that the next morning Kruger would be very busy repairing the only means of transport available, so I suggested that we forget the standard procedure of splitting sentinel duty and that on this occasion I stay awake all night and sleep at dawn the next morning, having my rest whilst he was working on the truck. Kruger again surprised me by saying he would partially go along with the idea but only on condition that I wake him at midnight, when he would do a couple of hours.

I awakened Kruger as arranged. Although the fire was still burning brightly, as yet the moon had not yet risen to its zenith, and the limit of visibility was only in the circle of light from the fire.

I curled myself up in my sleeping bag but it seemed that I had at the most slept only for a few minutes when I was awakened by the sound of a machine-gun, seemingly fired along the side of my head. Grabbing my PM, discarding the sleeping bag, I joined Kruger, whom I found only two metres away, blazing away with his second charger of ammunition. We were whispering for some unknown reason as I asked how many and where were the targets he was shooting at. He told me he'd heard the tins I had hung on the wire moving about and opened fire. By this time I too could distinguish noise and movement around the fence and decided to join in the firing myself. Only some five minutes had passed, and as I looked at my watch, I was surprised that it was almost two o'clock in the morning. Despite my unease, I must have slept for almost two hours.

All sound from the wire had now ceased, and now the light of the moon showed up objects to be seen at the periphery of the wire. With the aid of the moonlight, it was possible to see what appeared to be at least one body lying at the base of the wire. Kruger, naturally, being the senior man, elected to investigate and, as far as I was concerned, he was welcome. When he called me to join him, he said there were three bodies to move. My thoughts turned to the fact that this was surely going to mean a medal, a few days leave and a kiss from the colonel, and that I would probably shine in the reflected glory of Kruger.

The complete anti-climax was to find the bodies of three very dead dogs. My only thought then was that, if ever the rest of the section or company became aware of this incident, we would both be laughed out of the regiment and the Legion. We spent the rest of the night not sleeping but drinking coffee and beer and swearing each other to secrecy that our nervousness had resulted in the death of three dogs.

Next day the truck was repaired and we headed for the destination designated by the *adjudant* the day before, a very tiny Legion post at Maison Carrée.

During the journey from our bivouac area to Maison Carrée, Kruger produced from his sack his old corporal stripes and tossed them to me with the statement that, since we were heading for a base with unknown quantities, although they would be legionnaires, I should attach the stripes to my camouflage jacket and, as far as he was concerned, my summons to the corporal's training platoon meant that I was as good as a corporal. Wearing the stripes at a strange base would ensure that at least I would not be called upon to undertake any of the fatigues which were the normal lot of an ordinary legionnaire.

Despite the risk of punishment for promoting oneself, I thought 'To hell with it. Why not?' It was worth the risk to escape the inevitable guard duties and potato peeling and all the other dirty jobs I was sure to be selected for.

It was only after forty-eight hours had elapsed after our arrival at this small Legion fort that I realized Kruger had promoted me for his own selfish reasons. Without even saying goodbye, he disappeared, on his way to Bel-Abbès, to complete his further training, explaining to the captain that his corporal was fully competent and responsible and would therefore remain in charge of all the accoutrements of the regiment. Meanwhile the truck and its contents remained parked· adjacent to the parade ground. This had now become my bedroom, dining-room and washroom. I had become responsible for property belonging to the 3rd Regiment and was now completely surrounded by members of the 1st Regiment, who, given the opportunity, would have looted all the contents. I had a hell of a problem. If I left the truck for any length of time, I knew full well all the contents would evaporate into thin air, much to the displeasure of some very senior NCOs of the 2nd Battalion. Instead of a corporal's stripes, it would have been a different type of stripes placed on my back by those guardian angels of the *Compagnie Disipline* at Columb Bechar, where I would probably end my service.

For the next twenty days, that truck was guarded and protected as if the contents held all the reserves of the Bank of England and the Crown Jewels.

The regiment eventually returned from Bizerta after only three weeks, when I was compelled to listen to stories from the lying lips of my comrades of how they 'won the war'. Very few of them wanted to discuss the clipping from the British newspaper which I had received from my father, which told the story of British journalists who had been wounded near the cemetery roadblock. These journalists had refused to carry out the instructions that they should turn back, issued by members of the 6th Company – instructions not given in French but in English cultivated at Dulwich, so that there could be no mistake. Their error had been in instructing their driver to drive on. So the vehicle was fired upon.

Although David attended their wounds, he did not inform them that he too was British. Nor did he receive their thanks!

6 First Rung on the Ladder of Success

Only in exceptional circumstances were legionnaires from various regiments grouped together as a unit. Among these exceptions were the corporals' training platoons, where those selected by their captains would be sent for instruction. These platoons were located a short distance from Sidi-bel-Abbès and administered by the GILE (Groupement d'Instruction de la Légion Etrangère), under the auspices of the 1st Regiment.

At these platoons gossip and information are swapped about the activities of the various regiments. News of friends from early training days is gleaned, and sudden shocks are inflicted – learning of a death or a desertion. And it is here that the inter-regimental rivalry begins.

Little of the rivalry between the legionnaires of different regiments is venomous. First and foremost all are legionnaires, all belong to the same family. But rivalry certainly does exist. Legionnaires from the infantry regiments will declare that all parachutists are lazy bastards, and their only reason for joining the Para was that they were incapable of marching. They will also emphasize the point that it is only the Para who carry out combat operations against the Fell wearing steel helmets. When, defensively, the parachutists claim that the steel helmet is only to protect their heads from contact with the ground whilst jumping into combat, not from bullets, the infantry legionnaire will indelicately inform the parachutists that a block of wood dropped from an aircraft only a few hundred metres high and falling to earth like a feather in the breeze, will suffer no damage. Why then should the head of a parachutist require protection? Surely this was also wood? How else did he become a parachutist?

Infantry and parachutists alike will dismiss the cavalry as being completely bloody useless, and good only for motorized cavalcades with flags waving on ceremonial parades. The cavalry could not take their tanks into the mountains, and that was where the Fell were to be found. If tanks drive on the roads, the roads are rendered useless for other vehicles. Called upon to drive on the sands of the Sahara, they would be bogged down for eternity. Then, if they came under fire from the Fell, they would hastily clamp down the lids of their tanks, open a fresh beer and radio for help from the poor bloody infantry – who would come dashing to their rescue. They are then very impolitely reminded that, when they rid themselves of their mules, they lost their most valuable asset, not only because the mules provided an emergency meat ration but because it was legend that cavalry officers consulted the mules for advice prior to taking any positive action. For some reason, these comments were never well received by those legionnaires who served in either of the two cavalry regiments.

Not even the members of the Compagnie Saharienne (disbanded in 1963) were excluded from ribald comments, and they were the perfect target for all: adorned in voluminous baggy black trousers billowing until secured at the ankle, embellished with intricate filigree piping down the sides (all probably stolen from the Arab desert sheiks earlier in the century), brilliant white tunics, sandals (instead of boots), polished leather bandoliers worn bandit-style, crosswise across their chests, all of this topped off by a flowing, ankle-length cloak. They were all Hollywood legionnaires, patiently waiting in the remote desert forts for the arrival of an American film company to do a remake of *Beau Geste*, at which time they would be recognized as budding film stars by the film director.

I think that, like myself, most legionnaires not of the Compagnie Saharienne, were slightly envious and would dearly have loved to have their photographs taken in this picturesque uniform. But most, like myself, rarely saw a member of this desert brigade. During the whole of my Legion service I saw only one, and that was on arrival at the corporals' training platoon. When I shook hands with him and introduced myself, he was not in the least amused by my greeting of *Salaam aleikem, effendi*. But we did become friends.

When I entered the corporals' training platoon in 1962, along with some thirty-nine legionnaires from all regiments, we did not know at that time that we would be almost the last corporals' training platoon that would be completed in Algeria.

We duly lined up to be presented to our platoon commander, having arrived from Sidi-bel-Abbès, some thirty kilometres away, only an hour previously. We were all dressed in our 'Sunday best', walking out uniforms, some half of us from combat regiments, the other twenty selected direct from basic and specialized training – all of these were full members of the 1st Regiment, which was responsible for our training. We, the purported veterans, were attached to the 1st Regiment only for the duration of the instruction, after which we would return to our 'mother' regiments, for promotion to the rank of corporal or to prison in the event of our failure!

As we assembled, expecting to be addressed by at least a lieutenant, which was normal in the case of corporals' training, we realized it was not a lieutenant but a human fireball, who could bark louder and bite harder and had a reputation second to none in the Foreign Legion. It was reported that, when this individual shouted at his platoon and screamed at them to double march, other platoons up to a kilometre away would commence double marching out of fear, with their lieutenant white-faced and leading them in a frantic dash.

This was how we first met the daunting, intimidating, awesome and indomitable figure of *adjudant-chef* Schwanke. Prior to my arrival, I had heard many stories about him, most of them from sergeants in my own regiment, very efficient sergeants. They had told me stories about Schwanke and of their treatment at his hands, whilst carrying out their own corporals' training, assuring me that the chances of my training under the same man would be remote, so I would have nothing to fear. (Even I had noticed that the sergeants who told the stories of their suffering happened, by some remarkable coincidence, to be the best-trained sergeants I had known.)

As we stood to attention, all as rigid and upright as a series of steel beams, I found myself regretful that I had ever left my home regiment, and the warmth and cameraderie I had experienced whilst with them. This *adjudant-chef* standing some five metres away, directly in front of us, merely stared at us with a steely, icy look on his face, as if contemplating which legionnaire he was going to have barbecued for supper that evening.

Then he approached, still without having said a word, and slowly paced along the line, sometimes stopping in front of a legionnaire, slowly looking him up and down, his eyes boring into the poor bloody individual as if deciding this was the one he was going to have for supper, and wondering whether to have him flavoured with garlic or pimento. For some reason, as he stopped in front of me and looked into my face, I felt sure he was reading my mind. For a whole two minutes he stood only a foot away, eyeball to eyeball, studying my face, my features, my uniform and my boots. Still without saying a word, he glared into my eyes, challenging me to avert my gaze. (I still think today that, if I had averted my eyes, thereby refusing to accept his challenge, he would have returned me to my regiment the next day.)

After I, and some half dozen others, had suffered this penetrating gaze, he returned to his spot, completely relaxed and standing at ease, whereas we poor fools were still standing rigidly fixed. For the first time he spoke. In a very quiet and gentle voice, he stated that it seemed he had been given the job, almost as difficult as that carried out by Jesus Christ in turning water into wine, of turning forty pieces of shit into the cream of the Legion, qualified corporals. He felt he could not be compared with Jesus, neither would he ever qualify for sainthood, therefore it would be unlikely if more than twenty of us survived the training.

Then, with a change of voice that was as cutting and sharp as bullets being fired from a Schmeiser machine-gun, he declared: 'There is only one hero in this platoon. That is myself. All those legionnaires wearing citations, regimental insignia, *fourragères*, parachute badges and other cinema rubbish: get rid of them!'

Only one member of our newly formed platoon had arrived from one of the Saharan companies, fully decked out in all his desert picturesque glory. The *adjudant-chef* walked up to him and, again using his gentle voice (which we later learned to fear more than his shouts), enquired if he had made suitable arrangements for the stabling of his camel. Schwanke allowed us to share his joke for a matter of five seconds, then demonstrated the full power of his voice, dismissing us with the order to return in ten minutes, dressed in our olive drab fatigue uniforms.

The barrack rooms were 500 metres away, and none of us had yet unpacked our kitbags. After a mad, frantic dash, within the stipulated ten minutes we were all back in place, all in our drab fatigue uniforms, but looking like a shower of refugees from a Legion prison, with the fatigue uniforms unpressed and creased from being stored in the bottom of the kitbags. I had not had reason to wear mine for more than two years and hardly thought I would be required to wear it whilst at platoon. Consequently I looked far more disreputable than any of my colleagues. It did not help that I was also noticeable as one of the tallest men in the platoon. Meanwhile our barrack room, with the contents of forty kitbags strewn about, had been left looking like an abandoned brothel during a bomb scare.

By the time we returned, *adjudant-chef* Schwanke had been joined by the rest of his 'staff', whose job it would be for the next six months to produce a minimum of twenty corporals, each of whom would be an aspiring sergeant, as we had previously been informed, out of forty pieces of shit! The staff comprised an *adjudant*, second in command to Schwanke, three sergeants, and two full corporals. There was also a lieutenant whose only part in our instruction was to ensure that we were fluent in the French language on our departure.

Only later did we find that, of all the instructors, the two biggest bastards were the corporals. Each was in charge of a room containing twenty novices. Either of them, if taking part in an Olympic cross-country championship, would have qualified for the gold or silver medal. It was these two who were responsible for our physical training and, as I was to find later, much to my distress, both held black belts in judo.

It was these same two corporals who ensured that, although we may not have enjoyed it, we completed the early morning run promptly at 5 a.m., over a distance of fifteen kilometres, the last three in the platoon to return being the first three to be nominated for extra duties. Once again I found myself busting a gut to ensure that at least I did not return with the tail-enders. During my first few days at platoon, I found myself looking forward to Sunday with the same anticipation as a child awaiting Christmas Day. Sunday is a traditional rest day in the Legion unless one is on combat operations. I felt sick and ready to quit when I discovered that it was only in Schwanke's platoon that these runs continued even on Sunday. At the response to my 'drop dead' when requested to parade for sport, I received a practical demonstration of the judo corporals' expertise as I was thrown from my bed through the window.

As we assembled in front of Schwanke and his entourage, each of them very carefully studying us, I carefully studied them. A ratio of one instructor to five legionnaires clearly indicated that the odds were certainly not going to be in my favour, when and if I practised my usual expertise, carefully nurtured in the 3rd Regiment, of disappearing into space when extra bodies were required for fatigues.

It took only two weeks for the odds to shorten. The numbers in our platoon had already been reduced to twenty-eight. Some had formally requested a return to their regiments – these I envied. The others had been booted out by the formidable *adjudant-chef*, with the declaration that they would never make corporals even if they spent fifty years in the Legion, twenty-five of which as a colonel's batman. (One of those who returned to his regiment had served as a captain in the Italian Army.)

During this first two weeks, Schwanke performed his first miracle. He managed to convert the remnants of the platoon, despite all inter-regimental rivalry, into a unified body of men, with a determination that they would never be broken by this winsome character, despite all his shouting, the humiliation inflicted, all the threats of punishments already experienced, and those yet to be conceived. Despite Schwanke and all his cronies, each man was resolved that he would show that this platoon, and the regiments from which we had come, were a lot tougher than Schwanke expected – which, as I discovered later, was exactly what the bastard had been aiming at.

It was also during the first two weeks that two members of the platoon found they had been selected by the instructors for 'the treatment' – namely myself and Mario Mati. Mario was a tall, laconic gangling character, very athletic and a natural gymnast, the only man in the platoon taller than I. He had arrived from the 2nd Regiment of Parachutists.

On our first meeting, Mario and I struck an immediate *rapport*.

We were both enthusiastic and avid poker players, both highly skilled in the art of bending rules and regulations, both determined to become corporals with the minimum amount of effort, with the maximum amount of enjoyment. Both of us, however, had miserably failed in taking into our calculations the capability of *adjudant-chef* Schwanke. Of all the trainee corporals, Mario and I had spent the most time under operational combat conditions and had been accustomed to the easygoing and relaxed relationships between NCOs and legionnaires that is found during the stresses of uncertain combat and its unknown outcome. It was obvious that *adjudant-chef* Schwanke was fully aware of the relaxing of discipline on combat operations – even we had noticed that he had been decorated thirteen times, including the coveted *Légion d'Honneur*. My eyes had been drawn towards these ribbons during our first meeting, reducing my ego and making me wonder how many times during his service he had stuck his neck out to receive that lot. It was the most I had seen on any man's chest during my service. However, it was to be another three months before we found he could relax and that, even when he spat, it contained a sprinkling of human kindness and milk and honey.

Mario and I considered ourselves veterans – our first mistake! We were soon to learn that we had not yet even scratched the surface of what legionnaires are really made of.

It was the right of trainee corporals deciding to quit (through frustration, excessive physical effort or pure bloody-mindedness) to ask to see the captain and make a formal request to be returned to their regiment. It appeared that *adjudant-chef* Schwanke was determined to force both Mario and myself to make this request. Any legionnaire who quit platoon on a voluntary basis, irrespective of reason, and returned to his regiment would not be welcomed by those who had sent him there in the first place with anything less than eight days in prison, commencing within ten minutes of his return. Many of our platoon, however, had accepted this.

As far as Mario and I were concerned, the thought of facing our individual colonels, should we quit, was something neither of us would even contemplate. As far as I was concerned, I would rather have entered a cage of untamed lions than face my own colonel, telling him I had given up. As for Mario, he would have cheerfully jumped from an aircraft at any height without a parachute than have faced his colonel, who just happened to be the tallest damn colonel in the Legion. (Mario would not have had to jump without a parachute. His colonel would have tossed him out.)

We were therefore between the Devil and the deep, the Devil being *adjudant-chef* Schwanke, the deep our respective colonels. We had no option but to resign ourselves to the tender mercies of our *adjudant-chef* and pray that, if by any chance he should drop dead with a heart attack, we should both be allowed to witness it and savour the occasion.

Alhough we had resigned ourselves to the fact that, by hook or crook, we would finish our platoon, thus ensuring that, on our eventual return to our regiments we would be welcomed with a handshake instead of a kick up the arse, nothing had changed in our attitudes. We had both received sufficient education in the Legion to know the exact limit you could go to in an endeavour to drive NCOs frantic and crazy, without being accused of insubordination or insolence, dumb or otherwise. It is surprising how far it is possible to go without exceeding the limits.

The first month of training was devoted to reducing the morale of all who wished to wear the stripes of a corporal. If any man allowed his morale to be broken or reduced, he should not have volunteered in the first place. Not only is one selected for corporals' training: it is also a requirement that one volunteer.

The agonies of basic training and the punishments devised and designed at the disciplinary regiment at Columb Bechar are brought into play to provide entertainment for the instructors of a corporals' training platoon. Happily, they were of short duration – in our case just for the first month, then they got down to the serious business of training. But throughout the whole period of instruction, the instructors kept their hands in with the random allocation of the odd punishment, lest we thought they were becoming soft, or just to relieve the monotony. With any sort of luck, and if one had said morning prayers, it became possible to survive a whole twenty-four hour period without receiving a punishment. Then you would suffer a sleepless night, worrying that you were becoming weak in the head or losing your incentive in the failure to provoke.

Members of the 2nd REP leaving the helicopter in search of the enemy, south-east of Constantine, 1961

Airborne 'taxi services' at the height of combat operations adjacent to the Tunisian frontier, 1961

Emergency treatment and evacuation of Legion wounded at the infamous
'Bec de Canard' on the Tunisian frontier, late 1960

Napalm canister falling from a T6 aircraft on the Tunisian frontier, 1961

A very rare sight in the Legion – a live prisoner taken by the 2nd REP

Practising for a helicopter drop at Mers El Kébir, 1964 — unaware it was going to be made without a parachute

Practice jump at Cap Falcon in the sand dunes west of Oran, late 1963

57mm recoilless rifle about to be fired with evil intent by a Legion patrol, Tunisian frontier, 1960

Ceremonial parade of the 2nd REP – these dozen legionnaires are wearing a total of 107 awards for bravery

Members of the 1st Company of the 3rd Regiment of Infantry arriving in France from Algeria, late 1962

A very happy corporal on his way to the brothel at Bou Sfer, September 1963

Celebrating the 300th anniversary of the Legion's most popular beverage. (From left) Worden, Wilson, Murray and Carlson

The 'mafia' of chief corporals at Bou Sfer, 1965. (From left) Dieter, Michele, Wilson, Lauber, Worden and Kovacs

Exiting from a Dakota, August 1964

My first 'battle' with *adjudant-chef* Schwanke occurred only three days after our arrival, at morning assembly. The good *adjudant-chef* declared my uniform 'filthy' – it was spotless and immaculate but, being discreet, I decided it would not be in my interest to argue the fact. He instructed me to leave the parade and report back in a clean uniform in five, repeat five, *minutes*. It was a hopeless task: my barrack room was too far away, and anyway it is a physical impossibility to change a complete uniform in the time allowed, and he darn well knew it. Further he had opened the unwelcoming gate of the prison for me by declaring his instructions to be 'an order'. In the Legion there exists an adage, known to all in early training days, who try to clean a whole barrack block in a minimum of time: 'If it's damp, it must be clean.' So I quickly doubled away, ducked into the shower room of the sergeants' barracks only a minute away, turned on the shower, icy bloody cold, and stepped under fully dressed. I returned well within the five minutes stipulated, looking like a drowned rat, much to the merriment of my so-called comrades.

I duly presented myself to Schwanke in the correct military fashion, giving him my smartest salute, normally reserved for those of the rank of captain and above, and stated in the most formal manner – with water streaming from my head, face and uniform, and gathering in my boots: 'Your order executed, *adjudant-chef*. I received in return one of his specialized looks, clearly indicating that he was contemplating mayhem, murder or even the guillotine. Fortunately he realized that he had not ordered me to *change* my uniform, and even he was conversant with the Legion adage, 'If it's damp, it must be clean.' I know that for the next two hours he was enjoying life a lot more than I was. Upon reflection, I probably made that day a holiday for him.

I found it very difficult and extremely uncomfortable attempting to execute intricate drill movements with a rifle whilst dressed in a uniform soaking wet – and very, very troublesome around the crotch.

My gesture and protest could not be considered insolent. I had carried out the order, although not quite as he had meant me to. If he had ordered me to be marched to the cells, I would not have complained. It would have been worth it for the look of shock on the face of his second-in-command and the grins the sergeants had difficulty in repressing. I also learnt from that day on how to blend and melt myself into the background whenever *adjudant-chef* Schwanke was in the vicinity, and, if the opportunity arose, to be noticeable only by my absence. I did notice from that day on, that whenever he gave me an instruction or order he was very meticulous in his wording, and the crafty bastard cheated by having me repeat back to him, word for word, the orders received. (I was very thankful when I left the platoon that, as much as it is possible in the Legion, with the disparity of our ranks, we were friends and not enemies.)

It was here that we learnt what *Tenue Compagne* meant. It cannot really be described as a punishment, just a mindboggling, time-wasting, bloody nuisance. Four days *Tenue Compagne* could be inflicted on us even by the qualified corporals. A recruit at basic training will receive this 'punishment', perhaps one in a thousand chances, and many like myself would have neither experienced nor even witnessed it. For those at corporals' platoon, it was as regular as blowing your nose.

All that was required of the legionnaire awarded this 'punishment' was to report to the duty sergeant some 500 metres away, immediately after the regular nightly room and kit inspection ten minutes prior to the sound of the bugler sounding 'Lights out'.

However, there was a slight snag and handicap. The legionnaire is required to report wearing his dress uniform; over this dress uniform he must wear his raincoat, and over this raincoat his overcoat. On the shoulder straps of his overcoat he must have fixed the red and green tasselled epaulettes which, like the blue cummerband round his waist, would normally be worn only on ceremonial parades. He must also wear his steel helmet and liner (compliments of the US Army), tightly clamped to his head, and be adorned with ammunition belts and sundry paraphernalia. The legionnaire now looks more like a clown than a soldier, and a very fat clown at that.

But that is only the beginning. He is also required to take with him his complete kit, which, with any sort of luck and careful packing, will completely fill his kitbag. He will take with him his large bergen backsack, containing his groundsheet, half a two-man tent and the sundry poles, pegs and ropes, and his operation sleeping bag, both inner and outer. The smaller rapid-march lightweight sack called a *musette*, will contain a towel, soap, toothbrush and toothpaste, shaving brush and razor, all brand new, and any other odds and sods omitted from the other containers. It is essential that on arrival his boots are polished to a super-high gloss, even if it is pissing down with rain. (The rain in Algeria is little different from rain in any other part of the world, except at the training establishments in the Legion, where the raindrops seem a little larger and heavier and a lot more frequent, and on arrival at the earth's surface create the deep, red, thick mud unique to Algeria.)

The legionnaire is now almost ready to depart and pay his respects to the duty sergeant. All that is required is to pick up his iron bed, his mattress, his blankets, his pillow and his sheets (yes, we did have sheets at Legion training establishments) and make his departure. With the aid of one or two of his comrades, all of this will be piled onto his shoulder and he will stagger away. He is allowed to make only the one journey.

The legionnaire will probably announce his arrival to the duty sergeant by falling on his face, in his struggle to enter the office garnished with all his equipment. The duty sergeant, in the tradition of all Legion duty sergeants, will be found completely relaxed and at ease, leaning back in his chair, with his feet on the table, sucking beer from a bottle. This sergeant is likely to request you to abstract from your kit anything from a spare button to a safety pin. It is always advisable to produce the required item in double-quick time, or he will inflict a few extra days, just for fun.

Such are the ways of enterprising legionnaires that it took only a few days to resolve this nuisance. All members of the platoon contributed various items of equipment, and we established a permanent *Tenue Compagne* fully complete and on standby for any of the platoon to use. We even compiled a written list, giving the location of every item in the prepared containers. Boots were kept clean for the journey with specially made goloshes, cut down from a rubber groundsheet.

We could never understand why legionnaires in other platoons constantly griped about *Tenue Compagne*. Any member of our platoon could be in a position to present himself within ten minutes of receiving the 'punishment' and back in his bed ten minutes after leaving the duty sergeant.

Our NCOs became aware that we had made up a *Tenue Compagne* but frequent snap inspections of our rooms failed to show any surplus equipment, not even the spare bed utilized. Being such irreligious bastards, they never thought to check the chapel, but then, being NCOs, it is doubtful if they were aware of its location.

By the time we had finished our corporals' training, we had reaped the benefit of all the skills our instructors could impart. Each of us was capable of training up to forty recruits from the day of their enlistment to the completion of their basic training and their basic Legion education. Each of us was word perfect in the French manual of arms. Each could function as a drill instructor, weapons insructor or physical training instructor, not only for recruits but for a corporals' platoon. Map-reading had become easier than reading a book. The construction of booby-traps on vehicles, tracks, buildings and the barrack blocks of other platoons had proved both an education and a source of amusement. We had become so familiar with *plastique* explosive and detonators that a few of us were treating them with less respect than they merited. (It was inevitable that the odd accident should occur, such as the blowing-up of the toilets at the rear of the sergeants' mess, which luckily were unoccupied at the time. Mario argued at the time that it was a blatant waste of *plastique*.)

The monotony of training was regularly broken by weapon firing practice, not on a firing range but in some secluded valley a few kilometres away, preferably within hearing distance of one of the native villages, to remind them that independence would not be effective until early July that year and that it was not yet time to hang out the green and white flags.

Once Schwanke challenged me to fire an anti-tank grenade from a rifle whilst holding the rifle in the crook of my shoulder. Idiot that I am, I accepted the challenge and fired the grenade. The result was that I missed the target by a distance, and if it had not been for a small rise in the ground, the grenade would have finished up in the village. I ended up lying flat on my back, some distance away, with a broken forefinger and a shoulder that changed colour to blue-black and ached for a week, providing great amusement for my so-called comrades and great delight for the platoon instructors.

An American film had been shown at the camp, with an heroic American marine firing a 50-calibre machine-gun from the hip and, to the delight of the legionnaires watching the film wiping out thousands of the Japanese Army. It was inevitable that, at dawn the next morning, we were marched to the firing range, where to my horror I saw a 50-calibre Browning machine-gun which had been brought by two of the instructors. These weapons are usually fixed on aircraft, tanks or jeeps but on occasion are fired from a fixed tripod. Even prior to the lecture by Schwanke, I knew what was going to happen at the end of the lesson on the use of the weapon. He addressed the platoon and, although I cannot recall word for word of his speech, the content was: 'As you are all aware, Johnny, like his American brother whom you all saw at the cinema last night, was a wartime hero who beat the shit out of us peace-loving Germans who were only trying to defend our Fatherland. He will now demonstrate, like his American friend at the cinema, how to fire this weapon accurately from the hip.' He then invited me to instruct the platoon and demonstrate.

I did try. The targets were only a distance of 200 metres away. I think the nearest I managed was somewhere near fifty metres to the side or over or short. The gun, including 200 rounds of ammunition, weighs somewhere near sixty kilograms. It was all I could do to lift it, point it and fire it, yet alone aim the damn thing at a target.

Schwanke had, however, made his point: do not believe all you see at the cinema. Burt Lancaster had been reduced from an American hero to an actor playing with dummy guns.

Towards the end of our formal training, the numbers now reduced to only twenty-two, from the original forty, there was a complete relaxing of formality. The attitude of the instructors towards us all, with the certainty that we would qualify as corporals resembled the almost easy-going casualness of combat operations. It became so relaxed that Mario and I invited a couple of the sergeant instructors to join us for a drink during one of our poker sessions. They had suspected that a poker school existed but had no idea where it was established. Since we would soon be departing, we introduced them to our private bar. When they left the chapel, they had lost about £30 each.

It was also at the corporals' training platoon that we received

instructions in how to *marcher à la canard* – march like a duck.
This serves no useful purpose at all and, to the best of my
knowledge, was normally forbidden to be inflicted on recruits. I
think its main purpose was to encourage all the members of the
platoon to apply for an early return to regiment, thus enabling
the instructors to depart on vacation or, as most of them wished,
an early transfer to a combat regiment.

'Marching like a duck' is exactly what it means. You are
required to squat on your haunches, rifle in the position of
'shoulder arms', and attempt to march in formation and in step,
either quacking like a duck or singing the words of a new Legion
song just learnt. If one is out of step, out of tune or just out of
luck, a swift kick up the arse helps in regaining the tempo.

It was usually reckoned that a hundred metres was about the
limit of endurance prior to the knees becoming permanently
locked in the squat position, when assistance would be needed
before you could rise to your full height. A further source of
amusement for the instructors was to get truculent legionnaires
to run up and down a steep sixty-metre-high hill next to the
training area whilst carrying a backpack containing some fifty
kilos of rocks. If this task appeared to be causing only slight
distress to the legionnaire, the wide webbing straps supporting
the sack would be removed and replaced with field telephone
wire. Since Mario was the only parachutist in the platoon, to
demonstrate the toughness of the Para, he was required to do this
with his combat jacket removed. My mistake was laughing at my
best friend's distress, and I found myself invited to join him.

It was only a short time before I found that my laughter was
turning to tears. Mario was a stupid bastard, not showing any
signs of distress on his face each time we arrived at the base of
the hill, whereas I was feeling well and truly 'whacked'.
We managed to complete eight runs before I fell on my face in a
state of collapse, ready and willing to give up and go to Heaven,
when our favourite sergeant let us off the hook. Nothing,
however, could deter Mario. He told the sergeant that they did
the same thing in the Para, every morning before coffee, as a
normal sport. We consequently got the same dose for the next
three days.

I began to realize that I had made yet another mistake in
becoming friendly with Mario. Each time he received a

punishment, I would be selected to keep him company.

I was lying in bed, having just been served my lunch on a tray, smoking a cigarette and sipping my Kronenborg beer from the bottle, really enjoying life. I had an ample supply of magazines and a selection of Legion history books, whose study had become my hobby. I merely had to call an orderly and another beer would be produced. I was not required to attend parades, nor even to get dressed, just lie in my bed, relax and let the world drift by. I had finally achieved a legionnaire's conception of Heaven – not even the sight of an NCO.

I had arrived at this state of bliss because two days before I had had the good fortune to break my ankle and now found myself in Sidi-bel-Abbès – not in the Legion hospital but in the regular army hospital. When I arrived, there were two female nurses in the ward. Since my arrival they had been transferred and replaced by male orderlies. This demonstrates the lack of faith the regular army have in the Legion.

My leg had been sheathed in plaster from my big toe to just below the knee and suspended above the bed in a cradle. As far as I was concerned, platoon was finished, terminated and *kaput!* Once my foot was healed (and I had visions of three months at this paradise), I could return to my regiment, not in any disgrace but with a legitimate excuse for failure.

On the third day, disaster struck, in the form of a visit from our favourite sergeant, the cretin who could not let a day pass without making me undergo some sort of punishment. He was of Italian origin and was, without doubt, the greatest 'con man' ever to receive a promotion in the Foreign Legion. I learned later that he had been instructed by *adjudant-chef* Schwanke not to return without me, or he was dead.

He disturbed the very pleasant snooze I was enjoying with a shout like a clap of thunder: *'Vous!'* the abbreviated version of 'Attention!'. Without even thinking about it, and from pure fright, instinct and automatic reaction, I disentangled my leg from the cradle, almost leapt from the bed and attempted to snap to attention. Consequently I fell flat on my face. This upset the ward orderlies more than it did me, but with the aid of the sergeant, they got me to a sitting position on the bed.

It took this character only thirty minutes to convince me that my foot was not important. I would still be able to continue with the platoon, and the fact that my leg was encased in plaster would obviously exclude me from some of the more strenuous activities. He told me that *Adjudant-Chef* Schwanke had assured him I would be excused all sport, all marching and, in particular, the combat obstacle course.

He was a liar, *Adjudant-Chef* Schwanke was a liar, but when I discovered this, It was too late. I had already returned to the platoon.

It had been with this same bloody sergeant, only three days before, that I had arrived at a gully with random logs and rocks strewn on the bottom and a perpendicular drop of some six metres. We were passing the time leaping over natural obstacles, but here I had hesitated, with some fear and trepidation (fright), and this sergeant, some twenty paces behind me and unaware of the reason for my hesitation, very impolitely enquired: 'What the hell are you waiting for? Jump!' So I jumped. He was not aware of the depth of the gully, nor of the obstacles strewn all over it. Undeterred by both his and Mario's concern, which I could determine from the amount of laughter coming from the rim of the gully when they saw me sprawled on my face, I attemped to scramble clear lest both the bastards decided to use my body to cushion their landing, when they jumped.

The pair of them were still laughing when I shouted to them that I thought my leg was broken. Then they both climbed down to join me – neither jumped as I had, even though they were both parachutists. As they approached, I began rapidly scrambling away from them on my belly, determined not to give them any opportunity of practising their very elementary knowledge of first aid, not on *my* leg. I rolled onto my back, pulled out my bayonet and threatened them both with death if they even looked at my leg. They were still pissing themselves with laughter at my reaction to the branches they were holding when the medic and the stretcher arrived.

Then the bloody medic sliced my best combat uniform trousers with a knife and hacked a perfectly good ranger boot to pieces with a cut-throat razor. My only concern then was that the medic get me to the infirmary as quickly as possible, prior to the arrival of *Adjudant-Chef* Schwanke who, without doubt, would have ordered me to march to the infirmary. Broken foot, broken leg or broken back ...

I had, however, learned yet another very important lesson: when told to jump, think about it ... then faint.

Getting out of the hospital did not prove to be easy. It may have taken the sergeant only thirty minutes to convince me, but it took him a couple of hours to convince the doctor, who was a major, unfortunately for him, in the regular army. The major was horrified that I should leave the hospital and said I should remain for a minimum of three weeks to a month. I silently agreed with him but it is more advisable to agree with a Legion sergeant than to support a regular army major.

The existing plaster was therefore removed and replaced with a more forceful one, with a steel support fitted so that the whole of the weight was taken by the knee joint. It seemed to work and I thumped up and down the ward, demonstrating to the very concerned major that it was not causing me any pain. It did not but I was certainly aware that I was hoisting about a broken foot.

As we left the ward, it was somewhat disturbing to find that we were being applauded by the rest of the inmates, who were regular army and mostly conscripts. I do not know whether they were applauding the sergeant for beating the major, or myself in sympathy – probably the sergeant.

A further surprise awaited me when we left the hospital. I found that the sergeant had arrived in the captain's jeep, and Mario was there as armed escort. I found difficulty climbing into the jeep with my plastered leg, but my good buddy Mario solved the problem by picking me up bodily and tossing me into the back. I was already regretting that the major had decided to let me depart and cursing the stupid man for not asserting his rank and insisting that I should stay. But ... So we departed my temporary paradise on our way back to the loving care of *Adjudant-Chef* Schwanke, some thirty kilometres away.

It would have been a departure from tradition had we quit Bel-Abbès without a tour of the bars that abound the township. If it had not been for the fact that the captain was awaiting the return of his jeep, our favourite sergeant would have completely run out of funds.

It seems to be almost standard in the Legion that, when

legionnaires drink with sergeants, the legionnaire has either
sent all his pay home to his poor starving mother or lost it the
previous evening playing poker. As it was, the return journey
could have been completed in quicker time by the whole
platoon marching *à la canard*, than we managed with the jeep.

It was true that on my return to the platoon I was no longer
required to take part in the early morning runs. Instead I had to
clean the whole bloody barrack room every morning while the
rest of them were out jogging around the countryside, clearing
the stench of the barrack room from their nostrils and filling
their lungs with the pure, clean air of the early dawn.

It was true that I was not required to march with the platoon
to the lecture and drill areas, anything from two to five
kilometres distance. All I had to do was to 'thump, thump,
thump', following them, well to the rear, up hill and down dale
and eventually arrive utterly knackered.

The very next morning the good sergeant who had collected
me from hospital, the good sergeant whom we had allowed the
privilege of spending his money buying us drinks, requested
that I demonstrate the ingenuity of a legionnaire to the rest of
the platoon, by completing twenty push-ups, *avec musique* and a
broken foot. This was for my late arrival. From that day on, I quit
the camp thirty minutes early, arriving at the designated area
well before the rest of the platoon. It was their bad luck if I was
the acting duty corporal of the day: all would receive a mouthful
of verbal abuse and a minimum of fifty push-ups. This acted as a
salve for my foot and delighted the *adjudant-chef*, well pleased at
what a right bastard he was moulding.

It was necessary to return to the hospital every Sunday for the
next four weeks to have my plaster changed. This did not please
those on duty. Regularly at the end of each five days of 'thump,
thump, thump', the plaster would become broken and start
disintegrating. Even after three days, the plaster needed some
white paint that Mario had 'liberated' so that it looked tidy. By
the fourth visit to the hospital the plaster had become such a
damned nuisance that I arranged for the Legion medic to
remove it completely, strap my foot with an elastic bandage and
put it in a borrowed left boot a size too large. Although it
therefore gave the occasional twinge and I was always
apprehensive of resting my full weight on my left leg, it did heal.

It became a matter of principle, now I had discarded my iron foot to continue with the platoon in the normal way, even though with a slight limp handicapping me – when marching within the confines of the camp with a rifle perched on my shoulder, it had a tendency to pitch out of line. This did not please the instructors.

Only five weeks after I had damaged my foot, the platoon was required to complete a twenty-five kilometre forced march, with full kit, half running, half marching. This was a halfway training test for the survivors of the platoon, now reduced to no more than twenty-four.

The evening before this exercise I was informed by one of the instructors – though without doubt the message originated from *Adjudant-Chef* Schwanke – that it would be accepted if I declined to carry out the march. It was pure bloody-mindedness, plus a few gibes from my friend Mario that the infantry was useless, that made me determined, as the only British representative at Menton to demonstrate that the British, and the Legion infantry were as hard as nails and the British as tough as, if not tougher than, any other nation – the curse of pride, patriotism and loyalty!

As the march progressed, I realized that it was not bloody-mindedness that had forced me into the situation: it was simple-mindedness. It was only after some ten kilometres that the full impact of my stupidity hit me. It was a very hot day, and a hot day in Algeria is really hot. The outsize boot on my left foot seemed to shrink with every step. Sweat was pouring from my body, and I had not yet realized that it was not the sweat of strenuous marching but the sweat of a fever. Despite the perspiration, I was actually feeling cold. I had also dropped at least a kilometre behind the rest of the platoon, although Mario had kept pace with me for the first hour, encouraging me with verbal abuse. Then he had sped on ahead. It had become a matter of principle with Mario that he should always finish first (*Vive la bloody Para!*), and I had got him into a position where he would have to complete the remainder of the trip at the run. I was really feeling very lonely – the loneliness of the long-distance runner, except that I was at the back.

A jeep suddenly appeared alongside with the captain responsible for the training of all the platoons, accompanied by

Adjudant-Chef Schwanke. The *adjudant-chef* for the first time addressed me as 'Johnny' and said that enough was enough. 'Get in the jeep.' For the first time in the Legion I refused a direct order and declined, declaring I would finish the bloody march and, feeling lightheaded, told them in English to 'piss off.' They dropped back and allowed me to continue.

I think it was at the fifteen-kilometre marker that I met that great drinking friend of mine, the 'con man', who had collected me from the hospital. He was the fifteen-kilometre marker. Then the jeep again came up alongside, to collect him. I had reached the stage where I could no longer look ahead for any distance; my eyes could focus only on a point some twenty paces in front of me, and that point was my next target. My mind had blanked out completely, and each limping step was made with the silent voicing of, 'One step ... damn Schwanke, one step ... damn Schwanke.'

I was not aware of the surrounding country. I was no longer aware that I was in the Legion, or even in Algeria. The whole of my concentration was on keeping moving, and on the man I hated most in the world. 'One more step ... damn Schwanke.' I had become delirious and was later told that it was not silent voicing: I had been shouting it aloud in English.

Once again the jeep pulled up alongside (so I was told later), and this time the captain ordered me into the jeep. It appears that my response, in perfect but uncouth French, was that he could 'go shit on a candle'. This was not, and never has been, the correct way to address a captain.

I awoke the same evening in the sickbay. I was told that I had managed to complete almost twenty kilometres before the bliss of total collapse. I remembered nothing about it, only that on arrival at the sickbay my temperature had been almost 42°C, and that it had been Mario and Schwanke who had carried me in. *Adjudant-Chef* Schwanke came to see me the next morning, Sunday, and asked what I was doing, still lying about in bed. He also informed me that it would have been better if I had died on the road: then I would have been buried with full military honours. Instead of that he would now be looking forward to the future, from which he would derive much enjoyment, in the instruction of a legionnaire that the correct response to an order from a captain is not 'Go shit on a candle.'

My rest and recuperation in the infirmary lasted only forty-eight hours, which surely proves that the Legion attains minor miracles in maintaining peak physical fitness in all its members. Or perhaps it was the beer Mario managed to sneak into the infirmary that reduced my temperature.

Corporals training in the Legion are of necessity very tough, very hard and bloody mind-bending. But no man in the Legion ever achieves the exalted rank of *adjudant*, or *adjudant-chef*, without first enduring the rigours of a corporals' training platoon. With the completion of this first platoon, the most difficult rung on the ladder of promotion has been surmounted. Or has it? Before one can obtain the golden stripes of a sergeant, it will be almost back to square one. A sergeants' training platoon is not a great deal different from a corporals' platoon: the same punishments, the same tight discipline, the same inducement to try a little harder, the same encouragement with the same boot up the arse, and a hell of a lot more technical training.

When a Legion corporal walks away from his platoon at the end of his instruction, he is competent to command a platoon or section. (In the mid 1950s, in Algeria, a corporal took command of the company when all his officers and NCOs had been killed, and continued the combat.) Very few of those who have completed platoon will ever inflict on the legionnaires in his charge any of the mind-bending punishments he has endured, or the humiliation he has suffered. These are strictly reserved for platoon. However, should the novice corporal become an instructor of budding corporals at any time in the future, the little worm in his brain will tell him, 'Your stripes were hard earned. Now let these bastards suffer.' Then he will devise even more frustrating punishments to be passed on to posterity and help create yet another Legion tradition.

Adjudant-Chef Schwanke never did keep his promise to make my life a misery, although I gave him many reasons to do so.

On 30 April 1962, a day well celebrated by all ranks in the Legion, he brought his four children to the camp, the eldest no more than twelve, all dressed in miniature Legion camouflage combat uniforms, even to the ranger-type boots and the green Legion beret. Without the knowledge of Schwanke, and whilst he and his wife were having a drink in the sergeants' mess, I rounded up his kids and had the time of my life. Since they were dressed as legionnaires, I would treat them as legionnaires.

I marched them to a small parade square and commenced putting them through intricate drill movements, shouting and bullying them with a pretty good impression of their father's voice, making them do push-ups when they made a mistake, strutting about in imitation of their father's walk. The kids loved it. Members of my platoon who were deriving a great deal of enjoyment from my act were convinced I was putting my life at risk. But I intended to be long gone before Schwanke and his wife had finished their drinks. But I miscalculated the time, for the kids were enjoying it, I was enjoying it. (It was the first time for three years I had been surrounded by children.)

The youngest boy's shrill of 'Papa!' brought me back to reality. The *adjudant-chef* and his wife had been watching for at least five minutes. I should have realized this by the sudden disappearance of my platoon into the wilderness. He had returned to collect his children to take them to lunch at the sergeants' mess.

However, Schwanke had no chance against his children and their mother. He formally introduced me to his wife, who was very charming, and when the children declared that they were going to have lunch wih 'Johnny' and drink beer in the legionnaires' mess hall, that was the end of it. The children had adopted me, and with the *adjudant-chef*'s reluctant approval I called them to attention and marched them to the mess hall. They caused me only a minor problem when they tried to insist that, if they could drill like legionnaires, they should be allowed to drink beer like legionnaires. They did not win that battle and settled for coca-cola.

30 April 1962 will always remain a day fixed in my mind and heart. Prior to our departure, I had discovered something that a few months before I would have rejected as being ridiculous, that even *Adjudant-Chef* Schwanke was not above disregarding orders received from a superior.

Whilst commanding his section in the Aurès mountains, during the icy winter weather and the never-ending rain pouring from the sky, Schwanke had halted with his section on a hilltop designated by his company commander, with orders to remain for the night and sleep as best they might, but with the strict order that on no account were fires to be lit. This was after a fruitless two-day chase after a considerable number of Fell, also suffering from the effects of the punishing weather. After three hours of being utterly drenched, not even allowed to concoct a hot drink, his legionnaires depressed but not yet demoralized, *Adjudant-Chef* Schwanke concluded that by dawn his section would have to be evacuated by helicopter, direct to hospital, should they continue the night in such depressing conditions.

He then gave the order to light fires. His legionnaires leapt with delight to carry out his order and built the biggest bonfire ever seen on the mountain-tops of the Aurès. When the first flicker of his fire was spotted by other sections on other hilltops, they too decided, 'To Hell with it', and also lit fires. Within a matter of twenty minutes, some ten square kilometres of hilltops were ablaze with the light of flickering fires.

The busiest men for the next half hour were the radio-operators, kept busy by certain senior officers trying to determine who was the insubordinate clot who had flagrantly disobeyed the order that fires should not be lit. *Adjudant-Chef* Schwanke was never identified as the guilty party.

This was the first time that incident has ever been written about, and since the then colonel is now a general, it obviously did not affect his career.

Within two hours of the fires being lit, more than forty Fell for whom the regiment had been searching for more than two days had climbed out of the valleys, searching for the warmth provided by the fires and surrendering without a murmur. It was a very successful operation: forty weapons turned in, not a legionnaire wounded or killed, and not a shot fired in anger. (Well, not at the time of their surrender!)

The platoon finally ended. I was angered by being placed second. I had expected to be the bottom man, or at least in the last three. The knowledge that I had been placed second brought home the fact that it had only needed just a little more effort and I could have finished first. Typically of the *adjudant-chef*, when I shook hands and made my farewell, there was no 'Bonne Chance', only '*Hals und Beinbruck*' – 'Break a leg and neck!'

Upon reflection, I believe that what had prevented my being placed first in the platoon, which would have meant being promoted chief corporal instead of corporal was the visit to the platoon school of a British writer researching for a book he was writing about the Legion, a Major XYZ.

On his arrival at Menton, because of his rank he was handsomely received by our captain and afforded full honours. The captain was quite pleased to inform him that he had an Englishman at present completing platoon, and the author expressed a wish to meet him and pose question on life in the Legion. The next thing I realized I was in the captain's office, and the captain was asking if I had any objections to meeting him. I did, and over-reacted by informing the captain that if this gentleman wanted to find out what it was like in the Legion – and I quote: 'He can bloody well do the same as me and join the Legion – and I probably outrank the bastard anyway on the list of reserves.' My uncouth mouth almost got me into serious trouble with the captain, but he had a problem, in that he had already arranged an introduction.

The captain resolved the problem, and salved his conscience, by introducing me to the author as Legionnaire Wörden (pronounced the German way, 'Verden'), explaining that I spoke a little English and would act as his guide in the search to find Legionnaire 'Johnny'. It gave me a great deal of delight for the next couple of hours, escorting a civilian around the whole camp, enquiring of all we met if they had seen 'Johnny'. Even prior to our leaving the office, enough telephone calls had been made to alert all the sections what was happening. I eventually returned to the captain's office, along with our distinguished visitor, expressing my regret at our lack of success in a mixture of English, French and German. He gave me a guilty conscience by forcing upon me 100 francs for my efforts.

Upon my arrival at Bel-Abbès, I learned that almost the same thing had taken place during his visit there. British legionnaires were noticeable by their absence.

I had arrived at Sidi-bel-Abbès attached to the transit company (*Compagnie de Passage*), to await a suitable time for myself and other members of the 3rd Regiment who had been completing various courses of instruction traditionally held only at Bel-Abbès to be returned to our regiment once its whereabouts were known. At this time all regiments were preparing for the mass departure from Algeria. Independence for Algeria would be effective on 1 July 1962. All military personnel were required to quit Algeria in ninety days except the units that had been ceded a five-year period at the military and naval base at Mers el Kebir and in the south-west sector of the country at the oil-pumping stations. I was more than a little concerned that my own regiment would abandon me and leave me in the none-too-gentle hands of the 1st Regiment. (This was the only time in the Legion when I considered desertion. Left in the hands of the 1st Regiment, I would have resigned and left!)

By a remarkable coincidence, I found myself installed in the same dormitory as that I'd known when I had first arrived from France, as a novice recruit, except that this time we were only some eight legionnaires sharing a room that had previously held forty.

Although I had no love for Sidi-bel-Abbès, mainly because of the inflexible discipline I had experienced during my previous stay, on this visit one could sense a complete change in both attitudes and atmosphere. My built-in defence mechanism, natural aversion and instincts in the avoidance of any duties at this bastion of the Legion would normally have made me avoid visits to the main barracks, with the same precautions I would have taken in the avoidance of the plague, and after the rigours of corporal's training I'd convinced myself I'd earned a rest.

Despite this, I found that my inherent curiosity for the unknown and the obvious relaxing of formalities overcame any feelings of trepidation, and subsequently I found myself drawn to the *Quartier Viénot* (the main barracks) to see what was taking place.

Getting from the *Petit Quartier*, where I had been installed, to the *Grand Quartier* (main barracks), even at this time, during the large-scale evacuation and relaxing of formalities, required a certain amount of 'regulation bending', but being a legionnaire who had already done over three years of service, I found little difficulty in effecting my exit from the one to the other.

On my arrival at the main barracks, I was somewhat shocked. There appeared at first sight to be utter confusion. The 'Sacred Walk', the parade square of the *Quartier Viénot*, was overflowing with transport being loaded with packing cases – equipment, relics and all the accoutrements the Legion had accumulated during its stay of well over a hundred years. It required careful study to observe that this was not chaos and confusion but a well-organized and well-planned operation and that the Legion, with its usual efficiency, was evacuating the maximum with the minimum of transport allocated.

It was sad the Legion was quitting this base, which had been the pivot of all Legion activities since the arrival of the first legionnaires more than a century before – legionnaires had also been responsible for the foundation and construction of the town. But for some reason there seemed to be no air of despondency, but the impression of a holiday spirit. Along with this there was a certain feeling of apprehension that perhaps with some sort of luck the Fell would even at this late stage of the game attack the barracks, thus giving all departing legionnaires the opportunity to demonstrate that they were not leaving because of a battle or war that had been lost but were handing over because of the politicians in Paris and the surrender of the 'Grand Charles' at the conference table at Evian, the previous year.

If it had been at all possible, those legionnaires engaged in the task of stripping the barracks and loading the transport would cheerfully have volunteered their services for stripping and scraping the paint from the inner walls, rather than leave anything for the Fell, now officially known as the National Army of Liberation who, we were fully aware, would be taking over the barracks the moment the last legionnaire left.

Undeterred by all the activity taking place at Bel-Abbès, nothing had changed with regard to rumours. (The 1st was renowned for its creation of unfounded rumours.) The current most popular and most enthusiastically received rumour was that the Legion regiments were to be sold off in package deals to various emergent African states. The same rumour held that Legion pay was to be doubled and that on arrival in France each and every member of the Legion would be granted a thirty-day vacation. It was no small wonder that there was an air of festivity and celebration.

Only a day later I came across Jim Sinclair, now promoted to sergeant. Having a beer with him, I told him of the latest 'hot fire' guaranteed rumour circulating that was keeping a lot of legionnaires happy when they should have been miserable. He confessed that he, along with other members of the *Salle de*

Sport, all bloody parachutists, had engineered the rumour that had proved so successful.

It was from Jim Sinclair that I caught up on all the news about other 'Brits' whom I had met a few years before. I learnt that Donald, still with the 5th Regiment, had been promoted to sergeant and, with some regret, that Paddy Riley, promoted to chief sergeant, had been killed some ten months before. (Over twenty years before, 'Paddy', or Lou, an Irishman from Belfast, had been flying with me on Wellingtons in the Western Desert. It had been through him that I had joined the Legion.) It did nothing for my ego when Jim enquired what had taken me so long to become a corporal. He himself was due to leave the Legion, having almost completed his five years, and his regret was that he would not be able to celebrate the centenary of the Camerone due to take place the following year on 30 April.

I found that, despite my expertise on camouflage and avoidance of NCOs, the minions of Bel-Abbès had awarded me a duty. Along with other remnants of my platoon, we had each been allocated a dozen recruits, who had just completed their basic training, in order to assist various officers and NCOs in packing their household effects and crating them for shipment to France. These officers and NCOs, being married, did not live within the confines of the barracks but were scattered about on the outskirts of the town, in extremely well-built houses.

I had been allocated two very senior *adjudants*, along with my dozen novice legionnaires, to prepare packing cases as soon as possible, and prepare their evacuation, along with their family, as speedily as possible. Although both *adjudants-chef* were very senior, we found considerable difficulty in view of the shortages, in obtaining sawn planks, hammers, nails and saws, for the construction of the packing cases. Both *adjudants-chef* agreed with me that, because of the pressure of time limitations and because, ready or not, they were scheduled to depart within forty-eight hours, they would close their eyes if I utilized the traditional *Système D* in obtaining our requirements. (*Système D* in this case merely meant 'finding by stealing', not to be confused with stealing by finding.)

First I had to find a truck and a driver – very easy, and the payment was only a dozen beers. I loaded my dozen legionnaires and paid a visit to the *Salle de Sport* to see my great friend Jim Sinclair and all the other heroic parachutists engaged on permanent duty there, on a purely social visit. They too were busy crating their equipment, but by the simple expedient of inviting them for a beer (parachutists, irregardless of rank, will never refuse the offer of a free beer), they all jumped at the opportunity of downing tools and drinking at my expense.

Whilst drinking the beer, I listened to all their hardship stories, the trials and hazards they endured at Sidi-bel-Abbès, fully sympathizing with them, after the easy life I had been leading in the mountains. Some had been at Bel-Abbès for almost three years. The first hundred metres along the main road from the barracks, there were perhaps at the most only thirty bars. Bel-Abbès also had the biggest and best brothel – more brothels, in fact, than either Algiers or Casablanca. These poor parachutists had certainly been suffering.

Meanwhile my own bunch of novice recruits, having been pre-briefed, were fully occupied loading up our truck with all the timber and tools we required, which these foolish men I was drinking with had left unguarded. I was more than pleased to find on our return that the truck I had hired had departed well loaded.

For some unknown reason, when we returned from the bar and it became evident that a great deal of looting had taken place, their suspicions turned to me! It took a great deal of talking to reassure them that I, an ex-British officer and a gentleman, a recent graduate from corporals' training school, would never dream of stealing or being involved in any underhand thing against them. Jim assisted by pointing out that no Englishman would steal from another, meaning himself; it would be unheard-of. They all seemed satisfied with this and agreed that it would be infra-dig in the Legion for one Englishman to involve another Englishman in trouble. I was surprised that they had all known Jim Sinclair for a far longer period than I had known him and had not yet learnt that he was Scottish.

I had no principles at all as to the liberation of Legion property, to the great benefit of individual legionnaires, and both my *adjudants-chef* were old members of the 3rd Regiment and therefore part of my closest family. Anyway the stolen timber and tools had been the property of the 1st Regiment and would be put to a far better use aiding ex-members of the 3rd. When I said goodbye to Jim Sinclair, I was not offended when he called me a thieving, conniving bastard. In the Legion, this is only a term of affection.

My merry band of recruits, all now qualified exponents in the operation of *Système D*, had returned to the two *adjudants-chef*, stating that I would be following. I was told later that they had taken one look at the contents of the truck and both visibly paled, for my over-enthusiastic band of recruits had taken far more than we required – which proved that my corporal's training had been inadequate in the passing of meticulous instructions. However, both being very sensible *adjudants-chef* they had beaten a hasty retreat from the barracks with the truck, its contents and my legionnaires, to their family quarters. One had slightly more brains than the other, and he returned to the barracks to collect me, in a borrowed jeep.

When I arrived at the houses of the *adjudants*, my band of merry men had already unloaded the truck, which had departed. But having just finished their basic training, and still in awe of *adjudants-chef* they were actually lined up in the garden as if waiting for assembly and inspection.

They were very lucky recruits, for at this early stage in training they had the opportunity to learn that *adjudants-chef* are very human individuals: they could hardly believe their eyes to find them both with sleeves rolled up working alongside us, packing furniture, making packing cases and merrily sawing planks of wood. Between them the *adjudants-chef* had seven children, and my poor, bewildered recruits looked on with wide-eyed amazement to see a Legion acting corporal, armed with a bamboo cane, bullying and organizing the kids and getting them to help with the packing. They were not aware that both *adjudants-chef* were grateful that the children were being kept from getting underfoot and out of the way, and at the same time being entertained. I could never really understand that when I shouted in a loud bullying voice, slapped a bamboo cane down the side of my leg with a loud thwack and adopted threatening gestures, I could have legionnaires standing rigidly to attention but children of legionnaires would only laugh and clap their hands – which again proves that children are a lot more perceptive than Legion recruits.

It took just two days to pack the two homes, load them on a truck and arrive at the port of Oran. I also had the privilege of acting as armed escort for both *adjudants-chef*.

The terrain around the harbour at Oran looked a disaster area, cluttered with cars the departing colonists could not take with them to France because of the space restrictions on the ships. The cars had been deliberately crashed into each other, so that they could not be used by Algerians. I was happy to leave the harbour area and return to Bel-Abbès.

The evening prior to my departure from Bel-Abbès to my regiment near Algiers was celebrated with Jim Sinclair, a chief sergeant who had lost an arm whilst serving with the 3rd Regiment and was now on his way to France and retirement, and a few other legionnaires with the biggest 'piss-up' ever held in one of the few remaining bars still operating in Bel-Abbès, each of us with the knowledge that this would be the final drink we would ever have together at this most famous of all Legion bases.

All thoughts of *Appel*, the nightly rollcall for legionnaires, were thrown out of the window. If the regimental police appeared wanting to know what common legionnaires were doing in the Paradise Garden, drinking in a bar long after they should have returned to barracks, we would be protected by those exalted chief sergeants and *adjudants* who had now joined our company, with arms around each other's shoulders, almost tears streaming from their eyes, all singing in loud drunken voices the whole repertoire of Legion songs. If we were not protected, I could not have cared less. The way I was feeling, I would have fought the whole band of regimental police single handed, and personally castrated the chief of the prison. The owner of the bar was delighted to change five $100 bills I produced from my pocket, and to hell with beer: champagne became the order of the night.

To say that I got drunk would be the understatement of the decade. I became legless and as I was told the next morning, I sobbed my heart out between the songs, declaring that I would never leave Sidi-bel-Abbès but stay and fight the whole damned Algerian Army on my own before I would allow a single one to pass through those hallowed gates and place one foot on the Sacred Walk. (In effect, I behaved exactly like a legionnaire – and

I was supposed to hate Bel-Abbès!) My return to the barracks was made through the little-known secret entrance via the Legion cinema, slung over the shoulder of a drunken chief sergeant of the 3rd Regiment determined that he was going to prevent one of his own family spending the night in the cells.

That farewell evening was the only occasion on which I have ever fallen over, stupid drunk, in my life. I awoke the next morning with a headache so severe that my kepi hurt my head with its weight. Like all legionnaires, I took the customary oath that I would never drink again.

7 Farewell Algeria

Early in September the 1st Company of the 3rd Regiment of Infantry boarded an old Liberty ship at the port of Oran, destined for Marseilles.

I had rejoined my regiment from Sidi-bel-Abbès, to find them preparing for departure to Madagascar. Within two hours of my arrival I was marched into Colonel Langlois's office where, instead of the congratulations I had expected for successful completion of my corporal's training, I received a verbal rocket for my failure to finish in first position. When I explained that it had been somewhat difficult trying to compete against others whilst handicapped with a plaster cast on my leg, he dismissed this as a mere nothing and said that members of the 3rd Regiment should be able to march or run faster on one leg than any legionnaires from other regiments with two legs. I realized that I really had returned home.

The colonel then took the unprecedented step of presenting me with my corporal's stripes himself, along with the information that on arrival in Madagascar I would immediately undergo training for sergeant. It was this that induced me not to sign a further contract for six months, which would have qualified me for that trip to the Indian Ocean. Instead I opted to join the 1st Company, comprising mostly near-time expired legionnaires, heading for France to await the completion of their contracts.

The only tasks we were required to carry out were those of escort duty for the civilians and military units in the mass evacuations back to France. All the towns and villages had the new Algerian flag flying from their windows and rooftops. We had seen these flags previously only when searching the bodies of the Fell dead, most of whom had this green and white flag adorned with its red star neatly folded in their rucksacks.

Whilst engaged on these escort duties, we were instructed that our weapons must not be armed, or the chargers for them be loaded. This instruction was completely disregarded. There was no way any of us would have carried out even such simple duties with unloaded weapons through Algiers or Oran, where one could even smell the hostility of the local population.

Time pased with sunbathing and swimming in a waterhole we had manufactured by damming up the nearby river, just 150 legionnaires awaiting our own passage to France.

We were pleasantly surprised to find we were the only passengers aboard our Liberty ship, and that we were allowed complete freedom on board, only the bridge being 'off limits'. Although we were not fed on board the ship, we had ample supplies of field rations, bread and wine, and an abundance of hot water from the kitchen for making coffee.

We departed at midnight and arrived in France forty-eight hours later. None of us was sleeping as the ship left the port of Oran. Most crowded the ship's side, watching the coast lights of Algeria slipping away and reducing in size. Most of us saw Algeria disappear with reluctance, regret and a sense of loss at leaving this paradise of mountainous beauty. It was as if we had seen the death of a close comrade, had buried him and were now leaving the burial place forever. No violent cheers at the thought of entering France, just a complete feeling of emptiness in a hopeless situation. It needed only one bloody legionnaire to start singing *En Algérie* and every man would have cried his eyes out.

Chief Sergeant Kostron, who had his own methods of instilling discipline, generally with a fist instead of paperwork, brought the whole company back to earth (if the deck of a ship can be called earth) by the statement that we would now celebrate, and produced two jars of rum from one of the cases we were escorting to France. Most of the voyage continued with all on board in a state of mild alcoholic euphoria – including the captain and crew of the vessel. I know that when the manifest was checked on arrival at Marseilles, four cases, each containing a dozen jars of rum, could not be found – neither could five legionnaires who between midnight and the body count at 6 a.m. had decided to terminate their contracts.

I could not understand how they had managed to leave the

ship. Guards had been mounted at the gangplank and at those places where the ships' lines snaked down to the bollards on the harbour walls, with a very nervous corporal, unable to sleep, inspecting those sentinels every fifteen minutes.

It was only much later that I found out that my mistake had been in placing David on sentinel duty at the gangplank. As these now reluctant legionnaires walked down the path to freedom, he merely shook hands with each of 'em and wished them 'Good Luck.' It was his way of 'getting his own back' on Kostron, who, as the senior legionnaire on the ship, would take the ultimate responsibility. (Kostron had once struck David on the side of his head with the back of his hand and rendered him unconscious. It had been David's ego that had been hurt, rather than his head, at the thought of being 'laid out', with a backhander.) But the disappearance of the five legionnaires did not result in Kostron's carrying the can. Some very clever juggling with the documentation showed that these five had departed for Madagascar with the nucleus of the regiment.

For the next four months the eminent Chief Sergeant Kostron kept a very wary eye on me, and I was also well aware that he kept the list of legionnaires who had been on sentinel duty that night permanently available in his pocket. Those legionnaires were aware of it too. Until Kostron left the unit, they trod very warily indeed.

Kostron was a remarkable man. David's description was that he was built like a brick shithouse. He had the ability of halting a fracas between legionnaires and regular army even if they were twenty in number, by rendering them unconscious with a single punch thrown by either hand. Certainly not a man to trifle with, yet he was still blessed with a sense of humour.

There were audible sighs of relief as we disembarked when we were informed by Kostron that we would not be reporting to the 1st Regiment in Aubagne but would remain an independent unit and be proceeding to an old Legion farm between Aix-en-Provence and the Institut des Invalides at Puylobier. I think it was the first time Chief Sergeant Kostron had ever been cheered by legionnaires in the whole of his fifteen years service.

So we found ourselves at our new base, only some twenty kilometres from Aix, tucked away in the chalk hills of the Rhône valley. We were all glad that, along with our weapons, we carried our mountain sleeping bags, for without them, during the first week, the nights would have been very long and cold.

Although the farm had a few dilapidated buildings, they were very quickly renovated with building materials obtained from a new police station being constructed a few kilometres away. Since at a later date this building project was still found to be unguarded, we also utilized the bricks to construct a kitchen, showers and toilets. The newly renovated buildings were quickly converted to a company office, an armament magazine and a guardroom. Our first duty became the security of our camp site, lest any intruders attempt to steal any of our own equipment or newly found construction equipment.

We did obtain many supplies from the 1st Regiment, all very busy constructing the new Legion base at Aubagne: brand-new American-style eight-man tents, beds and even factory-made mattresses, plus a great deal of other equipment that had been lying around looking lost and disconsolate, waiting for adoption. This is probably why we also ended up with the best kitchen equipment, designed to feed 500 men but which served adequately well in feeding our own small company.

The establishment of our secluded camp had taken only a matter of two weeks and we were given ample opportunity to visit Aix-en-Provence, Marseilles and small towns in the vicinity.

It was surprising how quickly many of this company were visited by members of their families arriving from Italy, Spain, Germany and – happiest for myself – London. This resulted in our being excused duties, and twenty-four hour passes being granted with a minimum of fuss. My brother seemed somewhat surprised at my refusal to accompany him on the return journey to Britain and at my determination to complete the contract which I had signed so many years before, but at least he left me some clothes he had brought. At first I was quite appreciative of them until I tried on a sports jacket and found that the damn thing, which I had left behind in 1959, had been tailored for a near fat man and not for a lean and lithe legionnaire. I had taken the opportunity of opening a bank account at Marseilles with a residue of funds from my kitbag, and now I added to it a healthy cheque from London, which I felt was a gift conditional on my staying away for another few years.

It may have appeared quite strange but I felt only relief when my brother departed and quite happy to get back to being a bastard corporal. Some members of my company had succumbed to the entreaties of their families and girlfriends and deserted – we lost a dozen before Christmas, though none had more than a year's service to complete prior to becoming *libérable*.

Although we had not expected to be greeted by the French population as conquering heroes, we had hardly expected to be treated like carriers of leprosy, but we were. On our first visit to Aix-en-Provence, some forty legionnaires, we were adorned with all the trivia of the 3rd Regiment, bemedalled, sun-tanned, impeccably dressed in our 'Sunday best' and on our best behaviour, all with ample funds, interested only in finding a restaurant with crisp white tablecloths, gleaming silverware and food served on a plate, in lieu of the *gamelles* (mess tins) we had been eating from for nearly four years. But we were refused entry to hotels and restaurants for no other reason than that we were members of the Legion. We eventually found ourselves in a small bar, run by a one-armed veteran of the Second World War, who seemed delighted to have us. Without doubt, his takings that day exceeded the normal takings for three months from the local population.

Probably the citizens of Aix-en-Provence were unaware that the wrecking of their town had been deterred only by the persuasiveness of a British corporal who, despite his own feelings with regard to the wary attitude of these French citizens, which was greater than that experienced in Algeria, was only concerned lest his own men spend the night in the cells.

In the bar I had seen a legionnaire whom I did not recognize, damn near sobbing his heart out in frustration at the attitude of the local population. But it could have been his appearance that had denied his entry to the restaurants and hotels, for, with his deeply sun-tanned forehead and nose but his cheeks the colour of milk, he certainly looked as if he had the plague. It was only when he spoke to me that I realized that it was 'Bock', one of the most highly decorated legionnaires in the regiment that for over four years had been gaily in combat in the mountains of Algeria. Then he had sported the largest and bushiest full beard and moustache ever seen in the mountains, but he had shaved them off that morning for his first visit to civilization, in the hope that he might capture the heart of a beautiful French girl. He soon recovered his composure and usual aplomb, when I assured him that, if he had met a girl in this town, the only thing he would have captured would have been a dose of the clap.

Christmas approached, and we got rid of our boredom by carrying out night marches in the nearby mountains, for no other reason than that we wished to carry out night exercises. The citizens of Aix did not know that one of the exercises had been carried out in their own town, with a hundred legionnaires fully armed stalking the streets in the very early hours of the morning, leaving detachments at the *gendarmerie*, telephone exchange and railway station, planning the destruction of all. With the coming of the dawn, they melted out of sight without once having been spotted. It was an exercise thoroughly enjoyed by the company, especially since the *gendarmerie* entrance and exit, had been booby-trapped with a length of nylon cord and some practice grenades. They had been practice grenades because I had removed the real ones already planted by 'Bock', still suffering from a sense of grievance. Upon retrospect, even whilst writing this, I've often wondered whether or not I should have left the originals – perhaps my corporal's stripes had gone to my head.

It had been our small unit that had received the bodies of General Rollet, Prince Aage and Legionnaire Zimmerman, which had been flown from Algeria to be reburied with full military honours at Puylobier. General Rollet was the first Inspector General of the Legion and the most decorated officer in the French Army and Prince Aage, nephew of Queen Victoria, became a Legion officer in 1922 and fought in every battle in Morocco until the final peace. Legionnaire Zimmerman, an ordinary legionnaire who did not aspire to greatness, served for twenty years and died in his sleep. He is the Legion's unknown soldier except we know who he is and we also know who he represents: all those legionnaires who have died in obscurity in the Legion. We provided the labour for the digging of the graves and the provision of the honour guard. I claimed the privilege of digging the grave of Zimmerman for myself, although as a corporal I should have been supervising and not labouring. But this was not a labour of toil but a labour of love and respect. Anyway I had no chance of digging the graves of the General Rollet and Prince Aage, for I was outranked by other volunteers, many of whom had not only known them both but served under them.

As a Christmas present from the Legion that year, I received from the captain a beautiful watch with the face inscribed with the regimental crest of the 3rd Regiment of Infantry. It took David only some thirty minutes to persuade me that my existing watch, issued to all flying members of the Royal Air Force, had proved so invaluable that I should present my new watch to him. Since he only had five more months service to complete his contract, rather reluctantly I handed him the watch in exchange for yet another nylon sleeping bag, of which I already had two. So I lost the best souvenir present ever presented to me by the Legion, but I still had one Christmas to look forward to, whereas this was David's last.

Chief Sergeant Kostron asked me if I wished to learn to ski and in almost the same breath informed me that we would now be known as the first company of the 3rd Battaillon de Marche. When I enquired where the rest of the battalion were, and the other companies, he seemed to derive a great deal of pleasure from the statement that 'we were it'.

Kostron explained that the Chasseurs Alpins had invited two dozen members of our unit for a skiing vacation. Although somewhat suspicious, I said I'd be very happy with the opportunity of learning to ski. I little realized that the other members of this volunteer party had all been born on skis and that it was not a vacation but a mountain training course in the art of ski warfare. However, before I had discovered this, we were already in the overheated barrack blocks of the Chasseurs Alpins at Briançon.

Whilst the rest of the company were swanning about the mountainsides of Briançon, for the next two weeks, for eight hours a day, I found myself on the nursery slopes, the sole recipient of expert advice given by three sergeants of the Chasseurs Alpins and the caustic tongue of Kostron, at the completion of his rapid descents from the upper slopes.

It is still my contention that, if God had wished people to ski, they would have been born with these instruments of torture as an appendage of their natural form, and not added as a means of pitching a Legion corporal head first into deep snowdrifts from which he had considerable difficulty in extracting himself. Nevertheless, at the end of two weeks, in either frustration or despair, my instructors decided that I could be trusted to make a safe descent from the higher slopes. So I took my first cable-car run up a mountain, tickets duly paid for by the Legion. I found that on arrival at the landing stage we transferred to yet another car, climbing to even higher crests and seeming to be headed in the direction of the clouds. Since we were accompanied by a Legion lieutenant, Kostron and a couple of other sergeants, I realized that there was little chance of concealing myself under the benches of the car and completing the descent a darn sight easier than on skis.

On arrival at the highest point, I was delighted to find that there was actually a bar and restaurant and that easy access was afforded without the encumbrance of skis.

In this bar I was found some forty minutes later, busily quaffing large double brandies, both to keep out the cold and to provide the courage to make the downward journey. I had also been hoping that the rest of the company would have departed without me, thus allowing me to secrete myself in the cable car and arrive at ground level without a broken leg.

All my offers to buy the drinks, even the lunch, did nothing to thwart their determination to witness my newly acquired inexpertise. With great reluctance I strapped on my skis and looked down at the tiny spot below, unidentifiable, but which they informed me was Briançon.

The lieutenant was a gentleman. He explained that the descent runs were marked in various colours which denoted their degree of difficulty. Since this would be my first run, he said I should follow the blue markers, the easier route, and that he and the rest of them would follow me down. I was still hesitating, marking well in my mind the first blue marker, when I received a thump in my back. Needless to say, this was delivered by Kostron. It catapulted me forward like a bullet from a gun.

My first two minutes were spent only in trying to keep upright and spot the markers that were flashing by at high speed, and which with my twisting and turning, had changed from blue to orange, to yellow, then orange and red. Even in my ignorance, I realized that somehow I had really screwed up, for red in any man's language was danger.

I was definitely heading for disaster. I was no longer skiing on snow but down a narrow ice track. On arrival at the tree line, I realized that I must be at least two-thirds down. Many of these trees had low-hung branches which were trying to decapitate me. Eventually the small piste on which I found myself angled sharply to the left, whilst I carried on in a straight line and into space, thereby making my first and only ski jump – not a great jump, only some forty metres, but in a perfect swan-dive position into the deepest bloody snowdrift on that mountain.

I spent almost ten minutes in that drift, not a very nice experience, for it is difficult to determine which way is up. Happily the lieutenant found my body with the sharp end of his ski pole, with the inbuilt instinct of Legion officers and NCOs of finding that most vulnerable part on the anatomy of a legionnaire, his arse! Once I had recovered, with the aid of a cigarette which stilled my quaking heart, I felt quite pleased that my rapid descent had resulted in only the lieutenant and five other legionnaires managing to keep track of me. However, there was still one more obstacle to face. Some two hundred metres below us (and the descent was still very steep) was a very narrow bridge covered with snow, and on the other side of the bridge was a hostelry that would be serving the hot coffee and brandy which I sorely needed at that moment. I did manage the descent. I passed over that narrow bridge without seeing it (I had my eyes closed), and I managed to come to a halt at the door of that establishment by hurling myself into the deep snow piled outside.

It was only when we were ordering drinks that the lieutenant suddenly realized that he was now in charge of a corporal and five legionnaires who were the most recent deserters from the Legion. We were not in France but a few kilometres inside the frontier of Italy!

The lieutenant was not pleased when I remarked that, although I may have led this detachment to freedom and liberty, he was the man commanding and would therefore be held responsible by the powers that be. However, in exchange for his paying for the drinks and the taxi fare to the border post, I would guarantee not only that we would all return but that our straying would also be kept a secret. Rapid telephone calls for a taxi, more telephone calls to the headquarters of the Chasseurs

Alpins, and we arrived at our rendezvous with our army truck, with a very relieved lieutenant.

The story did not remain a secret for very long. The driver of the truck who delivered us to Briançon had been born with a tiny brain and a very big mouth. That same evening I was invited to have a beer with Kostron and almost doubled up with laughter, he bought all the drinks in exchange for my story of our descent and eventual arrival in Italy. When he and the rest of them had split away from us, he had been fully aware that it was a case of the blind leading the blind, especially with me leading the party, but his only concern had been that we would eventually arrive anywhere without injury.

Although invited, I declined further trips to the heights, and it was with some relief that I achieved the final long march of twenty kilometres on skis at a cost only of wearing out three pairs of socks and of a few blisters that I had not suffered from since my recruit days.

When I received my ski badge from the Chasseurs Alpins, it was buried deep in my kitbag along with the hope that any record of my ever having completed such training would be eliminated from my Legion dossier. (On our return it was a pleasure to pay for a case of beer for the company clerk for having all details of skiing instruction eliminated from my record.)

After twenty-one days we returned to our temporary home to find that it was almost abandoned. Those we had left behind had established a further temporary camp only a matter of a hundred metres from the main gate of the Institution des Invalides at Puylobier. The inhabitants permanently established there were Legion veterans, either pensioned or without a leg or legs, or without an arm or arms. This in no way deterred them from behaving exactly as they had in the Legion when they had been fully able-bodied. All were kept occupied on jobs at Puylobier, making ceramics and Legion souvenirs. All were still very proud men, as I discovered when I attempted to help a veteran with one leg up a flight of stairs and received a blow on the head with his crutch as thanks. We did later get drunk together, and I listened to stories of cavalry charges in Morocco on horseback, way back in 1925, which had cost him his leg.

All veterans love pomp and ceremony, all enjoyed the *Salute au Caid* sounded each morning by our company bugler on the arrival of the commanding officer at the main gate, and his inspection of the guard provided by our small unit. Those veterans at Puylobier considered us of the 1st Company nothing more than novice recruits. Perhaps they had good reason: among them was a very distinguished Russian legionnaire who had actually led one of the last Legion cavalry charges on horseback, way back in 1925. To buy a beer for that gentleman, you had to put your name on a list and await your turn.

We remained at Puylobier only six or eight weeks, providing for those valiant veterans the establishment of a *poste de police* and the manual labour to paint the chapel and everything else that did not move. It took us only a short time to realize that the establishment of a guardpost had been a serious error.

Our problem in establishing a guardpost at this small *caserne* hidden in the hills of the 'Domaine d'Anjou' (which produced some of the best wine that never left the Rhône valley) was that it is a requirement for the guard of honour to turn out for any holder of the *Légion d'Honneur*. These veterans would, after their lunch, decide to take a leisurely stroll outside the main gate to aid their digestion, having rummaged in their personal effects and dug out their awards of this, the highest decoration a legionnaire could achieve. Each would casually stroll towards the exit and extract delight at the panic to turn out the guard in his honour. It would not have been so bad if they had passed as a group, but the bastards were doing it deliberately and one at a time. That two-hour lunch-time guard became a nightmare as they paraded past with only the *Légion d'Honneur* suspended from their chests, watching the frustration of a poor bloody British corporal who was being driven mad and issuing contradictory orders, not sure whether the priority was to salute the *Légion d'Honneur* leaving or the one on its way in. My sigh of relief when I learned that the depot commanding officer had halted their games could have been heard as far away as Paris.

The veterans may have laughed at my antics at the guardpost, they may have been delighted at my panic in calling out the guard, but I considered it a privilege to share in their laughter and a beer in their *foyer* after the event. But they never let me forget that I had a further twenty years service to complete before they would call me a colleague.

During one lunch-time, instead of eating at our own company mess, some dozen of the volunteers engaged on painting the chapel were invited to share lunch with these veterans in their own dining-room. It was then that I was violently attacked by a screaming madman in a wheelchair who projected himself towards me and hurled himself from his chair with cries like a whirling dervish, causing the tray on which my lunch had been balanced almost to spatter the ceiling. This idiot, without legs, had his arms about my neck. Both of us rolled about on the floor, I trying to free myself from what I thought to be a gibbering idiot until I realized that his gibberish was 'Johnny! Johnny! Johnny!'.

It was Roig. The last time I had seen him was on a small hill near the Tunisian frontier, as he was being loaded into a helicopter for evacuation. He had served in my own section and received a full charger of bullets through his legs. David had accompanied Roig in the helicopter, and I had scrubbed the stretcher clean from all stains of blood. When David returned to the company, he expressed doubts that Roig would survive. I had therefore assumed that this raving lunatic had been dead since 1960.

Roig was an Algerian of Spanish descent. He had taught me a smattering of Arabic and lectured me on the Koran. Although we had not been the closest of friends, he had helped in my early days in the mountains, and we had shared many lonely nights on sentinel duty. We had been brothers in the same regiment.

When later that same evening I took pleasure and delight in telling David that we had been invited to the *foyer* at the Institute to drink with a 'ghost', and the look of utter bewilderment on his face at the appearance of Roig was nothing compared with his voiced comment, 'But you're dead!', which he blurted out without even thinking about it. It did nothing to spoil the evening, and Roig demonstrated that the loss of his legs had not in any way limited his consumption of beer, although where the hell he managed to put the vast quantities he consumed, I'll never know.

For the duration of our stay David and I would take Roig on our excursions to the local village and to the small town of Tretz, which we found far more hospitable than any other.

Almost each day would see the departure from our small company of yet another legionnaire who had completed his contract. Eventually, during March, with our numbers reduced to only a hundred, we upped stakes from Puylobier and once again found ourselves at the harbour of Marseilles, heading for yet another destination and short sea voyage. This time to Corsica.

As we climbed on board landing craft L9008, which had been left behind by American landing forces way back in 1944, and which was still utilized by the French Navy as a troop-carrier beween France and Corsica, we were bidden farewell by two civilians who only a few weeks before had been wearing uniform: ex-Corporal Pasquale Vetrano and Legionnaire Menon.

Pasquale, who with the help of the Legion, had obtained premises to open a dry-cleaning establishment in Marseilles, fully equipped with the machinery that he had received as a gift from one of the departing colonists in Oran. There had been no room on the ship bringing the colonist back to France for his equipment, but Pasquale had ensured that, appropriately labelled as military equipment, it departed with us aboard our Liberty ship.

They had both come only with the purpose of assuring Raphael, who still had three months service to complete, that upon his return he would find Menon awaiting with all arrangements for their departure to Argentina completed. Since both were aware of Raphael's sleepwalking tendencies, I also received instructions that he was now my complete responsibility for the next few months, and they threatened me with death if I did not look after him. (There had been no need for their threats, as for the next three months Raphael did nothing but eat and sleep, and I made bloody sure that he was exempt guard duties.)

Our voyage from Marseilles to Bastia in Corsica could have been made faster if we had all decided to swim. The journey took as many hours as had the trip from Algeria to France. However, the conditions on board this vessel were almost luxurious. Sleeping accommodation was air-conditioned, well-lit; the bunks themselves were almost too comfortable to sleep on. Like all others on board, I confined myself to our quarters. We had spent the first hour after leaving the harbour on the upper catwalk enjoying the sunshine and the sight of France and Monte Carlo seeming never to fade in the distance, but the pitching and rolling motion of the vessel, wallowing in the waves, with the line of the horizon changing its position from up to down, had the majority voiding the contents of their stomachs over the side, and then scuttling below to the tranquillity of artificial light, the dull throb of the engine and the security of the bunks.

As we entered the harbour at Bastia, still scarred from air strikes during the previous war (of which quite a few had been made from my own aircraft), our bugler high on the forecastle sounded the notes of Salute au Caid to signal our arrival. It was a complete waste, since residents of Bastia proved to be no different from those of Aix-en-Provence. I almost regretted that wartime instructions had been that only the harbour and shipping should be bombed or strafed. However, what had passed had passed, and one could do nothing to change past events.

We were eventually installed in a small fort south of the town, the Caserne St-Joseph, within easy walking distance of Bastia. After the first visit to the town, few of us returned for another, and I still regretted that the orders in 1944 had been so explicit!

Within a matter of only five days we were transferred to an old military airfield that lay between the new airport of Bastia and the town, which had been abandoned since the end of the Second World War.

The whole of April and May were spent hacking away at the undergrowth to establish a temporary camp, interspersed with nightly exercises in attacking members of the 1st Regiment, who were busy training recruits at Bonafaccio.

We made many discoveries whilst cutting away the undergrowth: slit trenches that still contained rotting rifles, ammunition and whole cases of abandoned Mills hand-grenades. At the extreme northern point of this abandoned airfield, elements of the 2nd Regiment of Parachutists installed a parachute training school instructing novice recruits in the art of parachuting, and this old airfield was utilized as a dropping zone.

We first met many of the NCO instructors whilst we were amusing ourselves burning whole cases of the wartime ammunition that we had discovered. They burned with a wonderful intensity and a noise that might indicate a small war had just started. We were also visited by the *gendarmerie* of Bastia, for the sound of 40mm shells and cases of grenades being exploded had even caused some alarm in the town. However, it was agreed by all that these very old stocks of ammunition and explosives, some of which even included rotting cartons of cardboard mines, would be a hazard if left in place, so, if we were willing to destroy them, 'the best of luck'.

The terrain which we now considered our home provided many interesting diversions. We had discovered that it was used by both the sergeants and corporal training schools being organized by the 1st Regiment as instruction sites for combat obstacle courses, and *pas Gymnastique* runs with full kit, around and around – even the sight of it made me giddy.

I found myself drawn to the parachute training school, observing the activities of raw recruits leaping from tall platforms, their parachute harnesses attached only to counter-weights that were never adjusted – the principle being: the smaller the man jumping, the easier would be the landing, whilst the heavier candidate, who would fall to earth like a sack of coals, should have gone on a diet if he wanted a softer landing. Protected partially by my corporal's stripes, I found myself not only being tolerated by the various instructors but even on occasion being invited to try out a few of the less hazardous perils which the recruits were required to endure.

There were times when a couple of these instructors, their arms ablaze with the golden stripes of their rank, would ask me to 'look after' these recruits whilst they themselves went to the toilet – which meant they were headed for their bar, to down a well-earned drink. Familiarity breeds contempt. These instructors, aware of my interest in parachuting, even invited me, a lowly infantry corporal, into their mess for a drink, promising they would try to explain the attractions of leaping from aeroplanes and the magic joy of serving in a parachute regiment. It was inevitable that I should become tempted, and the *adjudant* in charge of the instruction of these 'young lions' said that, conditional to my passing the required tests and medical, they would be delighted to accept me as a pupil.

My own company captain's reaction to my demand that I be

allowed to become a parachutist shattered my vanity. I was sure he would refuse my departure, since I was of the opinion that my own company had a far greater need of my presence. The speed with which he agreed to my undertaking both the tests and the training completely destroyed my ego, especially when my own *adjudant* informed me that the comment from the captain had been, 'Let him give it a try. He's sure to fail.'

Within a week, all the formalities completed, I found myself officially reporting to the parachute school as a prospective 'lion'.

I was required to undertake all the initial tests along with fifteen recruits who had recently completed their basic training, none of whom had more than five months service. My hard-earned corporal's stripes and my service in the mountains of Algeria counted for absolutely nothing now that this super band of instructors had finally got me into their hands. I discovered to my sorrow that the fact that we had been on Christian name terms whilst drinking in their mess allowed me no privileges. In fact, I found that my body was used for whipping with the flexible bamboo canes the instructors carried, and my arse again became a football.

The 2½ foot long, one-inch thick, semi-flexible bamboo canes, called 'Oscars', carried by all Legion para instructors were apparently a sign of their authority but, in reality were utilized as a means of encouragement to those legionnaires (even veteran corporals) slightly reluctant at leaping out of aircraft, from high platforms, from the upper branches of a tree or from a truck belting along at thirty miles an hour, onto a concrete runway, in a vain endeavour to complete a 'parachute roll', as defined in the Legion instruction handbook. The application of 'Oscar' to the buttocks or the back of a legionnaire invariably left a lasting impression that even the application of calamine lotion could not ease.

Instructors were strictly forbidden to strike recruits with 'Oscars', but they would explain in the bar during the evenings that I could hardly consider myself a recruit, and each time that magic stick whipped across my back, it was to *encourager les autres* – those young lads certainly did try harder.

After the first day of instruction, I returned to my own company and arranged for a double layer of canvas to be sown to the back of my combat jacket as a liner, so the constant whipping caused me no distress. The young recruits began to look at me as if I was Superman, since they knew nothing of my added 'protection' – neither did the bloody instructors. I wondered if my own company *adjudant* had asked for the special treatment so that I would 'drop out' and get back to where he could get his hands on me.

Each morning at the bright and early hour of 5.30 we did a morning run of some fifteen kilometres which to my distress would, towards its end, pass my old company lines – much to the joy of those I had considered friends, who seemed greatly amused at the sight of a forty-year-old corporal trying to demonstrate his peak physical condition. They would raise their mugs of coffee, whilst rubbing the sleep from their eyes and passing derisive and abusive remarks. Even worse was the sight of my own captain laughing at my obvious distress and calling, '*Révien à ta famille*, Johnny!' Not, as far as I'm concerned, the correct behaviour for a Legion captain, but I reconciled myself with the fact that it had been my own bloody fault anyway.

Like all good and bad things, training eventually came to an end, with six parachute jumps completed during daylight hours and the final one at night. The physical effort required to complete the ground training had once again reduced my weight by some five kilos.

The jumps proved exhilarating and enjoyable except for one, when I appreciated why the Para jumped with steel helmets on their heads. I managed to 'ring the bell' on that landing, and the helmet I was wearing absorbed the shock of impact with my head against a rock. If it had not been for the helmet, my brains (which older members of my company claimed I did not possess) would still be smeared over the rock, which had probably been planted by one of the instructors.

Legion parachute instructors all had the same sardonic sense of humour. During instruction it was emphasized that in the event of the parachute failing to open, and then the reserve chute also failing, the novice parachutist should raise his left hand directly above his head and salute with his right. This would indicate to the instructors waiting below that he had a slight problem. The fact that he would strike the ground whilst saluting would also indicate that the novice had been without fear. The left arm held straight up in the air would protect the novice's watch from damage, and from that day on it would be treasured by the instructor in memory of a brave young legionnaire.

The final briefing on this subject prior to our first jump had been enough to make one young hero refuse to go to the door of the aircraft and then refuse to step out or, in the manner of the Legion, hurl himself out. Legion policy had certainly changed from a few years before. There was no punishment for that young man: he was shipped out to the 1st Regiment the next morning.

Nothing was done by the instructors during our series of jumps to assist the slightly nervous. One dropped uniform trousers prior to a jump, to show that one's slip was of a spotless white (nothing could be worse than a novice parachutist arriving in hospital with a dirty slip). There was a further inspection on arrival on terra firma, to check that the slips had not turned a shade of brown. Certainly not a way of raising morale!

It took only some six weeks for me to complete my parachute training. I felt quite 'chuffed' that I had eventually become a 'lion', and more than delighted that my own company captain had asked to be allowed to attend the ceremonial parade and present me with my shiny new brevet.

After the award of the brevet, there was a party held by my own company, to which I returned the same evening, attended by all those responsible for my training. Their looks of surprise when I presented my old instructors with my specially padded combat jackets did nothing to assuage my feeling of loss that, during my absence, both David and Raphael had departed for France and the life of a civilian. Both had been very special friends for a long time. It was a shock to realize that our numbers had now been reduced to less than sixty, and there seemed a strong possibility that we would finally be absorbed into the 1st Regiment, from whom the captain had already received a request for NCOs as instructors.

I asked the captain for a leave period in Paris within days of my return, and he readily agreed, conditional to my going to sergeants' training afterwards. Reluctant or not, I would have agreed to anything at that moment for even ten days leave. But it was not to be. For some reason the 2nd Parachute Regiment had learned there was a recently qualified parachutist with the rank of corporal floating around Corsica wasting his time and had transmitted a signal demanding that he join them. The signal had originated from a Legion colonel, and my own company commander was only a captain. The battle had already been decided with the issuing of that signal. Like it or lump it, I had become a parachutist four years later than I had meant it to happen, so I would carry out my final months of service with a parachute regiment.

The captain allowed me to purchase all the stocks of beer from our own *foyer*, and the sergeants allowed me to purchase the stocks of their bar, leaving it dry – all paid for with a cheque on my recently opened bank account in Marseilles. Thus the first company of the 3rd Battaillon de Marche celebrated my departure with the biggest party ever. The noise from the grenades that most of the company had concealed in their kitbags, along with cases of signal flares fired at random in the air, once again brought a visit from the *gendarmes* based at Bastia, but they seemed satisfied that it was a belated celebration in honour of Bastille Day, which we had missed, and even stayed for the party.

So I took my leave of many of my comrades, with whom during the preceding years I had shared hardships, trials, tribulations, joy and fun – but never prison sentences.

8   The Old Lion

On 21 September 1963 I arrived at the main gate of the 2nd Regiment of Parachutists, bright-eyed and bushy-tailed, immaculate in a uniform purchased from a civilian tailor at Marseilles, the recently awarded parachute brevet polished to a golden hue adorning my right breast.

Parachute brevets were silver in colour when presented, but with constant rubbing on the side wall of the American-type tents the silver could be worn down to the base brass metal, producing a golden brevet. The tents being used as a polishing cloth would produce yet another hole to let in the rain, so it was a strict rule in Corsica never to rub a newly awarded brevet on the wall of the tent in which you yourself would be sleeping.

My journey to this new base at Bou Sfer, only three kilometres from the coast and at most thirty kilometres west of Oran, had not been uneventful, and was certainly not by the route planned by the Legion authorities. But though I arrived on time, my entry was denied!

The denial of entry was made by a gentleman, very tall, very lean, very wiry, with a somewhat mean-looking expression on his sharp, granite face. He spoke no word but merely pointed with a long finger to the barrier guarding the camp entrance. Although I had not expected to be greeted by a welcoming committee and a ceremonial band, I had expected to be met with the traditional handshake. But this character, with his long, pointing finger, clearly had no intention of allowing me to pass those hallowed portals.

This awesome figure, with the rank of *adjudant-chef* and with several rows of medal ribbons (none of which had been awarded for good conduct or long service), just glared at me with his steely, beady eyes as if challenging me to argue his authority.

There was no way I could understand his reason for denying me entry. My uniform was impeccable, my boots were polished to a high gloss, all thirteen pleats to my tunic shirt had been ironed to a razor sharpness. I knew damn well that I was a picture of a perfect legionnaire and that I would probably have qualified as a model for a recruiting poster but this bastard (who had obviously had his tongue cut out) was determined neither to explain nor to provide me with a bed for the night. Only when the short, stocky figure of a chief corporal bugler, standing some way behind the *adjudant-chef* began making a stroking motion with his forefinger along his upper lip did I realize that it was my moustache (which I had been carefully nourishing for four years) which was giving offence. Moustaches are forbidden in the Legion Parachute Regiment. They can add injury to insult whilst fighting to untangle a mass of suspense lines snapping round your head and face as you fall from the sky attempting to right the parachute. I knew darn well that this *adjudant-chef* was not going to make any concessions. Equally he had no intention of allowing me to find the washroom to shave it off. I had no choice but to find my razor in my small bag and hack at the first-class, fully matured military moustache that had been my pride and joy. It would have been a lesser pain to have had a couple of teeth extracted without an anaesthetic, but there was a consolation in the fact that I was allowed to enter the gate under the cynical eye of the *adjudant-chef* and, in the privacy of the guardroom, rapidly swallow the beer passed to me by the bugler. I was not in the least surprised to find that *Adjudant-Chef* Petrie was also in charge of the prison, very large and very prominent at the rear of the guardroom. There was also little doubt in my mind that, if I had retained my moustache, my only bed for the night would have been in the prison, with a rock for a pillow.

There had been a time whilst I was waiting at the gate when I had wondered if anyone had discovered that my route here from Bastia had included a visit to Paris, with a slight diversion to London, neither of which had figured in the officially prepared itinerary. Had he been aware of this tiny detour, this *adjudant-chef* would have incarcerated me in *his* prison for the next six months.

The captain had presented me with a letter for the authorities at Aubagne (the new French version of Sidi-bel-Abbès), with the recommendation that I be granted leave (my first) prior to my departure to Algeria. It had been only a few weeks before, that the captain had handed to me a registered packet that not only contained a passport, but even had the return address of the British Consulate at Ajaccio rubber-stamped on the back.

Obtaining this new passport had not been in the least difficult. An official application form received from London, duly completed, two photographs, a covering letter declaring that my original passport was being held in safe keeping by the Legion, a cheque and a note to the effect that the new passport was required for the purpose of my return to the UK on leave (albeit French leave). No problems, I had received the shiny new passport within twenty days of my application. (The captain had known that my father had suffered a heart attack in the month of June and had even arranged for his wife to telephone my home from Paris … he had been sympathetic and knew that if I managed to get to Paris, then my next stop would be London. *He had also been certain that I would return to the Legion.*)

Within five hours of my arrival at Aubagne, I had already been speeded on my way to Paris. Not only was the *adjudant* in charge of the transit company at Aubagne an old acquaintance, he had also been my old section chief back in 1960. He produced from thin air an official document for fifteen days leave in Paris. With the true confidence of a friend, he had guessed that I would be heading for London, and he too had been a hundred per cent sure that I would be coming back. (He also happened to be the same bastard that had sent me to Corporals' training school).

It had taken only thirty-six hours from my departure from the Legion camp at Borgo to entering the house of my family in London, to the great delight and happiness of my mother, and to the great relief of my father, when I informed him that I would only be staying for ten days prior to my return.

Less than an hour of the removal of my moustache, I found myself escorted by Oscar to the presence of yet another legendary colonel of the Legion, Colonel Caillaud. In the true tradition of the Legion I announced my arrival in my loudest voice, stating my length of service, the time I had held my rank, and my number, strictly in accordance with protocol, but reducing the voice to a murmur when I stated my age and how long I had held my parachute brevet. It did nothing for my ego when I overheard his muttered aside to the commandant: 'Where are they digging up these old bastards from?' Nevertheless, he did welcome me with a handshake, and offered the comment that I would find it difficult keeping up with the 'young lions', so I would be given a job with the 'old lions'.

He was another colonel of the Legion who knew every man in his regiment, and he had a smile on his face as he informed me that he already had four Englishmen, all of them 'good', and that he would expect me to do as well! 'Do as well'? Except for Bob Wright, all were regular visitors to the prison.

The speed with which I was introduced to my compatriots had me exhausted and a lot worse for drink by late afternoon. First I met Bob Wright, a British corporal who had been with the regiment since his enlistment four years earlier, then Legionnaires Bob Wilson, Kenny and Simon Murray – all this at the hands of Baccus, a portly chief corporal with more than fifteen years service, who had with the blessing of Oscar obtained a day off to show me around. Each introduction was accompanied by a few bottles of beer, and, although I had been well and truly indoctrinated in handling this potent beverage, I had never experienced the speed with which these men could empty a bottle.

Within twenty-four hours of arrival I found I had been fully equipped with brand-new items of uniform. My new parachute-type camouflage uniforms were immaculately tailored. (The old infantry type I had handed into the stores I had been wearing for almost three years in the mountains, repaired and patched but always scrubbed, and I almost feared when exchanging them that I was losing my identity.)

Bob Wright escorted me to every company commander, every senior *adjudant* and chief sergeant – not only of the company I would be joining but of the whole damn regiment. Although I did not receive a drink from officers I met, I was certainly liberally plied with it by those very senior NCOs. At the end of the second day of this initiation procedure, I was begging for mercy, and pleading with Bob to fix it so that I could have at least forty-eight hours in the infirmary resting. Then he realized he had not shown me the hospital.

Here was another chief corporal, Kovacs, and here I found

Baccus again. It may have been the hospital, but it had the biggest refrigerator I had seen in the Legion, and seventy per cent of its capacity was storing ice-cold beer.

Lest the reader is of the opinion that this was the hardest-drinking regiment of the Foreign Legion (it probably was), I had not realized that the day of my arrival was a Saturday, which, although not a 'day off', is normally devoted to 'make and mend', with a minimum of bullshit, and which is followed by Sunday, strictly a day of informality and rest, except for the poor slobs on duty.

The relaxed attitude at the hospital was quite normal. For some unknown reason, legionnaires will neither report sick nor even be ill on a Saturday or Sunday. Even those confined to the precincts of the hospital, with a broken arm or leg gained from an error of judgement at the DZ (dropping zone), will somehow struggle on these days to the bar of the *Foyer du Légionnaire*, to partake of liquid refreshments with their comrades.

So it was that I began my new life in the Legion, surrounded by these 'young lions' but quite happy to find that I had been well and truly accepted by the 'old lions', men of many ranks who had spent years of their lives in the Legion. Many had survived the black days of the defeat at Dien Bien Phu and had experienced more combat in that final fifty-four days than I had seen during mountain treks with my old infantry regiment or even during the five years of World War II.

Maybe I had been lucky to arrive at the week-end, for I found myself treated with courtesy by the *adjudant-chef* of the stores, who personally ensured that items of uniform were a perfect fit and well tailored, and by various NCOs, all of whom welcomed me even though I was obviously a bloody nuisance and disturbing their time off. Perhaps what impressed me most of all was that, even on a Sunday most of these veterans were at their place of work to ensure that a clean start could be made on the Monday. I was not a young and impressionable legionnaire easily influenced, but I got the feeling that, although I had left my old 'family' of the 3rd Regiment, this 'family' sincerely welcomed me.

The story of the loss of my moustache caused a great deal of amusement – and regret that my new 'brothers' could not have seen the look of horror on the face of *Adjudant-Chef* Petrie as he refused entry to the newest recruit to the regiment. These veterans informed me that the only person in the regiment who did not know he was called 'Oscar' (even by the colonel), was in fact the *adjudant-chef* himself, and it would be inadvisable for me to forget myself during any conversation with him.

Hearing the name, it recalled the bamboo canes, Oscars, wielded by para instructors. As I found out later, the nickname of *Adjudant-Chef* Petrie was apt.

It was not until four days after my arrival that I was introduced to my company commander. Then, for the first time in my life, I wished for a hole to appear at my feet and allow me to disappear for eternity, for he was one I had known well in the 3rd Regiment, Captain Rudolph X. Captain X had been responsible for David Fireman's carrying out over two years of combat operations without a weapon. He had hated David, first and foremost because he was a Jew, and secondly for his ability with the French language. I well remembered two occasions, one at night and one during the day, when David was caught in a crossfire. The utter despair and hopelessness of the situation had led to his calling 'Jim!' at the top of his voice – a voice that contained the tremor of a man already condemned to death. I cannot think of a more horrifying situation than being weaponless and in close contact with the enemy. David had as much courage as, possibly more than, most legionnaires, to have endured such a life for as long as he did.

I stood in front of this captain waiting for him to recognize me and resigned to the fact that my last nine months in the Legion were without doubt going to be very miserable indeed. Yet my guardian angel was still perched on my shoulder. He had not recognized me! I voiced a silent prayer of thanks to 'Oscar' for the removal of my moustache.

I recalled one operation against a small band of Fell when a girl had been captured, slightly wounded in the arm. This character, Captain X, had instructed David to dress her wound, and bring her to his rapidly erected two-man tent to be questioned. The rest of the company could not have cared less. Whilst he was indulging himself copulating like a rutting pig, the legionnaires were only hoping that she was not a virgin and would give him a dose of the 'clap'. It was this operation that ensured that a few legionnaires became moderately wealthy men. The girl had been 'paymaster' for a group of Fell, and two satchels that had been found contained banknotes of various currencies, probably for distribution in the Algiers sector. Although there was quite a bit of haggling over the French francs, there were no takers for the English pound notes and American dollars, and so it was with the compliments of the Algerian rebel army that, on our ejection from Algeria late in 1962, I opened a bank account at the Crédit Lyonnais in Marseilles with a healthy deposit of almost $2,000 and a cellophane packet containing £800.

As I stood in front of Captain X, so happy that he had not recognised me, it was difficult to restrain myself from bursting into laughter, at the thought that the girl he had had on that mountainside had been the most expensive he would ever have in his life. If he had acted like a captain, the officers' mess would have had some £15,000 in the kitty, instead of which at least twenty legionnaires of all ranks had reaped the benefit. Except between those who had accepted this 'manna from heaven' it was the best-kept secret in the 3rd Regiment.

I discovered that fortune had indeed blessed me, for my new company commander was Captain Racaud. (I often thought how fortunate the Legion was in finding such officers, the epitome of what every Legion officer should be: an example to all, fair-minded, always a gentleman, and with a sense of humour.) There was a smile on his face as he awarded me the first and only punishment that blotted my otherwise perfect conduct sheets, an even bigger smile when he awarded me the promotion to chief corporal, only a few weeks later. Then lady luck really went out of her way to help me. My section chief was a long-serving legionnaire, a veteran of Indo China (Vietnam) and of the battles at Dien Bien Phu. Chief Sergeant Karl Emmerich, rough, tough, rugged, during the battles in Algeria had led his section in some of the toughest actions and was immensely proud of the fact that he had never 'lost' one of his own men in the various combats – wounded perhaps, but never dead.

One of my most treasured photographs, which I was allowed to take during the ceremonial parade of Camerone in 1964 by special dispensation of Colonel Gaillaud, is that of Karl Emmerich receiving the much-coveted Médaille Militaire.

Karl was one of the most respected NCOs in the regiment, much admired by those legionnaires of all ranks who had known him for many years. He was a specialist and instructor in 'free fall', an exponent and part-time instructor in the art of 'Halo' (high-altitude drop, 5,000 metres, low altitude opening 200 metres or less), not in my view something that could be called a hobby but it certainly was to Karl and a few of the other veteran NCOs of the regiment. I was more than fortunate that I not only received from Karl friendship and an awful lot of instruction, but was promoted, through his efforts, to the exalted rank of chief corporal. Then later the bastard cheated by getting me drunk and, with the connivance of Bob Wright, had me signing on for another period of service.

Later, Karl offended me by giving me a severe kick up the arse, an indignity that made me refuse to speak to him for two days, or share a beer. The instructions he was required to give in his official capacity, and my response required in acknowledgement, were passed through a third party, Maurice Deville, a veteran sergeant and good friend, who after forty-eight hours of enduring a strained relationship, acted as a go between. He produced a bottle of scotch with a mouthful of verbal abuse direct from the gutters of Marseilles, saying we were making his life a misery and acting like regulars instead of legionnaires. Peace and harmony were restored and we all got drunk together. Karl probably had a reason for the kick. Even in the Legion, it is not the done thing to get rid of rats in a barrack room by shooting at them!

The Legion base at Bou Sfer, previously a vineyard, had been built completely by the muscular efforts of the legionnaires of the 2nd REP. It was a vast complex of single-storey prefabricated steel barrack blocks, all on concrete bases, all painted white, some even surrounded by flowerbeds, with a fifteen-metre wide black asphalt road running through the centre, almost two kilometres long. It was in complete contrast to what I had assumed at that time to be a typical Legion establishment: no walls surrounded this complex, no concrete pillboxes, no sandbagged outposts, just a couple of strands of barbed wire beyond which was the widest, deepest, tanktrap ditch I had ever seen. During my four years of service, I had seen only two of the traditional-type Legion bases, one at Sidi-bel-Abbès, the other at Saida. This new base, with only its brick toilets and showers lacking completion, gave me the impression that it must have taken at least two years to build, but in fact work had started on it only a year before my arrival. I was glad I'd not arrived earlier!

The builders of Bou Sfer's military airfield, only a matter of four kilometres away, had run out of materials during construction of the main runway. It was eighty metres short of the planned length. And why? Because the construction engineers were ignorant of the legionnaires' aptitude for spiriting away vast quantities of cement during night exercises. Instead of a legionnaire being punished for some minor infraction, he was 'fined' by his sergeant two or three bags of cement, with two results: acquisition of material required for construction work, and the legionnaire's gaining experience in evading sentinels during the nightly stealthy foraging expeditions. One idiot of a legionnaire in the 2nd Company, returning with his two sacks of cement, also carried the rifle of the sleeping French Air Force sentinel. Since the man who brought back the rifle happened to be British and stayed in the Legion and became an *adjudant*, I will not name him, but there are 3,000 legionnaires and ex-legionnaires who can!

My life in the para regiment did not prove to be what I had expected. At first I was somewhat dejected and dismayed to find that I had not been detailed to a combat company, but became responsible for the stores and sales of the *Foyer du Légionnaire* which had the longest beer bar in Algeria. The sight of a few hundred legionnaires queueing at this bar demanding rapid service, since all would be 'dying' of thirst, made me extremely grateful that my own work was behind the scenes, where I could remain unseen and uncursed.

My first few months with the regiment were devoted entirely to my work. The purchase of toothpaste was as important as the purchase of needles and thread, but the highest priority was that there be adequate stocks of beer. When stocks were reduced to 2,000 cases, it was a time to panic.

At first I found it difficult to adjust to the routine. Although I was happy to have a sedentary job, it came as a shock to find that this regiment also had a predeliction for early morning sport, in which there were no exceptions. Since the whole regiment seemed bursting with energy, they would indulge in weekly night exercises, going out at the normal time for sleeping and not returning until midday the following day. With all this activity, despite my desk-bound job, it was easy for me to maintain a high standard of fitness.

I had become the fifth British legionnaire to join the very exclusive regiment at Bou Sfer and, although we did not form a clique, being distributed between various companies, we did on occasions get together for drinks in the *foyer*.

Bob Wright, already a corporal in the regiment when I arrived, had also endured corporals' training school under the guidance of *Adjudant-Chef* Schwanke, so between us there was an immediate *rapport* and understanding. Although not quite born with a silver spoon in his mouth, Bob was the son of very wealthy and cultivated parents. He had had an expensive education and had lived in a large country house on the south coast of England, with the additional advantage of a well-appointed flat in the better part of the West End of London. Faced with the choice of either completing his university education followed by an assured career in the diplomatic service, or taking up the place he had been offered at the British Royal Naval college, he declined both and joined the Foreign Legion. A very good friend and drinking partner was Bob.

When we were not drinking in the *foyer*, he could be found at least three times a month at the regimental brothel. (He was the only legionnaire in the regiment successful in bedding Suzanne, who was not there to entertain, merely to manage – the lucky swine did not even have to pay!) It was Bob who told me that the leave I had taken prior to joining the regiment had *not* been entered on my record sheet, so the full amount of leave due to me still stood. I was never sure if this omission was a manipulation by my old chief at Aubagne or by Bob himself. Whoever had been responsible, I was quite happy.

The next Englishman I will slander has to be a Yorkshire lad who must have cost me a fortune in beer, and whom I will refer to only as Legionnaire Kenny. Tough and durable, only of average height but as strong as an ox, Kenny was much more mature than the other Brits, and prior to joining the Legion had served both in the British Army and at Hereford in the SAS.

It was normally the tallest men who carried the AA52 (light

machine-gun) in the various companies, but there was not a happier legionnaire than Kenny stomping through the mountains with this quite heavy weapon over his shoulder. He actually called it his baby, cleaned it, adjusted it, nourished it and, if he had been possessed of breasts, would have fed it milk. Any other man in the company who touched it, even if he was a giant, would likely end up with a mouthful of broken teeth from Kenny. You'd welcome him as a friend and drinking partner, but if he became your enemy, it would be time to take off for a regiment in the Pacific or Madagascar!

Only exceptionally tough legionnaires, thick of skin and even thicker in the head, were ever prepared to risk a second visit to the prison at Bou Sfer. Within nine months Kenny had been in prison three times.

Kenny never realized that it had been at my suggestion to Oscar and his lieutenant that he had become a member of the regimental police. This group were 'elite', very keen and under the direct control of Oscar. Kenny became a changed man, a greater disciplinarian than any of them and, although still only a legionnaire, once threatened me and two fellow chief corporals with prison as we entered the camp at 5 a.m. Talk about power and corruption! He drank for a full week at my expense. I respected Kenny for his tenacity and character and was well pleased that he was a friend.

Then there was Robert Craigie Wilson, a Scot, and prepared to let the whole world know it. To differentiate between him and Bob Wright, he was known to most of the senior NCOs as Bob No.1. (Why on earth he merited the classification of Bob 1, I could never understand. It could have been that it inferred Idiot No.1).

Bob was one of the three tallest men in the regiment, and a complete extrovert, an enthusiastic rugby player and a member of the dirtiest tricks rugby team in the whole of the French Army. The regimental rugby team were all officers, with the exception of three legionnaires. Bob represented the British element. Dirty players? they actually asked me to try out for their team but, after watching them play and damn near cripple fifteen members of the French Artillery, I wanted no part of that particular mayhem.

I wanted an even lesser part when I noticed that the 'trainer' was Mario Mati, my old buddy from *peloton* (corporals' platoon) days, now a chief corporal of the 2nd Company. As I watched Mario running from man to man of our team, with his bucket, towel and sponge, giving each man a swig of what I assumed to be water, bringing apparently dead men to life, I realized that, although Mario had been promoted, he had not changed in the least in his constant flouting of authority. The life-giving liquid he was providing to the team was scotch whisky, and he had a reserve of four full bottles concealed under a towel only a few metres from where the colonel was standing. Small wonder that the play was dirty! The 2nd REP not only had the toughest and roughest rugby team: it also had the hardest drinking team. At the completion of that match, most of the artillery team were in need of medical treatment at our base infirmary.

Bob Wilson was a happy-go-lucky character and, prior to joining the Legion, had served as a lieutenant and platoon leader in the Royal Artillery. Upon his enlistment and the completion of his documentation, on the line for 'Profession' he had written 'Soldier'. In the magical and mysterious ways of the Legion, this had been translated as *Soudeur*, and for the rest of his Legion career (lasting sixteen years), his civilian occupation according to Legion records was 'Welder'.

Bob and I would always agree on the fact that, although 'dining in' nights in a British officers' mess lacked nothing in the way of ceremony and pomp and circumstance, the food we ate as legionnaires was at least equal, if not better, and washing a meal down with our own *Piffe* (a very coarse, full-bodied red wine) was a damn sight better than the rejected Beaujolais from the vineyards of Northern France served to officers in the UK.

The fourth Brit was Simon Murray, a legionnaire on my arrival and a member of the regimental shooting team. Simon was the youngest of all, having joined at a very early age, and seemed to have a jaundiced view of the Legion. He was fortunate in the fact that he was quite a proficient piano-player, and he, with a few other legionnaires who could play musical instruments, would be rounded up to provide a dance band for the officers' mess soirées, thus avoiding the mundane duties of other legionnaires. But Simon did bring credit to the Brits, for he achieved first position in the corporals' training platoon early in 1964, achieving the grade of chief corporal, thus setting the precedent for Bob Wilson, who completed the second platoon, to have no option but to finish first. He had the eyes of the whole bloody regiment on him, waiting for him to fall by the wayside. However, Bob Wright and I completely agreed that, if they had taken their platoon under Schwanke, both would have finished last! (Which merely shows that both Bob Wright and I were not only prejudiced but also envious.)

When I also achieved the grade of chief corporal, a couple of months after Bob, it was probably due to the fact that I was the oldest corporal in the regiment – not in length of service, but in years, so that Colonel Caillaud bestowed this gift out of sympathy.

None of us realized that we had probably created history in the Legion, since without doubt it was the first time *ever* that three Brits were serving in the same Legion regiment all with the rank of chief corporal.

With the promotion and the fact that my pay was also graduated on the scale of how long I had held my corporal's stripes, the sum of £140 per month (in 1964) was more than sufficient to subsidize Kenny's unquenchable thirst and even, now and again to pay for his entertainment at the brothel.

Since our group comprised three chief corporals, a corporal and a first-class private, Kenny, it was suggested to Kenny that he too should undertake the rigours of corporals' platoon, obtain his stripes and, as a matter of principle, finish in first position, thus alleviating the strain on our pockets. The disrespect and verbal abuse that fell from his lips would normally have merited his paying a further visit to the regimental prison, and he would storm away to write yet another letter to 'Sea View Place' in Leeds.

In the way of simple legionnaires, and because small minds – particularly British minds – can be vastly amused by even smaller things, we would fall about in laughter at the fact that someone could actually name a street in Leeds as 'Sea View', slap bang in the middle of England and with absolutely no chance of a view of the sea in any direction.

We would always be forgiven, and after venting his wrath writing about the idiots by whom he was surrounded, Kenny would return to participate in the next round of beer. Although 'Sea View' caused Wilson, Wright and myself great amusement,

Kenny was not aware of the private joke, and there was no way I would have told him of it, for I once saw him throw a punch that travelled little distance, but with such speed that only I had witnessed it. The recipient was admitted to the infirmary with a fractured jaw, described officially as an accident sustained by being drunk, falling over and striking his jaw on the ground.

Life in the 2nd Regiment was not all boozing and whoring. When I had commenced parachute training, Colonel Chenel commanded the regiment. I had been looking forward to seeing the look of despair on his face at the arrival of the novice legionnaire he had rejected as a parachutist more than four years earlier, as being 'too old', and watching the tears roll down his cheeks in frustration. But almost three months prior to my arrival, the regiment had been taken over by Colonel Callaud. The construction of the camp had been almost completed, and now this dynamic character began to whip the regiment into shape, laying the groundwork that turned the regiment from a conventional parachute regiment into highly specialized rapid-intervention combatants, second to none in the world. He introduced experiments and techniques so original that they were copied by the NATO group as much as ten years later.

Among the veteran senior NCOs of the regiment were a very select few who had been in the first group of legionnaires to complete their para training at Setif in Algeria in 1948. They had become the nucleus of the 2nd BEP and then departed for Vietnam. (The 2nd Regiment of Parachutists inherited the mantle of the 2nd Battalion of Parachutists after their near annihilation at Dien Bien Phu.) It came as no surprise to me to learn from these veterans that our own Colonel Caillaud had been the very first officer to join this battalion, whilst still a lieutenant.

Karl Emmerich was one of these veterans, and many of them came to the office where I worked alongside him, old friends from the days they had been common privates together, now adorned with gold stripes and braid denoting their senior rank. On their dress uniforms, the odd Legion of Honour could be seen. They paid visits which I can only describe as regular 'bullshitting' sessions, reminiscing of days gone by, as they sucked beer from a bottle, reducing work to a minimum and providing a lot of entertainment. As Maurice Deville, also a veteran of Indo China, often remarked, 'They may hold up the work, but at least they pay for the beer.'

A few days before Camerone Day 1964, I obtained a long-playing record from France called 'Camerone'. To my surprise it was not a record about the battle of the Camerone of 1863, but a recording of the last grim days of the last stand of the remnants of the Legion at Dien Bien Phu, yet another lost cause fought by the Legion as they dropped in hundreds through exhaustion and continued assault. Attacked by 150,000 of the enemy, the Legion had been outnumbered by almost 200 to one. The slaughter had ended on 7 May 1954, almost ten years earlier.

On 29 April I asked Karl to remain in the office and listen to this recording after the *foyer* had closed, since it concerned events in which he had been involved many years before. He did stay behind, and he brought with him two of his old friends, one with the bars of an *adjudant*, the other an *adjudant-chef*. All three had served together at Dien Bien Phu, all three had survived fifty-four days continuous onslaught. None of them at the time of the event had held a rank higher than corporal.

None of these men was aware of what they were going to listen to, but I was placed under threat of death if it was rubbish.

I had prepared the setting well. A case of iced beer was readily available (my treat), the room illuminated only with the light of two candles.

So the recitation began, but to me it was far more than a recitation. It was four legionnaires sitting together sharing their beer, listening to a solemn requiem – and it was indeed a requiem. To the sound of Legion music in the background, accompanied by the quiet singing of the Legion choir, a very sombre and solemn voice began to tell the story of Dien Bien Phu. To the sound of falling shells, the crashing of mortar fire, the stuttering of machine-guns, the story unfolded. The atmosphere in that room became electric. One could almost see the waving searchlights and the bursting of the magnesium flares above the stronghold that was no longer a stronghold but a deathtrap. There was the fall of the defence post called Isabelle, then Beatrice and Dominique, then the others one by one, all of them called by girls' names.

I could almost feel the hairs on the back of my neck rising and a sense of feeling that we were actually back in time, and that I was sharing an experience with this band of very gallant men.

Midway through this requiem, whilst I was turning the record, feeling very humble in the presence of courageous men, I noticed in the candlelight that, in spite of all their efforts to restrain them, tears were trickling down their cheeks. These men, who between them sported a Legion of Honour, three Military Medals and more than a dozen other awards for bravery, had been crying.

When the recording ended, and the candles had been extinguished and the lights turned on, they began to talk. They were no longer exalted NCOs but the legionnaires of ten years before. 'Do you remember the time when Dieter did …?' 'Do you remember when Franz tried to get the wine from outside the wire?', 'Remember Grimault?', 'Remember Hartment?' Remember … Remember … Remember. So it went on until the early hours of the morning of the 30th. This was not a bullshitting session: each and everyone of them was paying tribute to the friends they had left behind, each remembering a Camerone Day of ten years before.

I learned about the battle of Dien Bien Phu not by reading about it but by listening to it falling from the lips of this gallant band who had created history.

I cursed myself for being such a lousy legionnaire and volunteered myself the dirtiest job in the Legion on Camerone Day, as corporal of the guard, much to the surprise of the idiot whose place I took, who looked upon it as a miracle from Heaven. I was not prepared to explain my reasons, not even to Oscar. Twenty-four hours of self-inflicted retreat …

That same year Bob Wilson, who had now completed his corporal's training, and remained at the small base at Lindles for even more specialized training, returned to the camp for a few days for various reasons I could never determine – probably for yet another rugby match, against the ever-unsuspecting French regulars. On this visit we had one of the biggest celebrations ever held at the *foyer* at Bou Sfer, and it climaxed in my only visit to the small village of Ain el Turk.

With his usual aptitude for discovering facts that would be ignored by others, Bob declared that we were all morons for having overlooked the fact that 1964 was the 300th anniversary of the creation of Hatt Brothers of Strasbourg, who had invented and produced the magical Kronenborg beer, the life-giving sustenance without which the Legion would not have survived and without which the 2nd Regiment of Parachutists would have died an agonizing death.

So we had a celebration, at first with only the British contingent, then joined by elements of the 'Mafia', then by veteran NCOs who had deserted their own mess when they learned of the party, and the reasons for the celebration. It became more than a party when we were also joined by three officers – who shall remain nameless, since one is now a general, one a colonel; the other, Captain C, was killed in an air disaster in Djibouti in 1981. It must be explained that our group of chief corporals, along with a few sergeants, had formed a 'mafia'. Between us we had the key man in every company within the regiment, each able to bend the rules and regulations. We could fix the loan of a jeep or motor-scooter, a leave pass, a parachute jump without authorization and the exemption from any onerous task by the simple use of the telephone and a whispered request. During this party stories of the hardships of earlier days and the battles in Indo China ten years earlier began flowing from the lips of an eminent *adjudant-chef*, recalling the frustrations of a newly promoted sergeant at Dien Bien Phu. Most of the legionnaires at Dien Bien Phu had been fully aware that they were fighting against odds of 200 to one. Most of them could not have cared less if it had been even higher. This *adjudant-chef* had at that time been a very junior sergeant. Attempting to rouse one of his legionnaires in the early morning to undertake his stint of duty he had been met with the response of, 'I'm out of this war. I killed the last of my 200 yesterday.' Then, with great delight, the *adjudant-chef* pointed a finger at a very popular chief sergeant responsible for discipline in one of the companies, and stated, 'That's the insubordinate bastard who should have been court-martialled instead of decorated and promoted.' And then, to the delight of all, he ended the story with the declaration that he had not killed his own tally of 200 until four days later and, when reporting the fact to his own officer, with the additional request for time off for achieving his ration, had found himself back to the rank of corporal! Such men as these have always existed in the Legion and always will.

Each company had a speciality in which they trained to the Nth degree: anti-tank combat, specialist tank-destroyers. The reflexes needed to throwing oneself between the tracks of a speeding tank and then somehow find a protuberance at its rear, grabbing it and hoisting oneself to a position to deposit a mine or bag of grenades, required a dexterity and athletic ability of a first-class gymnast. Even more impressive were the officers and veteran NCOs showing how it should be done.

The amphibious company trained in rapid embarkation onto landing craft, and even speedier departure whilst still twenty metres from the shore, fully equipped and armed, followed by a run of fifteen kilometres to get to their combat stations. They had not realized that they would also become exponents of the art of 'Halo' (p.178) night parachute drops in Mersa-el-Kebir harbour, in frogman's kit, armed with practice mines to destroy the French Navy.

Then there was the mountain specialist company, climbing vertical-faced cliffs that in the normal course of events should have been tackled only by world-renowned specialists, but which were treated as a day's vacation by the 2nd Company – they actually sang as they abseiled at high speeds from heights of more than ninety metres.

The whole damn regiment became enthused: sabotage groups, survival training, commando training, guerrilla warfare, night parachute jumps, forest jumps, forest jumps at night – when only your nose tells you how far away from the ground you are, and the smell of pine trees tells you when to take up the perfect tree-landing position – with one hand over your balls, and a silent prayer. (This is not in the Legion training manual, but who wanted to be rejected in the brothel?) There was sniper training and instruction in night-instinctive shooting for everyone, and jumping from helicopters into the sea only fifty metres from the shoreline from a height of only twenty metres, but which seems a thousand when the helicopter is belting along at eighty kilometres an hour. (I tried it once – the vanity of man! – then thanked God that Colonel Caillaud had not decided to experiment with the same exercise with the Dakotas that were readily available.)

The beginning of 1964 saw an uplift in the spirit of the regiment, a kinship I had not seen since the end of the Algerian 'police action'. This had become a regiment not of 'young lions' but of 'young warrior lions', even the most novice of the recruits exuding an air of pride at belonging to such a 'family'.

It mattered not what function a legionnaire carried out in the regiment – and in this instance I mean all ranks from the colonel to the newest recruit. All would participate in the daily routine of chasing through the countryside, wearing tracksuits for anything up to fifteen kilometres, at a higher speed than I had been able to maintain during my recruit days. This was known as '*dégraissage*' and took place each morning at the ungodly hour of 5.30, to sweat the booze out of your system. It might have been bearable except for the fact that each company commander appeared to be trying to impress the colonel with the vast distances his company had covered within the hour.

I was quite happy later to attach myself to the headquarters group of very senior veteran sergeants and *adjudants* who had no ambition to impress the colonel with their athletic prowess and were quite happy to jog around the periphery of the camp, whilst having an occasional puff of a cigarette.

A new senior medical officer offered scientific proof to the colonel that early morning sport did not produce supermen and that the ideal time for sport was four o'clock in the afternoon. I respected the colonel for being amendable to new ideas and adjusting this daily routine. I would willingly have kissed the arse of the new medical officer in full view of the whole regiment for having had such a brilliant notion, which meant that I could return to being awakened at 6.30 in the morning and served with my coffee in a civilized manner. From then on I actually looked forward to the afternoon sport and even frequently tested myself on the combat obstacle course just for fun.

There was no way I could ever have been classed as a 'good' legionnaire prior to my arrival at this new regiment. For a period of four years I had managed to get away with being contrary without being disobedient, incorrigible without being quite insubordinate, and perverse without being rebellious. It soon became clear that with the 'new look' of the regiment introduced by Colonel Caillaud, with Oscar as his staunchest supporter, I would once again have to walk a very straight line, adjust my way of thinking and make damn sure that Oscar was not going to welcome me to confines of his prison, unless it was for a social visit and the offer of a beer.

Baccus, the chief corporal bugler, and part-time second in command of the prison was a very good friend – who damn near got us both hanged.

It had been on a practice jump in the dunes at Cap Falcon. The colonel had joined the aircraft and taken the place of No.1, first out of the aircraft, a lead usually allocated to Baccus or myself. As the light appeared signalling that we were approaching the DZ the colonel took up his position at the door in the manner of the born parachutist. It was then that Baccus produced the mouthpiece of his bugle from his pocket and blew a blast that was a damn good imitation of the aircraft klaxon that signalled 'go'. So the colonel departed, landing some 200 metres short of the DZ and regrettably also some forty metres short of the beach, which resulted in a wet parachute and a somewhat irate, very wet, Legion colonel.

It had been my challenge to Baccus that he do this, but it had been meant as a joke and I never dreamed that he would actually do it. My own parachute had been hooked up as No.3, Baccus as No.2. I had struggled with Baccus to get him out to follow the colonel, but the maniac was still laughing. We did not jump out of the aircraft. Only a few seconds after the exit of the colonel, we both fell out, almost in each other's arms, both of us short of the DZ but at least on the dry beach. None of the remainder of the 'sticks' in the aircraft could ever understand why only the first three had heard the klaxon. We understood later that the captain of the aircraft was awarded eight days prison for his 'error of judgement'. Baccus and I did not mind his being punished – better him than us. Anyway, who would blow the whistle in the prison for the poor slobs undergoing the punishment of the *pelote*, if the usual wielder of this magic instrument was also 'inside'. The 'pelote' is an exercise for prisoners requiring the victim to run round and round in circles, preferably whilst the sun is directly above. The blast of a whistle indicates to the unfortunate legionnaire to crawl on his stomach, then march on his knees, hop only on one leg and so on. A boot in the right places ensures no slacking.

I have already written of the courage of Legion medics. The one I most respected, whom I felt it a privilege to call friend, was

Chief Corporal Kovacs, the most highly decorated man in the regiment below the rank of sergeant. The day one saw Kovacs without a smile on his face and happiness in his heart was the day when the sun rose in the west. He was an excellent medic, and I would have had no hesitation in allowing him to set any broken bone in my body or even remove my appendix. It would have probably been done without an anaesthetic but this would have been compensated with at least half a bottle of scotch whisky. (The other half he would already have drunk.) Medals won by medics are awarded not for the number of enemy they have killed but for the times they have risked their lives to give succour to their comrades.

Then there were Michel and Lauber, also chief corporals. Michel had won the French Army cross-country running championship the year prior to my arrival and could complete the traditional distance of the marathon in two hours forty-five minutes. Nothing special about that? Michel could do it with a sack on his back weighing fifteen kilograms, in camouflage uniform and ranger boots and carrying his weapon and 200 rounds of ammunition.

When he led the company on a fifteen-kilometre run in the early morning darkness, with myself and Lauber bringing up the rear, he would explain the semi-circular route he would be taking, thus allowing Lauber and me to drop out after a few kilometres, take a short cut bisecting his route, sit down and wait, have a cigarette and then join on the end of the now well strung-out column as they passed, at which time Lauber and I would really start running, overtaking the poor slobs who had almost been run off their feet trying to keep up with Michel. Meanwhile we would be shouting abuse and encouragement to near-exhausted legionnaires, most of whom were in their early twenties, and allocate the odd kick up the arse to speed them on their way. We would end the run at the head of the group, along with Michel, much to the delight of those very senior officers and NCOs awaiting our return.

Regrettably we were exposed when the cross-country runs were switched from an early morning departure in darkness to 4 p.m. The first of these, which we had no chance of avoiding, had Lauber and me throwing up each ten minutes, and at the end of that run we both swore off drink for a month. Our period of drying out lasted only five days, when we again succumbed to temptation. Then it was back to the brothel and pitch our tales of woe to Janine and Suzanne, from whom we received no sympathy, only gales of laughter.

Our group of chief corporals, Lauber, Michel, Baccus, Bob Wilson, Kovacs, Dieter and I, had formed a 'Mafia'. Although we were allowed the privilege of drinking in the sergeants' mess, rarely did we group together at this citadel of *adjudants-chef*. We would only pay courtesy visits and always be on our best behaviour. Perhaps the reason for this was that Oscar just happened to be the president of this establishment, and it was advisable to drink not well but very wisely. As far as Oscar was concerned, there were twenty-eight hours in a day, in all of which he was constantly on the lookout for customers for his prison – even three golden stripes on one's arm could not be enough for Oscar to make any concessions. During my whole period in the regiment, he allowed me to buy him one drink, but that, and the fact that he allowed me to drink with him, was something I bragged about for six months.

Life at Bou Sfer was ever-changing, a constant variation of new faces arriving, old faces departing, new training methods instituted, always variable, some of which were entertaining, many others that frightened the life out of me. When I enlisted in 1959, I was told that I would be required to work harder than I had ever worked in my life before. It was only at Bou Sfer that I appreciated that what had been said then had been true. But despite this, life with the 2nd REP could never be termed 'boring'. The whole regiment may have worked hard at developing novel skills but there was also 'playing' and relaxing to such a degree as almost to be undefinable.

Now I must at least mention the unmentionable. The regimental brothel. A brothel in the French language is a *bordel*. In the early days of my training, sergeants inspecting our barrack rooms would constantly refer to the state of our rooms as being a '*bordel* and disgrace', indicating that they were bloody tatty and that we were a bunch of idle morons. Since my departure from Bou Sfer, I have deplored an expression used by many of my civilian acquaintances, 'The place is like a brothel.' The brothel which holds some of my fondest memories was that at Bou Sfer, and it was exceptionally clean and sparkling, well organized and well run, a very profitable establishment, managed by two charming ladies, Janine and Suzanne. It was technically outside the precincts of the base, but still part of the establishment. The girls employed at this 'fun palace' might not have won beauty contests in London or Paris, but among them were a few who would have held their own in some of the smaller towns. Between the girls and the legionnaires at Bou Sfer (and by legionnaires I mean all ranks), there was an affinity, a kinship, brought about perhaps by our belonging to two of the oldest professions in existence since the creation of man.

Since the early days of my youth, I had always guarded the advice proffered by my father when I first departed to fight in another war: 'Treat a whore like a duchess, and a duchess like a whore'. Until my arrival at Bou Sfer, this advice had never produced the results I had dreamed of. But here, when I treated the girls with politeness, courtesy and even respect, and always as ladies, this brought about some amazing results.

At a conference of members of the 'Mafia', we introduced a few ground rules to ensure that we would reap the benefits of a relationship steadily maturing. The first rule was that we would use the brothel for the purpose for which it had been instituted only from the twentieth day of each month, a date at which most of the regiment would be low on funds, because of their constant previous visits. The girls would then be as fresh as daisies and would welcome us with open arms. Rule 2 was that we would visit this place only as an ensemble and that we would all book for the night. The result was that once a month the brothel became almost a private club. Very few legionnaires can say that they had been invited to dinner at a brothel and been received by girls attired in flowing Parisian evening gowns, but we had. Today serving legionnaires refer to a regimental brothel as 'the Poof'. Little do they realize that the expression was devised by a small group of legionnaires at Bou Sfer in 1964 in its original form as 'Puff', the definition in Bob Wright's dictionary being 'a short, quick blast'. We may have achieved nothing exceptional in the Legion but at least we contributed to the language …

In February 1965 I returned from London (officially known as Paris) after twenty days leave so flush with money (after a dog-track win) that on arrival at Bou Sfer I promptly telephoned

Janine at the 'Poof', booking the whole establishment for the following evening for the 'Mafia'.

On the 24 February, three days before the regiment received their pay, I hosted the night's entertainment at the 'Palace of Pleasure'.

We had all celebrated my return too well and unwisely and were all very jolly and happy when a sudden count of heads revealed that we had one more chief corporal than there were girls to be distributed equally. Now the champagne flowed almost faster than the bottles could be opened, each of us determined it would not be he who would be the first to fall over drunk and therefore be eliminated from an evening of delight. The first man to succumb to the curse of alcohol was our great friend, a man for whom we would have all laid down our lives (except in a brothel), Bob 'No.1' Wilson. He was very unceremoniously bundled out of the window and into the fresh air, thus allowing him to recover his wits and return to his room, whilst we carried on with the party.

The next morning, at the unhealthy hour of 5.30, we, the seven lucky ones, took our departure from the brothel, all in tracksuits and running shoes, our dress uniforms left behind for sponging and pressing. (We may have been a band of morons, but we were not quite stupid!) Our tracksuits had been deposited the previous day, so that any officer or senior *adjudant* seeing us jogging at that unearthly hour towards our quarters would only express his admiration for this band of veterans setting a first-class example to the younger element of the regiment, little realizing that we were all half dead from our night's excesses.

Bob, in his wisdom, upon my return, requested twenty-four hours absence from duty. We little knew when we tossed him out of the window that he had dropped into a very large empty drum that served as a rubbish bin. There the prisoners detailed to clean the area had found him, still dead to the world at 9 a.m., when the whole of the regiment was a hive of activity. Luckily for Bob, among the prisoners were two legionnaires from his own company who, with an eye to the future and blessed with a modicum of common sense, placed the drum on a wheelbarrow and wheeled him back to the safe arms of his company. Upon their release from prison, those two legionnaires had their beer bought for them for a month, which I made sure Bob paid for. For us it had been a night to remember, for Bob Wilson a night he was not allowed to forget for the duration of his sixteen years service.

It was also at Bou Sfer that I again met Delgado, one of the knife-wielding experts at Sidi-bel-Abbès, and Jim Sinclair's *chef de section*. Although we had a beer together and talked of times past, he put me off him for life when he voiced disgust that I had not yet completed sergeant's training. I voiced my opinion that corporal's training had been hard enough, and once bitten twice shy, and that only an idiot would volunteer for a second helping of hell. I further waxed loquaciously on the fact that all instructors of corporals' and sergeants' platoons should be hung from the highest tree by their balls. I did not know at the time that Delgado was an instructor at the corporals' training school at Bou Sfer. I was not therefore in the least surprised to find that both Simon and Bob really had to work hard for their stripes. (I often wondered if it had not been the fact that Delgado was Jim Sinclair's best friend at Bel-Abbès that also aided their success?)

After Bob Wright returned from leave in Paris, where he had spent fifteen days with his family, we both found an interest in photography. Bob had a beautiful new Japanese camera that he had received as a gift from his father. I had a primitive Retinette IA purchased in Corsica. We both decided to study this subject under the guidance of the official regimental photographer, and to learn the art of developing and printing. Bob became an expert, whilst I, in my usual fashion of failure, ruined far more film than could be expected from even a novice.

Three months after I joined the regiment, as the parachute jumps now came thick and fast, Bob and I carried our cameras slung around our necks, and attempted to photograph each other or our comrades on our descents. Our early experiments – or rather my own experiments – were not at first successful. The first twice I tried, I omitted to remove the lens cover, then on the third jump half the exposures of the photographs which I had taken were marred by the appearance of the two very large parachute boots that had been on my feet. However, as time progressed, my photographs became better. Then I discovered from some of my drinking companions that, although they were delighted when I took their photographs in the bar, during a parachute jump they would do their utmost to ensure that when we boarded the aircraft they would not be required to jump either immediately in front of or behind me.

I had discovered that even the military-type parachutes could be easily steered in any direction by pulling on the nylon suspense cords with one's hands. However, whilst descending, both hands are required for holding the camera. To help me, Karl Emmerich had demonstrated how to raise myself in the harness, elevating a boot into the suspense cords, and, by forcing down with the boot, to steer the parachute in the direction of the foot. Whilst this did allow one to travel at an angle of forty-five degrees from the vertical, it also increased the speed of descent. I was never sure until much later who was the more frightened, the person whose photograph I was attempting to take, belting towards him at a high rate of knots, or myself when I raised my eyes from the camera and realized how close I had got!

Once I collided with Lauber in mid-air – it was his own bloody fault: he had been shouting at me in German instead of French. We landed together like two sacks of potatoes, tied together, but happily the parachutes behaved themselves and did not decide that one of them should wrap itself in the other, thereby causing our untimely demise. It was then that I decided that mid-air close-up photographs of parachutists should be left for those more expert than myself. I do, however, still have some quite good photographs, most of them taken from the ground, of those descending.

Since I have previously written of one 'unmentionable', I think I should also write of the second, the prison at Bou Sfer. It was really not much different from any other Legion prison. It should be said that all legionnaires develop an enormous sense of pride in their cleanliness, their smartness and their bearing. They are always fresh shaven, always alert, with their heads held high, prepared to look any man direct in the eyes, without fear or anxiety.

Imprisonment means the removal of all things most important to the legionnaire, principally his sense of belonging to an 'élite' force. It is designed to humiliate him, to reduce him to the status of an animal, to deny him cleanliness, which he holds most dear, to deny him the right to salute and to look another man in the eyes. Physical punishment in a Legion prison is rare. There is abuse, yes, but the principle is that it is a legionnaire being punished, and as a legionnaire he should have known better, but his captain will want him back in his company after eight days – without a bruised face.

I cannot write first hand about life in a prison (thanks to my guardian angel), but I know of the experiences of those who did suffer. (Since most of the sentences were for drunkenness, I had little sympathy for the offenders.)

It is a requirement that Legion prisons or stockades be strict and severe, the principle being that, once endured, the culprit will not freely volunteer himself for a second helping. The first thing a prisoner encounters is the removal of the hair on his head – *boule à zéro*, not a short back and sides but shaved. (Because of my baldness, I would shave my own head once a month. Consequently strangers often assumed that I had either just left prison or would be going there after lunch!) All prisoners also lose their pay for the period of their sentence. This pay is not returned to the French Government but credited to the regimental funds for the benefit of legionnaires who keep their noses clean. (The thought that perhaps a couple of *adjudants* and sergeants could suffer the indignity of *huit jours en tôle* would have the ordinary legionnaire dancing with joy.) There is another penalty for those in prison: their time in this haven of rest is added on to their contracts. Receive a hundred days prison during one's five-year contract, and the result is a contract longer than that anticipated.

A man returning to his company after an eight-day confinement, would normally be given twenty-four hours to re-adjust, probably standing under a hot shower for a minimum of two hours, cleaning his teeth for the first time for a week, meanwhile gulping down the beer brought to the shower by his comrades. He would probably burn the stinking fatigue uniform he had worn continuously during his *séjour*, carrying it to the fire not in his hands but on long sticks, holding it as far away from his nose as he could. His officers and NCOs would wipe from their minds the fact that this individual had been a recent prisoner, and it would be as if it had never happened – until the next time.

1965 brought many changes. Bob Wright had departed late the

previous year, and Simon left just a few months later. Early in March we received four more English-speaking recruits, three of them British and a young American who insisted on being called 'Rusty'. He insisted that he had served in the US Para Corps and had been an experienced parachutist prior to his enlistment. However, his landings were frightening to observe. He was the only man I have ever seen who, instead of landing on his feet, would deliberately allow his arse to make contact with the ground first. The Legion, in their wisdom, very quickly shipped him back to France, to the safe arms of the 1st Regiment.

One of the Brits became a medical orderly, the other two were placed in Simon's old company. For some reason they seemed unable to relax in my company. It took me a while to realize that this was because I was wearing the inverted gold stripe on my uniform denoting that I had already completed my first five years of service, and that those recruits had the fear of a chief corporal's black kepi that I had suffered in my early days. Nor had I realized that my regular companions were either the 'Mafia' or some of the senior NCOs of the regiment. Kenny had now become a feared figure in the regimental police and, when he did join the illustrious gathering for a drink, made it quite clear that it mattered not what grade we were wearing on our arms, for he and his good friend Oscar wielded the power, I never saw the bastard pay for a drink from the day he was made a policeman.

I was upset to learn from Oscar and Baccus that two of our young British recruits had deserted, attempting to get to Morocco, and had been picked up by the Algerian police and returned to the regiment. Worse: prior to their desertion they had stolen a radio and suitcase. Until that time, all the British in the regiment had been fairly respected, Bob Wilson being perhaps the most popular of all, though Kenny also had merited a lot of respect, and many of the regiment remembered Simon and Bob Wright with affection. Now these stupid young men had knocked the reputation we had worked so hard at establishing.

When I was given the details by Oscar (drinking a beer he had actually paid for, which really showed that he too was upset), I casually remarked that there was only one way to punish Englishmen, and that was to shame them. I also voiced my doubts that either of the bastards was capable of marching ninety kilometres, let alone attempting the distance to Morocco. I casually stated that I would chain them up and let the whole regiment see them.

I was surprised to find the next day that both had been chained to a telegraph pole, either side of the main road through the camp and bang in the centre. Each had a notice displayed on his chest, in French and in English 'I AM A THIEF'. They were released each day when the sun reached its highest point, one carrying the stolen radio, the other the stolen suitcase, to demonstrate their ability to maintain the rate of a forced march for the distance between Bou Sfer and the frontier of Morocco. Both later agreed, when they were released from prison, that they would have died on the journey, and they confessed this to me as I bought them beer along with Bob and Kenny a few days later. I have not named these young men. I have no reason to, for I have no axe to grind.

Shortly after I left the regiment, one of them, with a whole fresh look at the Legion, undertook the rigours of corporals' training and became a popular corporal in the regiment.

The Legion never failed to surprise me, not even in March 1965, when into the office walked one of the newest recruits to the Regiment, for this was no ordinary recruit but a man who had already completed fifteen years service and yet still wore the single stripe of a first-class private, aiming for his target of twenty years. There was more than a handshake between us – there was lots of embracing and almost tears at our reunion. More than two years had elapsed since I had bidden farewell to 'Minnie' on his departure to Madagascar, along with the 3rd Regiment. Minnie had taken me in hand when I joined that regiment as a novice recruit and had probably been more than responsible for my learning how to be a legionnaire.

Minnie told me he had no wish to be a parachutist. His only jump had been along with 699 other members of the Legion who, without any training, had volunteered to jump into Dien Bien Phu, where like other survivors of the defeat they had been led away to over fourteen months captivity. Subsequently these men had been awarded their parachute brevets. Now idiots at the 1st Regiment in Aubagne had started sending all legionnaires wearing a brevet to the 2nd REP. Minnie had completed his two years in Madagascar and, despite the fact that he should have had a choice of regiments on his return, had been shipped to the 2nd REP. This was one time the Legion screwed up.

I introduced him to Captain Racaud, explaining his background, his one and only jump, and how he had taken care of me for over two years as my acting corporal. So Minnie was grounded before he even had the opportunity to jump, found medically unfit and, in a matter of weeks, returned to France – still with honour, still wearing his brevet, but now classified as *modèle huit*, unfit to be a parachutist or first-line infantryman. (Minnie ended his twenty years as a chief corporal motor technician with the cavalry.)

It was a well-established fact in the regiment that the most hazardous jumps at the dunes of Cap Falcon were those carried out by the 2nd Company, but not in the opinion of members of that company! They would descend singing not a Legion song but the current No.1 hit broadcast from Monte Carlo, much to the annoyance and dismay of officers and NCOs in attendance.

In the normal course of events, the most dangerous objects falling from the sky and raining down on those on duty at the DZ, apart from the parachutists, were the rubber bands that had secured the straps and nylon cords in the parachute packs. Then a member of the 2nd Company instituted the practice that each member should secure in his vest a full bottle of beer. To prove what an efficient parachutist he was, and how much better this company was than the rest of the regiment, the bottle was to be opened during the descent, the beer to be drunk during the trip down, and the empty bottle presented after completion of the jump, to show how bloody clever he was. The shower of bottle tops deluging the DZ resulted in my ending up with a black eye, having looked up in admiration. I was thankful they had not been dropping their empty bottles as well. Happily this somewhat unorthodox practice was terminated before they realized how much more fun they could have had by dropping the bottles – with the assurance that they could have made direct hits, many would have been content to drop a full bottle, providing the target wore a black kepi.

1965 was also the year in which my guardian angel left me for another. Karl Emmerich had decided to leave the Legion.

Seventeen years were OK, but his wife was complaining about his target of twenty. After he left, I found myself with a *chef de service* who in no way matched his proficiency and ability, and who even left me requesting a change of service. On 15 April 1965 I made my last parachute drop with the regiment.

I had many times requested the opportunity of participating in 'free fall', and although at that time it had been neither accepted nor rejected, I had been allowed to jump without the sound of the klaxon or the monitor's boot up my arse. I would stand in the doorway of the aircraft watching for the designated 'target' and launch myself into space, in the hope I would prove to the experts that I knew what it was all about. On my last jump the target was an abandoned farm, just a few miles from the camp. I looked down from the door of the aircraft, watching it approaching my right boot, then launched myself out as the farmhouse left my sight under my boot. It had been a very good departure, with first-class judgement. Although it required quite some juggling and steering, I felt the king of them all as I slowly negotiated my way to the farmhouse yard.

It had been too bloody good. Only in the last fractions of a second, when my heart was trying to make its way out of my body through my teeth, did I realize that I was going to smash into the side of the building. I did – not into the wall but straight through the aperture that had once been a window. It did not hurt much. It was only equal to dropping a man from shoulder height, flat on his back. It did not hurt much – it near killed me. Part of my parachute was still draped on the guttering of the farm, and although I managed to free myself from my harness and struggle into the courtyard, I was grateful to those who had been waiting in an open field only fifty metres from the farm, when they came to my aid. Although my back did cause me pain, I thought that within a few days it would wear off and then I'd be back to normal.

Ten days after this event, I participated in a night march, only a matter of some twenty kilometres and considered a very simple exercise. On our return to the barracks, I found that the pain was now so severe that I could not bend down to take my boots off. I did not report sick but depended on Kovacs to give me pain-killing injections in my back to enable me to carry on with my work. After ten more days of pain and injections,

Kovacs, my best friend (and concerned only with me), confessed to the doctor, who, after checking me over, declared, 'You are as good to this regiment as a dead man' and shipped me off to hospital at the naval base of Mers-el-Kebir. It was there that the bastards tortured me for some six weeks, placing me on a rack and trying to extend my height to two metres, twisting my legs till I screamed in pain. They had such admiration for my spinal column that they X-rayed it every other day.

The greatest sadists at that hospital, who seemed to hate members of the Foreign Legion, were those over-muscled, big-breasted nurses who all had moustaches and were of the opinion that the war between Napoleon and Wellington had never ended, and so were getting revenge for the battle of Waterloo. After six weeks they gave up and sent me back to the regiment where for three days I slept on planks, tied down by Kovacs. Then I was shipped out to the Hospital Laverne at Marseilles, to a new form of torture: they wrapped me in plaster from my upper thighs to my chin. This did nothing for me, except to prevent my bending over, thus preventing the spasms of pain that had caused me distress. It also made me an expert at manipulating myself to the toilet, where I required a mirror to aid my sense of direction!

I remained at the Hospital Laverne at Marseilles for some six weeks, visited by Lauber, who had decided to become a civilian and get married, and subsequently borrowed some £200 to pay the expenses. Then I was visited by David Fireman, who had left the Legion after my departure to the REP and now came to see me at the behest of my parents. At least David's visit got me out of the hospital for a day. The doctor was most impressed that an ex-Legionnaire had travelled from London just to see a patient of his. The next day he became unimpressed, when my outing resulted in a ginormous hangover and a broken plaster cast, from falling down the stairs on my return to the ward (the result of a visit to the Crazy Horse bar).

Then I received a visit from Captain Most, of the 1st Regiment at Aubagne. He had brought along a document for me to sign for yet a further year's service, so that I could continue my medical treatment. He became somewhat annoyed when I refused and said I wished to leave on my due date (six days hence), return to London and see what Guy's Hospital could do in the way of treatment.

It took considerable pleading with the authorities both at the hospital and at Aubagne for me to quit the Legion with the aid of an aluminium crutch. Regrettably I found that I had missed the traditional farewell from the Legion. I had not even received the beautifully illuminated certificate, or the handshake from the colonel.

I was driven from Marseilles to Dover, with frequent stops to alleviate the pain in my back and with the rigours of a plaster cast forcing my head up. Eventually, arriving in London and at Guy's Hospital, I produced the medical documents issued from the Hospital Laverne, written in French. They meant nothing to the doctor there, who merely arranged for the plaster to be removed and told me to return in two weeks.

My back was cured within a week of my visit to my local golf course. All the golf-playing fanatics who suffered from back trouble, due to their attempting to play off a six handicap instead of their regular fourteen, suggested that I visit an eccentric organ-player orthopaedic specialist in Bromley. For the sum of £5, I spent one hour lying on my stomach with electric rubber plugs injecting mini shocks into my back, then thirty minutes with the bastard trying to break my back by doubling my spine the wrong way until a flash of pain hit my brain and I fainted. I came to with a glass of brandy at my lips. Prior to my fainting, I had heard a crack, and really thought that my back had been broken.

This Irish organist had achieved a miracle. All pain had gone, I could bend down and touch my toes, I could twist the trunk of my body violently to the left or right, without the slightest twinge.

Within two months of leaving the Legion, I completed my first parachute jump as a civilian, by courtesy of the 44th Para Hospital TA unit.

Epilogue – Family Ties

Since my departure from the Foreign Legion, through the Amical des Anciens Combattants de la Légion Etrangère de Grande-Bretagne (the British Foreign Legion Association, initiated over thirty years ago by John Yeowell, a well-decorated ex-legionnaire), I have met many of those who also served in the Legion with *Honneur et Fidelité*, friends from years ago, some of whom served for more than fifteen years, some indeed still serving. Each month, on receipt of the Legion's own publication, the *Képi Blanc*, I scan the pages looking for old friends, and watch their progress through the ranks of the Legion. Some who joined with the lowly grade of second-class private have reached the exalted rank of colonel. I also search the obituary columns – these too can produce a sense of shock.

During the past fifteen years, there have been many books written about the Foreign Legion by British authors, most of them professional writers. The exception among them is Simon Murray, himself an ex-chief corporal who in his book *Legionnaire* wrote of his own experience in the Legion.

During the short period of time we spent together in the same regiment (eighteen months in the Legion is a very short time) we did share a few beers together. Perhaps our different views on life in the Legion can be explained by the fact that he looked upon it through the eyes of a very young man, whereas my own view was that of a somewhat cynical forty-year-old who had already served in a war.

All the books have included material on Camerone, the Mexican battle that took place on 30 April 1863, and its importance to both serving members and ex-members of the Legion. The professional writers usually say that the '*Récit du Combat du Camerone*' that is read aloud to all serving legionnaires on the anniversary of that date is too long to be included in their books, and then give their own translation and interpretation, using three times as many words – *and get it wrong*! (Although Simon Murray did not give the names of the last surviving six legionnaires who made the final charge, he did get the facts right that there were indeed six.)

Those six, without a round of ammunition between them, charged against more than a thousand of the enemy with the bayonet. These gallant few were: Lieutenant Maudet, Corporal Maine, Legionnaire Catteau, Legionnaire Wensel, Legionnaire Constantin and Legionnaire Leonhard. Only three of them survived.

Even today members of the Mexican Army present arms when they pass the monument erected to the exploits of the company of sixty-three legionnaires who took part in the battle.

Towards the close of the 'Algerian Affair', the effective strength of the Foreign Legion was in excess of 25,000. If one could have traced more than fifty British serving with the Legion during that time, it would have been a miracle! The winds have changed during the past twenty years, perhaps due mostly to the exploits of the Legion at Kolweizi in 1978, when for the first time ever the British popular Press lavished praise and applauded the exploits and courage of the Legion. Then perhaps the efforts of the British services in the Falklands have evoked a new sense of pride among the British, and a uniting of the nation not seen since the days of the Blitz during the Second World War, so that many young Englishmen have volunteered their services to the Legion, looking for adventure and the opportunity of proving themselves 'Men among Men'.

The Legion of today is greatly reduced from the numbers maintained during the fighting in Indo China until 1957 and the Algerian campaigns until mid 1962. Today there is a force of fewer than 10,000 highly trained and specialist soldiers, but of these one in twelve is now British, and in the most select and élite regiment in Europe today, the 2nd Regiment of Parachutists, twelve per cent are British.

We the veterans gather together in London for the reunion of Camerone, with members arriving from all over the UK. Many of our members also attend gatherings of ex-Legionnaires in Germany, Belgium and France. Tell me, reader, if life in the

Legion is so terrible and horrifying, full of brutality and hatred, why do we gather to talk of old times, of long-gone days, and still remember word for word our old Legion marching songs? Why are we joined by younger members, who have just left the Legion?

To those who have a son, a brother, a nephew, a cousin or a sweetheart in the Legion, I say: do not fear for his wellbeing, hold your heads high and be proud that you know a man who is serving alongside men. Life in the Legion is hard, but life is hard anyway. Although legionnaires are themselves hard, they are also among the most tolerant men to be found in any military society in the world.

Memories of the Legion are treasured. There have been many who say that, 'Time erases bad memories': I disagree. I have found that the bad times are remembered as well as the good. But then again, all things are relative – what others would consider 'bad times', I could shrug off with a laugh. What I consider 'bad times' bring guffaws of laughter from others at reunions.

I have attended Legion reunions in strange places – such as a tiny village tucked away in the hinterlands of Mauritania, where Dr Blanchard, an ex-Legion medical officer in the cavalry at Bou Sfer, celebrated the Camerone with me, for three successive years, in the heart of the southern Sahara desert.

There was a time when I was at Jeddah in Saudi Arabia, along with Bob Wilson, I flying off to London for the reunion of Camerone, Bob on his way to Djibouti to celebrate along with the 13th Demi Brigade. To ensure that I could return to London with my 'duty free', I had booked via Paris, and my Air France plane had broken its journey from Abu Dhabi, both to refuel and to pick up six more passengers. When the stewardess placed me in the seat allocated, I found myself next to ex-Chief Sergeant Delgado, who had been responsible for the training of corporals at Bou Sfer.

Once we had both recovered from the shock, his first enquiry was, 'Have you ever seen *le grand* Bob?' When I told him that Bob was awaiting the next flight to Djibouti, he could hardly believe that we were actually working for the same group of companies. (In 1980, after completing sixteen years, Bob had joined me working in Saudi Arabia.) He was even more shattered to find that there was actually another ex-member of the 2nd REP running the fire service. During that flight to Paris, the aircraft ran out of champagne.

I have been fortunate indeed. Jim Sinclair, David Fireman, Bob Wright and Bob Wilson have all visited me since our days in the Legion, and I maintain a lengthy correspondence with ex-legionnaires in Canada, the United States, Germany, France, Italy and South Africa, and even one in Japan.

In the latter part of September 1986, as this book was reaching its end, I and four other British members of our association attended a reunion at Lille in France, where for the first time since departing the Legion I met our old colonel of Bou Sfer days now General Caillaud. It was a happy reunion, and we greeted each other with more than just a handshake. However, I continually blotted my copybook by addressing him as '*mon colonel*', instead of '*mon général.*' He took no notice of this breach of etiquette, but quite a few VIP guests seemed shocked. I was highly delighted when another veteran joined the illustrious company for a drink, who had known the general far longer than I, and addressed him as '*mon lieutenant*'.

Such is the way of the Legion that a general in the French Army can let out a booming laugh when an insignificant ex-chief corporal declares that he cannot understand how General Chenel and the current General Commander of the Legion, General Roue, achieved their exalted grade, since they had both shown a perceptible lack of perspicacity in their refusal to allow him to become a parachutist!

Vive la Légion!